Defending the Left

AN INDIVIDUAL'S GUIDE
TO FIGHTING FOR SOCIAL JUSTICE,
INDIVIDUAL RIGHTS, AND
THE ENVIRONMENT

David E. Driver

The Noble Press, Inc.

Printed in the United States of America.

Library of Congress Cataloging-in-Publication Data

Driver, David E.
    Defending the Left: an individual's guide to fighting for social justice, individual rights, and the environment / David E. Driver.

        p.   cm.
    Includes bibliographical references (p.   ) and index.
    ISBN 1-879360-12-8 (pbk.) : $11.95
    I. United States—Politics and government—1981–1989.   2. United States—Politics and government—1989–   3. Liberalism—United States.   4. United States—Economic policy—1981–   5. United States—Social policy—1080–
6. Environmental policy—United States.   I. Title
E881.D75   1992
320.973—dc20   91-51221
                                                                  CIP

Noble Press books are available in bulk at discount prices. Single copies are available prepaid direct from the publisher:

Marketing Director
The Noble Press
213 Institute Place, Suite 508
Chicago, IL 60610

Contents

Preface   *xi*

ONE   *To the Progressive Left*   1
Our Children's Future   2
The American Psyche   3
Defining the Left   5
The Progressive Left   9
Common Cause   10
The Progressive Counterrevolution   15

TWO   *The Rise and Fall of the Right*   19
The Rise of the Right   24
The Emerging Majority   28
Running out of Steam   29
What was the Message?   33

THREE   *America: The World's Leading Capitalist*   39
The Cost of Capitalism   44
Reaganomics   47
Corporate Welfare   55
Progressive Economics   57

FOUR   *Class, Race, and Gender Bias*   67
Class Warfare: From Haymarket Square
to Reaganomics   72
America's Class Makeup   77
Gender Bias   79
Racism   84
Eliminating Class, Race, and Gender Bias   87

FIVE   *Environment and Poverty*   91
Poverty in America   92
The State of the Environment   95
Eradicating Poverty   100
Restoring our Environment   105
Act Locally   109

SIX   *Foreign Policy and the Third World*   111
Third World Policy: In Whose Interest?   113
Economic Weapons   114
To What End?   118
Building a New Third World Policy   121

SEVEN   *Disinformation*   129
Manufacturing the News   132
The Impact of Disinformation   135
Liberatory and Multicultural Education   139
Censorship   142
Defeating Disinformation   143

EIGHT   *Grass-Root Politics*   147
Community Government   148
The Flourishing Grass-Roots Movement   150
Putting Progressives in Office   155
Becoming a Political Activist   156

NINE   *Dollars for Change*   165
Socially Responsible Consumers   166
Socially Responsible Investing   174
The Decency Decade   178

TEN   *Resource Guide*   179
National Progressive Organizations
with Local Branches   180
Alternative Political Organizations and Third Parties   181
Progressive Research and Advocacy Organizations   183
Legislative Information and Candidate Ratings   189
Resources for Socially Responsible Consumption
and Investing   191
Alternative Media   194
Alternative Radio   196
Local Alternative News Weeklies   197

Acknowledgments

THE COMPLETION OF THIS PROJECT WOULD HAVE not been possible without the assistance of my colleagues in publishing, as well as the aid and support of my family and friends. First, thanks must be given to my editor, Lisa Mirabile, who despite having her first child in the middle of this project, worked tirelessly to see this idea become reality. I also must thank my good friend, Caroline Smith, for her help in compiling the necessary research, and for her special support and encouragement. Angela Oliver, my sister, also deserves thanks for her support and patience, as do the staff of the Noble Press, who kept the company moving forward during my frequent absences.

Special thanks must also be given to the many progressive researchers, writers, and advocacy organizations whose research and insight made the writing of this book possible. The most notable of these include Barbara Ehrenreich, Robert Kuttner, William Greider, Holly Sklar, John Kenneth Gailbraith, Helen Caldicott, Robert Reich, and the late Michael Harrington.

CHAPTER ONE

To the Progressive Left

FOR THOSE WHO VALUE JUSTICE AND EQUALITY, the past twelve years have been a painfully wrenching time. We have endured twelve years of extreme conservatism, of the American political system at its worst: government by the rich for the rich. Today, the spirit of national community has been lost and the ugly divisions of race, sex, and class are wider than at any time in recent history.

The well-to-do profited greatly during the past decade, but the fruits of their gain can be seen only in their beautifully maintained, high-security suburban communities. These economic winners are safely tucked away from the collapsing cities and disintegrating rural communities where the economic losers face the daily struggle of just getting by.

It has been a period of political and social fascism, as a small group of ruling-class white males has attempted to redefine American culture, morals, and attitudes in its own image—partly because this group believes it knows best, but mostly as a way to keep the economic losers divided while American democracy, long skewed in favor of the elite, was impaired even further. Political leaders made hollow promises to appease the electorate while they shaped public policy to meet the desires of "major economic organizations and concentrated wealth and the influential elites surrounding them," as author William Greider puts it.

For those on the Left, it was a time of anger, as hard-won gains in women's rights, environmental protection, minority advancement, individual liberties, and economic equality were attacked with a viciousness not seen in America since the communist-crazed days of Joseph McCarthy. Legions of hungry, homeless, and illiterate Americans wandered aimlessly through the squalor of the nation's once-proud cities, and cries for peace were overwhelmed by the sound of death and destruction in Nicaragua, Panama, Iraq, and elsewhere.

Despite these setbacks, the poor, the environment, civil rights, and freedom did not suffer the greatest losses from conservatism. America and its future did. America today is a nation divided not only against itself, but also against the world. It is a nation full of skepticism and distrust among the races and between the sexes. It is a nation that is suffering, and its only recourse has been to blame someone else, be it feminists, welfare mothers, northern liberals, unions, or the Japanese.

OUR CHILDREN'S FUTURE

The Reagan/Bush years not only left the nation full of skepticism and doubt, but also left a heavy burden of debt. Our children will someday have to pay down the national debt, currently estimated at $3.7 trillion. In addition, our children will have to pay roughly $200 billion to clean up nuclear waste at 14,401 military weapons sites and as much as $750 billion to clean up nuclear and hazardous waste sites. Our children may also be responsible for untold billions for the future bailouts of federally insured banks, savings and loans, pension funds, and insurance companies, all severely weakened by years of Reaganomics.

Our children will also have to pay for the neglect of our nation's cities. Billions will be required just to save cities like Philadelphia, New York, and Detroit from bankruptcy. Even more will be required to make them habitable again—to rehabilitate everything from their roads and bridges to their education, mass transit, and health care systems.

Our children will also have to pay for the failings of our business leaders. America, once the world's leading manufacturing and trading nation, has rapidly lost ground to Japan and Germany. Largely as a result, America, once number-one in per-capita income, has fallen behind Sweden, Denmark, and Switzerland, as well as Germany and Japan. Decent paying jobs, even for the college educated, have become harder and harder to find, while once prosperous corporations such as Macy's,

Wang Computers, U.S. Steel, Eastern Airlines, and Chrysler either cease to exist or struggle to survive.

And unless the direction of this country changes, the quality of our children's lives will suffer from more than just economic blight. They will also have to breathe air and drink water many times more polluted than it already is; global warming will be a reality; and AIDS will have increased tenfold. They will have nowhere to dispose of their garbage; there will be no government scholarships to help pay for college; our daughters will have lost their right to choose whether to continue an unwanted pregnancy; and our sons will be required to fight wars in the Third World to protect American corporate investments overseas.

THE AMERICAN PSYCHE

Fortunately, the dangers of an extended period of ultra-conservative rule are becoming obvious to more Americans. The number of Americans who approved of President Bush's overall job performance dropped from a high of 89 percent, during the Persian Gulf War, to the mid-thirties slightly more than a year later. Bush's drop in the polls suggests that many Americans have learned that false national pride—especially when it comes from beating up on a fourth-rate army—does not replace having a job or financial security. And possibly, the drop in Bush's popularity suggests that the average American has finally discovered that trickle-down economics only works when the elite at the top decide to turn on the faucet.

While the change in Bush's fortunes has given the Left reason to cheer, that cheer should be a cautious one. The Reagan revolution was not only economic, but philosophical as well. Over the past decade, the Right has subjected American minds to powerful propaganda. Its well-framed messages have confused many about the value of compassion, fairness, and community; about the proper role of government and corporations in American society; and about America's role in the changing international landscape.

In the place of good conscience, the Right's propaganda machine substituted social Darwinism and libertarian values—a modified version of Ayn Rand's Objectivism, which says "Capitalism and altruism cannot coexist in man or in the same society. . . . The cross is the symbol of torture; I prefer the dollar sign."

The Reagan Revolution encouraged greed and conspicuous consumption by the affluent. At the same time, it removed the burden of guilt—Ayn Rand's cross—by rationalizing poverty and the lack of equality in American society. Conservative sociologist Charles Murray proclaimed that the best way to help the poor was to *completely* eliminate unemployment insurance, welfare, Medicaid, and all other federal income-support programs. Conservative economist George Gilder declared that the poor needed the "lash of their poverty" to keep them working. While New Right leaders, such as Jerry Falwell and Phyllis Schlafly, exclaimed that feminist were to blame for everything from welfare dependency and the increasing divorce rate to "America's rapid decline as a world power."

The Right's attack on the American psyche led many to question not only whether equality and human dignity should be government concerns, but even whether they were appropriate human concerns. It also led many people to question their allegiance to groups that were working in their own interests. For example, while surveys showed that the majority of women supported the feminist agenda, very few women would admit to being feminists. In fact, surveys showed that the majority of Americans supported the liberal position on most issues— protecting the environment, abortion, affirmative action, the need for greater spending on social programs—but very few would admit to being liberals.

This paradox is puzzling, and for activists, frustrating, for it limits our ability to generate the mass support needed to bring about positive change. The late writer and political activist Michael Harrington expressed his frustration at this social contradiction well:

> [America] is, in social terms, the most left-wing nation on the face of the earth. We often fail to recognize that fact because the United States is, in political and legislative terms, the most backward of advanced societies. It is the only developed capitalism without a significant socialist movement; its welfare state was not only the last to emerge in the West, but remains the meanest and cheapest, the only one without a national health system. . . . And in foreign policy America too often plays the role of Moscow under the Czars."

For economist and political strategist Robert Kuttner, the problem lies in the contradiction between American society's political wants and its political beliefs. Kuttner points out that most Americans believe in liberalism in spirit and in application but are ideological conservatives: "The United States, as a liberal society, has often turned to social-democratic remedies, but rarely to a social-democratic ideology."

Kuttner's and Harrington's observations suggest that the Left must do more than just propose new "fairness" programs. It must dedicate itself to consciousness-raising and it must provide a new vision, a vision that offsets the lingering confusion caused by divisive and self-indulgent conservative ideology and replaces it with a belief in national community, fairness, and compassion.

DEFINING THE LEFT

The ideological label "Left" carries with it a variety of perceptions and definitions. For many, the prevailing image of the Left is liberalism and the Democratic party. For others, it is the American Marxist, socialist, and social democratic movements. For some, the label evokes memories of the Left's great accomplishments, such as Franklin Roosevelt's New Deal or the social advancements of the 1960s. For still others, the Left describes the environmental, peace, women's rights, civil rights, and other social justice movements in America.

The Left is all of these things. It is a collage of people, issues, and ideals. It includes people who care dearly about world peace, the homeless, clean air and water, living wages, and free speech. It includes advocates for animal rights, nuclear disarmament, civil rights, stronger unions, an environmentally sustainable economy, and greater government support for the nation's children. It includes liberals, social democrats, feminists, environmental and social justice activists, organized labor, Marxists, and progressives.

The Left and its many segments have long been at the forefront of social advancement in America. According to political scientist Leslie Dunbar, "In our era, [the Left] has taken up the causes of women, civil rights, labor unions, the environment, children. In earlier times, it had other special concerns: the entrepreneurs, public schools, men's suffrage, the abolition of slavery."

The Left's rich and diverse history shows a mass movement in constant transformation. During the 1930s, labor and unemployed workers' movements, often inspired by Marxism or socialism, provided the grass-roots catalyst that helped inspire the New Deal, a series of legislative initiatives that included unemployment insurance, Social Security, the National Labor Relations Act, and minimum-wage and child-labor laws.

The New Deal was a boost for the American worker, but it also benefited the young, families, farmers, and people of color. It created the Civilian Conservation Corps—the "tree army"—which trained millions of the nation's youth and put them to work in city and country forests and parks. A massive public housing program for the poor and working class was begun. Federal deposit insurance was instituted to protect citizens from banking failures. Agricultural assistance programs were developed to help farmers. Through the Wheeler-Howard Act, Native Americans were offered education, self-determination, and self-government. The Works Progress Administration, a program to help the unemployed, gave almost 30 percent of its jobs to African-Americans. This, and the fact that "ultimately, virtually every New Deal agency contained Negro officials or Negro advisors," according to Stanford historian Carl Degler, led to "the political allegiance of blacks [shifting] dramatically from the Republicans to the Democrats."

The next great period for the Left came in the 1960s. This period, according to Harrington, "coincided with the high point of the greatest advance in living standards that history has ever known." The political activism of the 1960s was fueled by a growing awareness of the civil rights movement, an unprecedented student movement, the ascent of Martin Luther King to national prominence, and John F. Kennedy's election to the White House. Like the New Deal, the Left of the 1960s produced legislative advancements—Medicare and Medicaid, the Voting Rights Act, Head Start, the Civil Rights Act—that have become an integral part of society today. Just as important, the 1960s produced powerful social movements for women's rights, environmental protection, gay rights, peace, civil rights, and social justice.

Today's Left is all of its past. It is a labor movement that ranges from progressives at the Labor Institute to the union elite at the AFL-CIO. It is a movement for equality for women, people of color, and gays and lesbians that ranges from the aggressive tactics of the gay activists of ACT-UP to the moderate leadership of the NAACP. It is an environmental movement extending from the confrontational tactics of Earth First! to the Washington lobbyists of the Sierra Club. It is a peace movement that ranges from young students in SANE/FREEZE to the clergy of the Religious Task Force on South America. It is a social justice

movement that runs the spectrum from grass-roots neighborhood activists to limousine liberals.

THE PROGRESSIVE LEFT

Today's Left is vast and diverse. That is its strength, and its weakness.
But although the Left looks—and sometimes acts—unwieldy, it does
have a center and a unifying objective. Its center is what is increasingly
referred to as the progressive movement, and its unifying cause is the
call for a new economic order in America.

The progressive movement is to the left of mainstream liberalism
and to the right of Marxism and anarchism. Progressives mediate between the often extreme and uncompromising positions of the far Left
and the inability of the liberal elite to confront a political and economic
system in which their own entrenched interests lie. The progressive
movement has no head, but plenty of voices. These voices include Social
Democrats such as Vermont senator Bernie Sanders and author Barbara
Ehrenreich; party Democrats such as Jesse Jackson, Pat Schroeder, and
Jim Hightower; and activists and writers such as Lois Gibbs, Ralph
Nader, Helen Caldicott, William Greider, and Robert Kuttner.

The progressive movement envisions a society in which racial and
gender bias cease to exist, but the richness of diversity is celebrated; a
society in which the working and middle classes are not exploited by
capitalism, but enriched by it. It envisions a society in which the health
of the environment, the state of the country's children, and the welfare
of the disenfranchised replace world domination and the enrichment of
the elite as the government's leading policy objectives.

Progressives look to a future in which the people of the Third World
are not exploited by America but are friends and neighbors. Their goal
is a democracy in which America's direction is not determined by corporate and affluent interests but by a true majority of the people. The progressive movement envisions a fairer and more just America. If national
surveys are correct, it is a vision that is shared, if not by the majority,
then by a large percentage of the American people.

All of these progressive concerns—women's equality, environmental preservation, world peace, affirmative action, Third World auton-
omy, social justice—are impeded by the current economic order and the
elitist power structure it sustains. Accordingly, a new economic order is

the predominant and unifying concern of the progressive movement. Progressive economics, far from radical, envisions an American economic system more in concert with the rest of the industrialized world—for as we shall see later, the current American system is the most capitalistic in the industrialized world.

Today, as in the 1960s, it is economics that separates progressives from their mainstream liberal counterparts. Despite the abject failure of Reaganomics, Democratic party leaders, for the most part, continue to prescribe trickle-down economic policies to cure the nation's economic woes. *New Republic* editor Mickey Kraus argues that liberals should not try to curb the excesses and failings of capitalism. "You cannot have capitalism," writes Kraus, "without 'selfishness,' or even 'greed,' because they are what make the system work."

It was capitalistic "greed," however, that helped create not only the Great Depression, but also today's multi-billion-dollar crisis in the banking and savings and loan industries. The capitalist myth that corporate prosperity will trickle down was again disproved under Reagan. Responding to these realities, Harrington, in *The Next Left*, warns mainstream liberals of the folly of hoping that economics as usual can lead to social justice:

> Mainstream liberals—the heirs of the Kennedy-Johnson years—
> [believe] if there was a little more growth and lower exchange rates
> for the dollar . . . the nation could get back to happier times. This is
> the liberal equivalent of Herbert Hoover's faith that, between 1929
> and 1932, prosperity was around the corner.
>   . . . A rising tide lifts all boats is no longer operative (and
> never was as universal as Kennedy and economists of the sixties
> thought). . . . The economic and political basis of the Western Left
> for the past half century—the link between economic growth and
> social justice—is, in its traditional form at least, going, going, gone.

The economy grew in the 1980s, and few benefited. In contrast, although the economy stumbled through most of the 1930s, the redistributive programs of the New Deal still worked to improve the lot of the poor and the middle class. Unfortunately, this lesson seems to be lost on most of the Democratic elite. They choose to champion economics as usual instead of heeding Robert Kuttner's call for the Democratic party to return to the New Deal's "broad, embracing, expansive visions" that "provided redistribution and social justice *via inclusion.*"

A progressive economic order would encompass the words and ideas of the past and present visionaries of the progressive Left. This includes embracing Patricia Schroeder's belief that "morality should matter to economics: equity is just as important as efficiency," and recovering, as Schroeder suggests, the wisdom of the old Navaho proverb: "We do not inherit the earth from our ancestors; we borrow it from our children." It includes adopting Illinois senator Paul Simon's view that "the nation's highest commitment—our most important national goal—must be to guarantee a job opportunity for everyone who wants to work" and endorsing Jim Hightower's call for a new "percolate-up" economics that invests in "grass-roots economic development." And it includes embracing not only Martin Luther King's call for racial justice, but also his belief that "an edifice which produces beggars needs restructuring."

The progressive movement is more than just high ideals, however; it is also action. Although progressives are currently a tiny minority in national government, a number of members of Congress are working to create a Progressive Caucus." These self-proclaimed progressives and a number of legislators who have been pursuing a progressive agenda include Bernie Sanders, Social Democratic congressman from Vermont; Democratic members of congress Patricia Schroeder of Colorado, Barbara Boxer and Ronald Dellums of California, and John Conyers of Michigan; and senators Paul Simon of Illinois, Paul Wellstone of Minnesota, and Tom Harkin of Iowa.

These and other legislators have proposed or supported a number of progressive legislative reforms such as a 50 percent reduction in military spending by the year 2000; a Peace Tax Fund that forbids taxes collected from those opposed to war to be used for military purposes; a more progressive tax code; and programs to rebuild the nation's cities and provide for the American family. They also support a foreign trade policy that imposes additional import duties on goods imported from countries without adequate environmental standards and new agricultural programs to detoxify the food supply, support family farms, and promote sustainable farm practices and organically grown foods.

Progressive legislative initiatives also include campaign financing reform to remove the undue influence of wealth from politics; legislation to secure equality for women, including the Economic Equity Act and the Freedom of Choice Act; and a new foreign policy that includes debt relief, economic assistance for Third World children and women, and the redirection of foreign aid, according to Harkin, to benefit "the world's poorest people, not the world's generals, bureaucrats, and despots."

While the growing presence of progressive ideals in national political and intellectual thought is impressive, the real strength of the progressive movement is at the grass-roots level. Regional and local groups such as the Progressive Vermont Alliance, local Green affiliates, local Rainbow Coalitions, California's Peace and Freedom party, and Wisconsin's Labor/Farm party are bringing about legislative change in their states and local communities. Even more, a host of progressive organizations are empowering ordinary people to stand up and make a difference in their own neighborhoods.

With the support of progressive organizations, citizens have successfully fought discrimination against people of color and against gays and lesbians. They have prevented the location of toxic waste dumps and other environmentally destructive industrial projects in their neighborhoods. They have lobbied to maintain access to legalized abortions, and to pass state and local laws against stalking, domestic violence, and sexual harassment. Through socially responsible consumption, they have pressured exploitative corporations to amend their abusive practices. And through the establishment of nuclear free zones and sister city relationships, they have worked to educate their neighbors about the plight of people in the Third World and the dangers of militarism.

Today's progressive movement is the core of the American Left. It is the vehicle that can unify and focus the Left. It is the catalyst that will empower millions of people, from legislators to students, to dedicate themselves to the ideals of true democracy and social justice. It is the engine that will propel the vision of an equitable and sustainable society beyond rhetoric to reality.

COMMON CAUSE

When President Ronald Reagan nominated Judge Robert Bork for a seat on the Supreme Court in July of 1987, he unknowingly did more to light a fire under the Left than any leader in recent history. Fearful of Bork's extremely conservative interpretation of the Constitution, progressive citizens nationwide raised their voices in alarm. Within days, an unprecedented array of liberal organizations had banded together to fight the Bork nomination.

The possibility that someone of Bork's extreme conservative ideology might ascend to the Supreme Court shocked the entire progressive and liberal movement into action. Over three hundred organizations joined together to form the Block Bork Coalition, including the AFL-CIO, Planned Parenthood, the National Council of Churches, the Organization of Chinese Americans, SANE/FREEZE, Friends of the Earth, the NAACP, Catholics for a Free Choice, the Association of Retarded Citizens, the National Gay and Lesbian Task Force, the National Lawyers Guild, the Sierra Club, the YWCA, and the ACLU. Through their combined efforts, Bork's nomination was defeated.

The Bork defeat demonstrated the power of a combined Left. It showed the social and political force that can be amassed when the disparate elements of the Left look beyond single-issue concerns to embrace a larger cause. It showed the strength that comes from accommodation and collaboration for the sake of a broader goal.

After the Bork defeat, the triumphant Left was hopeful that it could maintain its newfound unity. Unfortunately, it was not be. The strains of class, sex, and racial division, along with each group's separate agenda, pulled the coalition apart.

Hence today in Berkeley, California, white, middle-class environmentalists, feminists, peace activists, and "new agers" shamelessly "cross a picket line of mostly African-American and Latino workers" at Whole Foods Market, a health-food store. The Berkeley Left, once a driving force for progressive radicalism, appears to be yet another victim of the self-interest and class divisions that afflict all of American society.

In a 1991 article for *The Nation* titled "Tofu Politics," L. A. Kauffman investigated why Berkeley's "Birkenstock set" refused to support the workers' strike. After interviewing a number of Whole Foods shoppers, Kauffman wrote that many saw "their individual purchasing decisions as thoughtful efforts to 'make connections' with what's happening elsewhere on the globe."

In an attempt to answer the obvious question, Kauffman wrote: "What kinds of 'connections' are Whole Foods shoppers making, after all, as they pursue a politics based on purchases? Clearly not connections to the African-American and Latino working-class picketers. . . . Nor are they making connections to the unionized workers at other food stores in Berkeley, who stand to see their own wages go down because Whole Foods is depressing area standards."

"Fifteen years ago," Lee Goodlee, secretary of the Berkeley Commission on Labor, told Kauffman, "Berkeley would have shut Whole Foods down. . . . But the Berkeley environment has changed." Unfortunately, the rest of the country has changed too. For much of the Left, self-interest and divisiveness have become the order of the day.

The divisions on the Left are symbolic of the splits throughout American society—race, gender, and class division. For instance, critics have accused the environmental movement of racism. But the environmental movement doesn't exclude minorities and the poor: it just doesn't speak to their needs. Being largely middle-class and white, the environmental movement tends to address issues of concern to its predominate constituency.

Women's organizations such as the National Organization for Women (NOW) and the National Women's Political Caucus have mostly a middle-class, professional, white membership. As a result, according to activist and author Sheila Collins, they tend to focus "almost exclusively on issues of paramount concern to them: pay equity, passage of the Equal Rights Amendment, sex discrimination in education, and reproductive rights,"while tending "to ignore or downplay the survival needs of working-class and poor women and racial minorities for adequate housing, health care, child care, and income maintenance."

The civil rights movement also faces a number of divisive issues. These include the open hostility of some civil rights groups to the movement for gay and lesbian rights, and their at best lukewarm support for the feminist movement. However, the major divisive issue in the civil rights movement is internal: the disparate interests of the upwardly mobile and the poor.

As more and more minorities move up the educational and professional ladder, some civil rights organizations have become less influential in shaping public policy to benefit the poor and the working class, and have, according to Collins, "increasingly functioned to enhance the individual careers of the black middle class."

One example of this class conflict was the 1984 defection by minority organizations from the long-running labor boycott of beer maker Adolph Coors. This defection, according to Yale political scientist Adolph Reed, Jr., was initiated by Operation PUSH, the NAACP, and several other black and Hispanic organizations. In exchange for their support, Coors pledged to support minority capitalism and "redirect" some of its investments into minority-owned businesses. This compromise, however, was a slap in the face to workers, both white and African-American, who had put their livelihoods on the line to combat union busting and other unfair labor practices by anti-union employers such as Coors. It was a setback to the rest of the Left as well, since the Coors family is one of the leading financial backers of far-right organizations.

Labor unions have also helped to divide the Left. The former leadership of the AFL-CIO provided financial support to help destroy leftist unions in El Salvador and Grenada. In general, unions have not welcomed women or minorities. And in many areas of the country, environmentalists and peace activists have met union workers head-on over mining, logging, and defense jobs versus weapons cuts and environmental protection.

These divisions within the Left, coupled with the individual pursuit of self-interest, have led to changes in the progressive movement. Community organizer Ellen Ryan coined the term "boutique politics" to describe the current state of the movement:

> Much of what passes for progressive political action today is little
> more than exhorting people to take a position on one or more
> issues: abortion, affirmative action, saving the whales, the latest Supreme Court nominee, etc. There are numerous causes and organizations for environmentalists, labor unionists, farm activists, feminists,
> and world hunger activists to choose from depending on their particular tastes—these are the activist boutiques."

Given the depth of the differences among various liberal causes and the narrow focus of much of the Left, it is not surprising that the Left keeps losing. Winning in the political arena by changing public consciousness requires mass support. And mass support comes from a broad-based agenda that speaks to the needs and beliefs of a diverse public.

SOLIDARITY

The Left can create a broad-based agenda by going beyond specific issues to their underlying causes. One obvious example is the imbalance of political and economic power enjoyed by America's corporate elite.

Environmentalist Brad Erickson, of the Earth Island Institute, agrees: "We can't solve any problem without revealing fundamental power imbalances and changing them. . . . Winning environmental regulations in the US without controlling the movement of capital leads to the relocation of industry to the developing nations where corporations avoid paying equitable wages and are able to keep environmental and labor movements at arm's length. And civil rights victories in the absence of the redistribution of wealth and economic power do not prevent widespread poverty."

Interestingly enough, it is the youth of the Left who appear to have grasped the wisdom of fighting for a broader agenda. At a 1990 convention sponsored by the Student Environmental Action Coalition (SEAC) at the University of Illinois Champaign-Urbana, several members explained the organization's broader agenda to the *Utne Reader*. "The environment must not be separated from the social. Saving the planet means fighting economic injustice, racism, sexism, imperialism, and all oppression," said Charles Betz of the University of Minnesota. SEAC coordinator Beth Ising agreed: "Everything is connected—environmental degradation, poverty, hunger, homelessness, and racism. What we want to do is make a difference in every aspect of the environment."

A broad-based agenda has also been the key to success for many grass-roots groups around the country. One of the most notable was the Progressive Vermont Alliance, a coalition of peace activists, environmentalists, social justice activists, and Democratic party left-wingers. Together, they have elected "Rainbow Democrats" and independents to a number of local and statewide offices, and even Socialist Bernie Sanders to the U.S. Congress.

Across the country, banners proclaiming "Jobs with Peace" and "Build Homes Not Bombs" herald the increasing cooperation between peace activists, civil rights groups, city mayors, social activists, unions, environmentalists, and liberal clergy in support of peace and economic equality. One such campaign, the Citizens Budget Campaign, included more than a hundred diverse organizations. This national campaign's primary focus was on lobbying for new priorities in the federal budget; in 1990 it endorsed the Congressional Black Caucus's Quality of Life Alternative Budget. These same peace and justice coalitions are also very visible on the local level. Through their efforts, eighty-five cities had passed Jobs with Peace resolutions by 1990, up from six in 1982. A number of cities, with the support of peace activists and unions, have also passed measures to reduce their dependence on defense-industry related employment.

Labor and the environmental movement have also begun to work together on important issues. The two groups have banded together in an organization called Citizens Trade Watch Committee to oppose Bush's proposed free trade agreements. They are also collaborating to promote the development of a "workers' superfund"—a corporate-sponsored fund to "support and retrain workers displaced by environmental regulation or shutdown."

Even more important than collaboration on issues of mutual interest is for progressives to realize that one of the keys to social change is a change in social attitudes. It would be naive for peace activists to assume that a society that is indifferent to Americans dying of hunger or AIDS will be responsive to concerns about bystanders killed in Iraq or Panama, just as it would also be naive for equal rights activists to assume that a society that tolerates discrimination against women will be responsive to appeals for equality for gays and lesbians.

Nor can we trivialize the importance of one group's agenda versus another. It is not a matter of whether children in American ghettos are more or less important than children in the Third World or whether dolphins are more important than dogs used for laboratory testing. What is important is the prevailing moral climate and social philosophy toward life and nature. Peace, equality, and social justice will come only when the attitude of the nation is transformed from one of self-interest and apathy to one of compassion and generosity.

THE PROGRESSIVE COUNTERREVOLUTION

The 1990s revolution, armchair liberals will be happy to note, does not include riots, police confrontations, or even mass demonstrations. Our weapons are not guns or rocks; instead, we will use the technological weapons of our time: computers, faxes, letter writing and telephone campaigns, stockholder resolutions, publicity, litigation, lobbying, consumerism, education, voter registration drives, public awareness building, boycotts, referendums, community action, and the ballot box.

Our revolution will be civilized, but it will require action. We will have to mobilize political forces to replace Republicans and Democrats alike, both nationally and locally, with progressive politicians; to campaign for the passage of local referendums; and to support incumbent progressives. Public awareness projects, from door-to-door canvassing to national media campaigns, will need volunteer support. Consumer awareness campaigns to promote socially and environmentally responsible companies will require widespread participation. Letter writing, fax, and telephone campaigns will also require assistance.

The revolution will require committed citizens acting on their ideals and vision. It will require time, money, and effort. It will require collaboration and a sharing of concerns, priorities, and possibilities. It will require action to translate the Left's ideals and visions into sweeping political and economic change and a renewed America.

TIME FOR A THIRD PARTY?

Ralph Nader says that the Democratic party is "so bankrupt it doesn't matter if it wins any elections." Democratic Socialists of America co-chairperson Barbara Ehrenreich agrees: "The Democratic party is run by the money people." As a result, says Tony Mazzocchi, secretary-treasurer of the Oil, Chemical, and Atomic Workers union, the Democratic party "is not going to challenge the major corporations in America." Progressive Democrat Jim Hightower argues, however, that "it's more productive and easier to take over the Democratic Party than to create a third party." Progressive author Frances Fox Piven agrees. "It could be terrible," says Piven. "So long as [Jesse] Jackson seems committed to the Democratic Party, third-party efforts will split progressives in the United States." To the contrary, NOW's former president and third-party advocate, Eleanor Smeal, argues that since the national Democratic candidates "won't talk about [feminist] issues...and always fails anyway...we have nothing to lose" by forming a third party.

And so the debate as to whether the progressive Left should go it alone or work through the Democratic party continues. While the Democratic Socialists of America and most of the Rainbow Coalition continue to pursue their political agendas through the Democratic party, other members of the progressive Left have decided to explore the creation of a new political party. NOW has launched the 21st Century party. Progressive labor leaders are currently organizing a new labor party. The Rainbow Coalition has spawned Campaign for a New Tomorrow. And the Green party continues to grow, with statewide ballot status in California and Alaska and active chapters in fifteen other states. The New Party, a recently launched social democratic party, is hoping to have an impact in state and local elections beginning in 1993. And statewide third parties such as the Progressive Vermont Alliance, Wisconsin's Labor/Farm party, and California's Peace and Freedom party continue to make political inroads in their regions.

Behind all this feverish third-party activity is the widespread belief that both the Republican and Democratic parties predominately represent the interests of their major corporate donors. With elite interests dominating both parties, the environmental movement, labor, people of color, women, and the poor have little, if any, influence on public and economic policy. "The feeling is that Democrats have promised (the people) and not delivered," writes Martha Burk, head of the Center for Advancement of Policy, while "Republicans have promised (the corporations) and delivered, and both outcomes are bad for the average American."

American progressives have watched with prideful envy as the Canadian social democratic party, the New Democratic Party (NDP), has racked up tremendous political gains. With growing support among a broad Canadian constituency—labor, people of color, women, farmers, and environmentalists—the NDP is now the controlling political party in the provinces of Ontario, British Columbia, and Saskatchewan and in the Yukon Territory. NDP usually wins about a fifth of the national vote; in late 1990, it held 43 of the 295 seats in the Canadian parliament. Largely as a result, Canadians now enjoy national health insurance, equal pay for women, a nationalized pension plan, government-subsidized college tuition, a comprehensive unemployment insurance program, and strong labor unions.

Unfortunately, the United States, unlike Canada and the European nations, has no mass socialist or progressive political party. Largely as a result, the American social-welfare state is among the weakest in the industrialized world, the American corporate elite hold an awesome influence over government policy, and the American electorate, alienated by its lack of real political choice, abstains more and more from participation in the political process.

The progressive answer to the American political dilemma is the establishment of a progressive political movement that, by addressing the needs and concerns of everyday Americans, can arouse the electorate to participate and thereby make a difference. The more difficult question, and the subject of continuing debate on the Left, is, How do we accomplish this goal?

Political developments will answer the question in time. Will the Democratic elite continue to move to the Right if they win the White House? Will an increase in the number of women in Congress increase the power of the forty or so progressive Democrats in Washington? And how successful will NOW, the Green party, and the Rainbow Coalition be in building a national political organization?

CHAPTER TWO

The Rise and Fall
of the Right

NOT VERY LONG AGO, AMERICA WAS MAKING
huge strides in social advancement. After a two-hundred-year struggle,
women and people of color had obtained full equality under the law.
Americans of all stripes were allowed into the mainstream of society.
New government initiatives were created to meet the needs of the poor,
the disabled, and the nation's children. And true democracy was prac-
ticed, as average citizens banded together so that their voices and demands could be heard.

The 1960s were a time when America had heroes of monumental
stature, such as John F. Kennedy and Martin Luther King, Jr. They were
joined by others with equally strong commitments, from Gloria
Steinem and Ralph Nader to Eugene McCarthy, Tom Hayden, and Malcolm X. During this historic but turbulent period, African-Americans,
white college students, Hispanics, women, Native Americans, war veterans, lesbian and gay activists, and the disabled participated in a drive
to restructure the economic, political, and social structure of America. It
was a movement to shift political power from the elite to the majority,
to redistribute wealth from the haves to the have-nots, to reorient
America's relationship with the Third World, and to provide the equal
opportunity guaranteed by the American Constitution to all Americans,
regardless of sex or race.

The movement had high goals, and although it fell short of some of them, it did achieve several notable successes. These included obtaining voting rights and affirmative action remedies for women and people of color and making a national commitment to help the poor and other oppressed Americans. The movement ended back-alley abortions, hastened the end of the Vietnam War, and put the health of the environment on the national agenda. Most important, the movement showed ordinary people that they did have political power.

In spite of its success, the movement ended as quickly as it had begun. The New Left, as the movement was called, thought it could change the world. But it quickly discovered that it had to fight not only against bigotry and imperialism, but also against the liberal elite— moderate and liberal corporate and political leaders whose power and wealth emanated from the status quo. By the early 1970s, according to Sheila Collins in *The Rainbow Challenge*, "most Movement activists felt as if they had been, like Sisyphus, pushing a boulder up a steep hill only to have it roll down again." Within a few years, the New Left was exhausted and demoralized, and the political climate of the country had shifted 180 degrees.

In the 1980s Ronald Reagan, Oliver North, and Donald Trump replaced heroes like Kennedy and King as national symbols. Practicing racism became acceptable again, even for presidential candidates. Eventually, extreme free enterprise produced economic decay the likes of which has not been seen since the 1930s, and the positive spirit and sense of community that prevailed in the 1960s were replaced by individualistic greed and self-interest.

In attempting to understand how America's political and social climate could have shifted so far so quickly, journalists, historians, and political analysts have offered varying theories on political and social change. Often cited among these is the concept of backlash, which concludes that the forces that moved America to the right stemmed from a negative reaction to change and its perceived cost.

Authors Thomas and Mary Edsall in *Chain Reaction*, and Susan Faludi, in *Backlash*, present a persuasive case for this backlash theory, the Edsalls for a backlash primarily against racial progress, Faludi for a backlash against women's rights.

The Edsalls see the backlash as the reaction of white Americans to the impact that social advances for minorities has had on their lives. In the Edsalls' view, school busing, neighborhood integration, affirmative action, and criminal rights, mixed with a deteriorating economy and an increasing tax burden, pushed a large number of white Democrats to the Republican party. "At the extreme," they write, "liberalism inflamed resentments when it required some citizens—particularly lower-income whites—to put homes, jobs, neighborhoods, and children at perceived risk in the service of bitterly contested remedies for racial discrimination and segregation." This resentment was "increasingly amplified and channeled" by the Right.

Faludi sees a backlash among males, especially the New Right leadership and the downscale "younger, poorer brothers of the baby boom" against women's equality. Faludi argues that many in media, political, and intellectual circles have attempted to pin the blame for social and economic ills, such as unemployment, declining wages, increasing divorce rates, and even crime, on the movement for women's equality. She cites, for instance, a 1982 Ronald Reagan speech in which he said that "part of the unemployment is not as much recession as it is the great increase . . . in women who are working today." "To some of the men falling back," writes Faludi, "it certainly has looked as if women have done the pushing."

Another author and social critic, Barbara Ehrenreich, also sees America's move to the right as a form of backlash. Ehrenreich, however, describes a backlash of educated middle-class liberals, from university professors to politicians, against the student left's desire to see the liberals' "cherished institutions in flames." The student left wanted to change the system, and middle-class liberals were part of the system: the student left saw the system as a core part of the problem, while middle-class liberals saw the system as the source of their status and economic well-being. As Ehrenreich puts it, "an elite can still be liberal in its attitudes toward those who are less favored. But an elite that feels beleaguered . . . is not likely to remain liberal for long."

Other social commentators, such as Harvard political economist Robert Reich and Berkeley psychologist David Barash, see liberalism's failure to spread the costs of affirmative action and poverty programs equally throughout society—exacerbated by increased competition for jobs and educational opportunities—as the cause of the movement toward conservatism. According to Reich,

> the extraordinary growth of the American economy in the 1960s made it possible for the nation to wage a war on poverty, and then

another on North Vietnam, while enjoying a broad rise in living
standards. . . . As the economy began to slow in the 1970s . . . [how-
ever], it was no longer possible for some groups to benefit without
the burden manifestly falling on others.

Barash states, "it is one thing to favor equal opportunity . . . but it is
quite another when people begin to feel they are being penalized so as to
improve opportunities for others."

Together, these explanations point to one very compelling reason
for the abrupt shift in the nation's political climate. First and foremost,
civil rights and affirmative action remedies, by not addressing the
imbalance in the nation's distribution of wealth, produced intra-class
warfare by heaping the cost of inclusion on already economically hard-
pressed working- and middle-class whites. Affirmative action, by opening the door for more women and people of color to participate in the
"mainstream" labor force, in effect increased the supply of labor. Unac-
companied by meaningful full-employment programs, large-scale
government work projects, coordination with industry, or any other
mechanism to address the newly expanding work force, affirmative action pitted white male workers against the new entrants: women and
minorities.

Asking the white working class to share its already meager slice of
America's economic prosperity was inequitable and politically unwise.
Many working-class whites' economic situation was little better than
that of minorities. In addition, according to Reich, the Left provided "no
convincing story to explain why this burden should fall so heavily upon
the shoulders of working-class Americans." For it was not white workers and their families who had benefited from slavery or the exploitation of Mexican, Chinese, and African-American laborers: business
interests had. And during the next two decades, it was business that
benefited again. The increase in the number of workers put downward
pressure on wages, while the resulting race and class conflicts increased
business's already immense political power by fracturing the consensus
of its opposition.

In effect, liberalism, while morally and politically motivated to assist the socially oppressed, had ignored more widespread economic oppression. In doing so, liberalism had ignored the white working class.
Although the social advancements of the 1960s were impressive, they
did not include national health insurance, full-employment programs,

progressive taxation, greater union power, and plant-closure restrictions.

Working-class women, for instance, who were given new choices through affirmative action and the feminist movement, found that without more sweeping changes these new choices actually made life more difficult for many. Even working women still bore primary responsibility for housekeeping and child-rearing, and the social changes they needed to lighten their double burden—better and more accessible child care, family-assistance grants, and family leave—were never put in place.

The failure to address the concerns of the entire working class extended beyond affirmative action policies to President Lyndon Johnson's Great Society and War on Poverty programs. Even though many of these programs—legal aid, college assistance, youth employment and job training programs, child development and nutritional programs, and income assistance—offered benefits to the poor and the middle class alike, they were presented as programs to eradicate the "culture of poverty" from America, programs established specifically for the poor. Even Michael Harrington, a committed poverty activist, described the poor as "internal aliens," people with a language, a psychology, a world view, and "a culture that is radically different from the one that dominates society." These characterizations, both from the Left and the Right, defined the War on Poverty programs not as insurance for "us" against economic setbacks, but as programs for "them." Despite the fact that two-thirds of the poor are white, "the early rhetoric of antipoverty policy," Reich says, "which linked the movement for black civil rights to the plight of the poor," conspired to make "them," in the eyes of the white middle-class, African-Americans.

This was a grave error, because the success of the New Deal approach to social justice and income redistribution had come, says Robert Kuttner, "via inclusion." Unlike the War on Poverty programs, Social Security, low-cost housing, and college loans were not presented as anti-poverty or welfare programs. "They defined needs," according to Kuttner, "that applied to a substantial majority of the electorate. They engendered a sense of egalitarianism and empathy and political cohesion . . . [which] built both civic and political community." Johnson's Great Society programs, however, became, to white Americans, just another expense that they had to bear on behalf of minorities.

In summary, although the backlash against the social gains of the

1960s was inflamed by the Right, the issues themselves are not without merit. In their desire to create a more equal society, the Left's leaders focused on race and gender and ignored economics. They failed to address the broader social question that Martin Luther King, Jr. asked in a 1967 address:

> One day we must ask the question, "Why are there 40 million poor people in America?" And when you begin to ask that question you are raising questions about the economic system, about a broader distribution of wealth. . . . One day we must come to see that an edifice which produces beggars needs restructuring.

Many of the social changes in the 1960s were implemented by the liberal elite, and not surprisingly, this elite did not question the system itself. The liberal elite was willing to work for positive social change, but not at the expense of challenging the free-market system. Unfortunately, legalistic progress—progress that does not address a power structure that allows the top 1 percent of the population to accumulate more wealth than the entire bottom 90 percent—will continue to lead to social discord as the various segments of American society fight for their shares of the economic pie.

THE RISE OF THE RIGHT

While the Left certainly made great progress during the 1960s, the seeds of conservatism's new popularity were sown at the same time. According to University of California sociologist Jerome Himmelstein, "the early 1960s witnessed an explosion of conservative activity." Contributions to the John Birch Society and other major right-wing organizations jumped from "only a few hundred thousand dollars a year in the late 1950s" to $7 million a year by 1964. New conservative organizations were formed, such as the Young Americans for Freedom and the American Conservative Union. And right-wing columnists such as William Buckley became mainstream—by the 1970s, Buckley had become one of the mostly widely syndicated columnists in the country.

During the late 1960s, the Right received an important and unexpected boost: the defection of a number of prominent liberal intellectuals, coined "neoconservatives," to the conservative cause. Alarmed by the New Left's desire to restructure America's political-economic system, the emergence of a popular antiwar movement, and the increasing emergence of participatory as opposed to representative politics, neoconservatives began a scathing attack on the principles and workings of liberalism.

The neoconservatives, who included Daniel Bell, Irving Kristol, George Gilder, Nathan Glazer, and Jeane Kirkpatrick, added a sense of intellectual legitimacy to the Right's viewpoint. "The first accomplishment of neoconservatism," says *Washington Post* journalist E. J. Dionne, "was to make criticisms of liberalism from the Right acceptable in the intellectual, artistic, and journalistic circles where conservatives had long been guarded with suspicion." Oxford political scientist Gillian Peele shares Dionne's opinion of the significance of neoconservatism. "The arguments of the neo-conservatives," writes Peele, "contributed greatly towards making the candidacy of Ronald Reagan and the kinds of policies which the Republican Party advocated in 1980 much more acceptable... and ensured that the Reagan assault on the White House was not dismissed by the media in the way that Barry Goldwater's was in 1964."

The writings of the neoconservatives, according to Peele, served to "remold [the] climate of opinion" in a number of areas important to the Right. Michael Novack, George Gilder, and Irving Kristol wrote passionately about the virtues of capitalism. Nathan Glazer and Daniel Patrick Moynihan, along with Novack, Kristol, and Daniel Bell, wrote at length about the growing number of professionals, the New Class, who were profiting from the growth in government-funded social programs. Their writings also vigorously analyzed the perceived failures of affirmative action programs, Johnson's War on Poverty, and other government attempts at social engineering. Jeane Kirkpatrick, Norman Podhoretz, and Kristol wrote extensively about the need to combat the spread of communism and support friendly Third World regimes unconditionally.

In addition to the intellectual assistance of neoconservatives, the conservative movement also benefited from an influx of right-wing corporate sponsors and the birth of the "New Right." During the 1970s, wealthy business people and their foundations poured money into existing and newly created conservative and extremist organizations. Among the largest contributors were the Coors family; Mellon Bank heir Richard Mellon Scaife; the John M. Olin Foundation, headed by former secretary of the treasury, William Simon; Richard DeVos, president of Amway Corporation; Robert Krieble, retired chairman of Loctite Corporation; Michael Valerio, owner of Papa Gino's Restaurants; and Smith Richardson Foundation, founded by the Richardson-Vick Company.

During the 1980s, as the reactionary viewpoints of the Right's think tanks were made legitimate by neoconservatives and the media, the Right's funding sources expanded to include much of corporate America. The Heritage Foundation, according to Jerome Himmelstein, received major financial support from the Chase Manhattan Bank, Dow Chemical, Pfizer, Reader's Digest, Mobil Corporation, and Smithkline Beckman. The American Enterprise Institute, where both Robert Bork and Jeane Kirkpatrick are resident scholars, received donations from six hundred corporations, including the Ford Motor Company, Times-Mirror, *The New York Times*, the Philip L. Graham Fund (*The Washington Post*), Weyerhaeuser, and General Electric.

With this substantial new funding, ambitious far-right organizers created and expanded a host of organizations for the purpose of political lobbying, such as Jesse Helms's National Congressional Club; for the development and promotion of far-right public policies, such as the Heritage Foundation; for politicizing evangelical Christians, such as the Moral Majority; and for single-issue advocacy, such as the anti-ERA Eagle Forum and the anti-union National Right to Work Committee.

The rapid formation of these new far-right organizations was led by a small band of reactionaries. Most notable among these was Paul Weyrich. Weyrich, who according to the *Washington Post* was an ally of German pro-Nazi politician Franz Josef Strauss, was involved in founding many of the New Right's organizations. With funding from Joseph Coors, Weyrich founded the powerful Heritage Foundation in 1973. Within the span of a few years, he also founded the Free Congress Foundation (originally the Committee for the Survival of a Free Congress) and assisted in the founding of the Moral Majority, International Policy Forum, Coalition for America, the National Pro-Family Coalition, Intercessors for America, and the House Republican Study Committee—a group that at one time listed 80 percent of Republican congressmen among its membership.

Interlocking board memberships allowed an elite few to wield control over the various elements of the New Right and to keep its various groups—anti-feminist, religious, pro-business, pro-military, pro-censorship—united. The New Right advocacy group Council for National Policy (CNP) is an excellent example of this integration. CNP lists among its current or former officers and board members Richard Shoff, former Indiana Ku Klux Klan leader; Paul Weyrich, founder of the Heritage Foundation; Pat Robertson, of the Christian Broadcasting Network; billionaire and former John Birch Society leader Nelson Bunker Hunt; Jesse Helms associate and "former" segregationist Tom Ellis; U.S. Senator William Armstrong (Colorado); Richard DeVos, president of Amway Corporation; Reed Larson, head of the National Right to Work Committee; Moral Majority leader Jerry Falwell; Don Wildmon, a leader of the censorship movement; and anti-feminist Phyllis Schlafly. In addition, other current or recently nominated CNP members include Robert Brown, publisher of *Soldier of Fortune*; James Quayle, Vice President Dan Quayle's father; and a host of former ambassadors and retired military officers, including Oliver North.

With generous funding and a strong organizational structure in place, the Right went to work on influencing the minds of America. Its think tanks produced reams of research on everything from the evils of government regulation to the harmful impact of feminism and affirmative action. A number of pro-conservative books, underwritten by right-wing financiers, were published and highly publicized. The most notable of these were sociologist Charles Murray's *Losing Ground*, funded by the Olin Foundation and Manhattan Institute, and George Gilder's *Wealth and Poverty*, funded by the Smith Richardson Foundation. Not only did these books—which praised free-market capitalism and advocated an end to social-welfare programs—receive widespread media attention, but they also, according to Himmelstein, "inspired conservative cadres within the administration."

The Right also launched an extensive lobbying and propaganda campaign. In Washington and in state capitals, right-wing lobbyists argued their positions with legislators while their political action committees (PACs) financed ultraconservative candidates and targeted liberals and moderates for defeat. At the same time, a sophisticated flood of direct mail poured right-wing literature into millions of American homes. The media were besieged with articles, studies, and surveys supporting the right's position on numerous social issues, and many of these found their way into news reports, talk shows, and editorial pieces. According to Susan Faludi, these themes even found their way into television programs and movies.

In addition, the Right had, in effect, its own broadcast network, the electronic church. Of the top six television evangelists, four—Pat Robertson, Jerry Falwell, Jimmy Swaggart, and Jim Bakker—preached the anti-individual rights, anti-abortion, and anti-ERA rhetoric of the Right, and numerous other right-wing ministers preached the same message on thousands of radio stations across the country.

THE EMERGING MAJORITY

During the early 1970s, America was in social decline. The Vietnam War had split the country apart. Foreign-policy liberals lamented the fact that America had engaged in such an immoral war, while conservatives lamented the fact that America had lost. The Vietnam debacle was followed by Watergate, which disgraced not only Nixon but the country as well.

By the mid-1970s, the economy had begun to deteriorate. Unemployment, plant closings, inflation, and crime were all on the rise, while workers' wages were in decline. In the late 1970s, a second OPEC oil shock, the invasion of Afghanistan by the Soviet Union, and the Iranian hostage crisis suggested to many that America was becoming increasingly impotent in world affairs.

In this environment, the Right's message blaming the Washington liberal establishment, people of color, women, and homosexuals for the nation's problems found a willing audience. Many social conservatives, evangelical Christians, and Catholic voters responded eagerly to the Right's call for the restoration of school prayer and an end to abortion, the ERA, pornography, "nontraditional textbooks," and gay rights. Financially beleaguered blue-collar voters embraced the Right's call for an end to affirmative action programs. Some homemakers, intimidated by the feminist movement, eagerly supported the Right's "Stop ERA" campaign. Foreign-policy hawks of all stripes, dismayed by the country's setbacks in international affairs, responded to the call for a massive new military buildup. And the business community and wealthy individuals applauded the Right's stand on tax relief and reduction in governmental regulations.

Through the construction of a "populist" platform, the Right shrewdly managed to persuade lower- and middle-income voters to abandon their class interests—higher wages, progressive taxation, and union protection—and join in an unholy alliance with business and the affluent in the Republican party. By the presidential election of 1980, the Right had assembled a broad coalition of high-income economic conservatives, evangelical Christians, midwestern social conservatives, and former blue-collar Democrats who had supported George Wallace's bid for the presidency in 1972. It was this unlikely coalition that led Ronald Reagan to victory over Jimmy Carter in 1980.

RUNNING OUT OF STEAM

For a short time, the conservative movement was able to bridge the wide class and economic differences among its voters. The nucleus of this unifying strategy was a Reagan administration agenda that, at least on paper, included tax relief for all, deregulation, the restoration of school prayer, the elimination of legal abortion, the dismantling of affirmative action, reductions in government spending, and military expansion.

Over time, however, the wide gaps in the interests and priorities of the members of the conservative coalition began to take their toll. Segments of the business sector were the first to abandon the alliance. Many corporate leaders who supported trade and arms control with the Soviet Union saw the Right's "evil empire" rhetoric and rapid military build-up as irresponsible and dangerous. Large real estate investors, concerned about the impact of deteriorating urban areas on the value of their developments, also jumped ship. In addition, many in the financial services industry had serious concerns about the exploding budget deficit and also abandoned the Reagan camp. By 1983 a substantial number of business leaders were lining up to provide financial support to the Democratic party's presidential candidates.

The business community's support for détente and a nuclear freeze forced Reagan to moderate his militant stance toward the Soviet Union, and in 1987 Reagan met Gorbachev in Moscow. The INF disarmament treaty that resulted threw the far Right into a monumental uproar. Howard Phillips, leader of the Conservative Caucus, branded Reagan a "useful idiot" of the USSR. Indeed, détente with the USSR, according to Jerome Himmelstein, "contradicted every conservative impulse."

Many of Reagan's more moderate supporters were also becoming alarmed, not by his shift in foreign policy, but by the presence of Nazi sympathizers and other radicals in the conservative camp. In 1984 *The*

Wall Street Journal published a story exposing a fund-raising letter signed by Ronald Reagan for white supremacist Roger Pearson. Pearson, who had served in editorial capacities at both the Heritage Foundation and the American Security Council, was famous for his 1969 monograph titled *Eugenics and Race*, in which he stated: "If a nation with a more advanced, more specialized, or in any way superior set of genes, mingles with, instead of exterminating, an inferior tribe, then it commits racial suicide."

In 1988 *The Philadelphia Inquirer*, *The Washington Jewish Weekly*, and *The Boston Globe* published stories about the Bush presidential campaign's use of Nazi sympathizers. According to the newspaper accounts, some of the Bush campaign's "ethnic advisors" were former officials of fascist groups such as Romania's Iron Guard, Latvia's Legion, and Hungary's Arrow Cross, who had collaborated with the Nazis during World War II. Another Bush advisor, Fred Malek, was forced to resign after *The Washington Post* reported that Malek had compiled a list of federal employees with "Jewish sounding" names while serving in the Nixon administration.

Another cause of alarm to some members of the conservative coalition was the rising influence of Christian Reconstructionists and others with reactionary religious beliefs. Christian Reconstructionists, who advocate replacing the American Constitution with a literal interpretation of biblical laws, served with Jerry Falwell and Phyllis Schlafly on the board of the Council for National Policy (CNP). One CNP board member, R. J. Rushdoony, whom investigative journalist Russ Bellant describes as the "ideological leader" of the Christian Reconstruction movement, advocates the abolishment of democracy, which he describes as a "heresy." Rushdoony also believes, according to *Christianity Today*, that, "true to the letter of Old Testament law, homosexuals . . . adulterers, blasphemers, astrologers, and others will be executed." Perhaps most remarkably, he also advocates instituting the death penalty for children who "disobey their parents."

Two other religious cults whose members rose to positions of prominence in the New Right were the Unification Church, led by Reverend Sun Myung Moon, and the Word of God (WOG). Followers and supporters of Moon—who, according to Bellant, "have called for the abolition of American democracy"—held leadership positions in the Heritage Foundation, Christian Voice, National Association of Christian Educators, and the Council for National Policy.

The "shepherding" cults, such as WOG, also had members in leadership positions in New Right organizations. These cults, according to Bellant, strive for total domination of their members by insisting that control of "one's personal life, choices of recreation, choices of spouse, weekly schedule of activities, and other matters must be approved by an appointed shepherd." WOG and other shepherding cult's members held leadership positions in the Heritage Foundation, the Free Congress Foundation, the Coalition for Revival, the Christian Voice, the National Pro-Family Coalition, the American Coalition for Life, CNP, and Intercessors for America. One notable WOG supporter, Connie Marshner—who Susan Faludi describes as "the highest level woman in the Heritage Foundation"—is also on the steering committee of the Coalition on Revival. The Coalition is a group that, according to Bellant, advocates replacing democracy with a totalitarian Christian republic and that has "developed detailed plans for taking over government, law, education, media, economics, and entertainment in the U.S. and Canada."

While the "more moderate" fundamentalist Christians may have been appalled at the growing influence of the religious cults, they were grappling with their own internal problems. By the late 1980s, the Moral Majority and a number of other right-wing religious organizations had folded, weakened by the moral failings of their leaders. In 1987, it emerged that pro-family minister Pat Robertson had lied about his wedding date to hide the fact that his child was conceived out of wedlock. Two other influential political evangelists also received highly embarrassing media scrutiny: Jimmy Swaggart for his involvement with prostitutes, and Jim Bakker for adultery, bribery, and fraud. Viewership of the Religious Right's television broadcasts nose-dived, and with it the influence of right-wing television evangelists.

Other highly publicized events were also working to splinter the conservative coalition. The Iran-contra arms-for-hostages scandal was only the largest of a long series of scandals in the Reagan administration. Twenty senior EPA officials, caught in a long-running scheme to favor corporate polluters, were either indicted, fired, or forced to resign. Wedtech brought to light the bribery, influence peddling, rigged contracts, and gross overcharges that were commonplace in the weapons procurement process; it also led to a federal grand jury investigation of Reagan's attorney general, Edwin Meese. Reagan's press secretary, Michael Deaver, under investigation for illegal lobbying activities, was convicted of perjury. In addition, the public was starting to catch wind of the magnitude of the theft and influence peddling rampant in the savings and loan industry. And persistent rumors in the media of widespread fraud in the Department of Housing and Urban Development would later be found to be grossly understated—the agency and its administrators had misappropriated an estimated $8 billion of taxpayers' money. By the end of Reagan's second term, according to journalist Haynes Johnson, 138 administration officials had been investigated, indicted, or convicted.

The persistent and recurring scandals, writes Haynes Johnson, "led even some of Reagan's staunchest supporters to turn on him." After the full extent of the HUD scandal began to hit the newspapers, conservative columnist James Kilpatrick solemnly wrote:

> For conservative pro-Reagan Republicans (I count myself among them), these have been disheartening times. Since the first of the year, it has been one damn thing after another. . . . The scandals within the S & L [savings and loan] industry were bad enough. . . .
>
> What is more deeply disturbing is the unfolding story of scandals within the Department of Housing and Urban Development. The more one hears of this rotten affair, the worse it gets. . . . Let it be said up top: The primary responsibility for this debacle lies squarely in the lap of Ronald Reagan.

By the time Bush assumed the presidency, the strong conservative coalition of the early 1980s was only a shadow of its former self. Many New Right organizations were in financial disarray. The New Right's leading direct-mail fund-raiser, the Richard Viguerie Company, had gone bankrupt, while the National Conservative Political Action Committee, once the wealthiest PAC in the country, was deep in debt. Even the venerable John Birch Society, the secret society for upper-income bigots and fanatical anti-communists, was rumored to be in financial trouble. As Himmelstein put it, "the New Right's day [had] passed."

As Bush struggled through his first term, a nagging recession and continuing media reports of the economic mess Reagan left behind— the budget deficit, the S & L bailout, the increasingly unequal distribution of wealth—caused many middle-class voters to question their support of conservatism. Indeed, Bush's overall popularity, as measured by presidential approval ratings, plunged over fifty percent from its high during the Persian Gulf War. In addition, Bush's tax and free-trade policies had contributed to a loss of faith among many of the hard-core members of the Right that culminated in a symbolic challenge in the 1992 Republican primary from the ultra-conservative Patrick Buchanan.

WHAT WAS THE MESSAGE?

Throughout the Reagan presidential reign, the national media, the Right, and even many of the Democratic party elite trumpeted the new Reagan "mandate." It was a mandate, declared by the voters, it was said, for less government, lower taxes, increased military spending, a reduction in social programs, and a halt to affirmative action. To many political analysts, Reagan's landslide victories signaled a realignment of lower- and middle-income voters away from the economic liberalism of the "New Deal Coalition" toward Reagan's free enterprise principles. Columnist James Kilpatrick, writing for *The Nation's Business*, called the election of Reagan and of several other conservatives to Congress "the clearest mandate for change since Franklin D. Roosevelt licked Herbert Hoover in 1932." Political scientist and Mondale advisor William Galston declared that Americans "wanted to get government off their backs. Ronald Reagan's simple message was their wish was his command."

With advice like that, it is not surprising that Democratic presidential candidate Walter Mondale was trounced in 1984; the prevailing analysis of Reagan's landslides was dead wrong. White middle-class and working-class Americans had not become Reagan-like conservatives. They had voted for Reagan for three reasons. First, because he had an ideology—he stood for something—and the Democrat candidate did not. Second, because many working-class white voters had come to perceive the Democratic party as the party of special interests—minorities, the poor, feminists—and neither Carter nor Mondale had offered any compelling new message to counter this perception. Third, because the voters liked Reagan personally. Working-class voters, Robert Kuttner wrote, "liked Reagan's patriotism, his optimism, his faith in them, and they forgave his more bizarre positions on social and foreign-policy issues." Even a writer for the left-leaning *Nation* had nice words for Reagan's persona. "Compared with Lyndon Johnson, Richard Nixon, Gerald Ford, and Jimmy Carter," wrote Mark Green, "Ronald Reagan is stable, decisive, charming and damn nice."

In fact, voter exit polls showed that many people voted for Reagan *in spite of* his conservative ideology. In the 1984 presidential election, according to data from the University of Michigan National Election Surveys, Reagan's conservatism reduced his overall appeal among a substantial number of those who voted for him.

Conservatism's lack of popular appeal was also evident in the 1986 congressional elections. Without Reagan on the ballot, the Democratic party regained control of the Senate and widened its majority margin in the House. Even more significant, two groups who were formerly part of the New Right coalition—white Catholics and union members—had swung solidly back into the Democratic column.

Numerous polls taken during the decade also suggested that the vast majority of Americans were still practicing liberals. In 1982 a *Los Angeles Times* poll found that the public heavily favored government regulation of industry. When asked whether they favored "keeping" or "easing" regulations that President Reagan "says are holding back American free enterprise," a majority favored keeping regulations regarding the environment (49–28%), industrial safety (66–18%), the teenage minimum wage (58–29%), auto emission and safety standards (59–29%), federal lands (43–27%), and offshore drilling (46–29%).

The American public was also strongly in favor of more government. By 1985 polls found that Americans thought that the government was not spending enough on health, education, the environment, and fighting crime by margins of almost ten to one. By margins in excess of four to one, those surveyed also thought that the government was spending too little on public transportation, energy, and solving urban problems. A CBS News/*New York Times* poll found that 74 percent of the public supported a jobs program, even at the expense of increasing the size of the federal budget deficit.

In 1986 Harris polls found that only 19 percent of the American public felt that the business sector paid its fair share of taxes, while only 28 percent felt that business executives could be counted on to behave legally and ethically. A Gallup poll taken the same year showed that only 13 percent of Americans favored increases in defense spending. In addition, Harris polls showed that in 1986, 62 percent of Americans were opposed to aid to the Nicaraguan contras and 67 percent of what the Harris poll described as the "white Moral Majority followers" reacted negatively to Falwell's characterization of South African Archbishop Desmond Tutu as a "phony."

Despite the racist, sexist, and hypocritically moralistic tendencies of the Reagan administration and many of the Right's leadership, surveys suggested that this bigotry and intolerance was not shared by a majority of the public. According to a 1986 Gallup poll, only 13 percent of the public favored the banning of all abortions. In the mid-1980s, a Harris poll indicated that 73 percent of white parents whose children had been bused to achieve racial balance said that the experience was "very satisfactory." In another Harris survey, 85 percent of those polled agreed with the statement, "after years of discrimination, it is only fair to set up special programs to make sure that women and minorities are given every chance to have equal opportunities in employment and education."

What these surveys, exit polls, voting patterns, and sociological studies suggest is that the majority of Americans, including most of the white working and middle class, did not become Reagan conservatives. Instead, it suggests that the Left and the Democratic party, which have historically been aligned with these groups' economic and social beliefs, no longer met their needs.

The Left, impassioned by the moral high ground of achieving equality for women and minorities, saving the environment, helping the homeless, and bringing about world peace, had forgotten about the concerns of the working and middle classes: progressive taxation, job security, health care, better roads and mass transit systems, education, affordable housing, and fighting crime. In effect, the Left became a vehicle for upper-middle-class liberals' cultural interests, while the lower middle class was left out in the cold. E. J. Dionne, author of the aptly titled book *Why Americans Hate Politics*, writes, "When government was seen to fail on the basics . . . the broad American middle gave up on government. This message was misread by conservatives as a demand for less government when, in fact, it was a demand for better government."

The misreading of the middle class by both the Left and the Right has not only led to the flawed assumption that its political attitudes have changed, but it has also blinded the Left to this group's legitimate grievances. As Dionne points out,

> The revolt of the middle class against a growing tax burden was not an expression of selfishness but a reaction to the difficulties of maintaining a middle-class standard of living. Anger at the rising crime rates was not a covert form of racism but an expression of genuine

fear that society seemed to be veering out of control. Impatience
with welfare programs was sometimes the result of racial prejudice,
but it was just as often a demand that certain basic rules about the
value of work be made to apply to all.

But today, more than ten years after the working and middle classes
cast their votes for Reagan, much of the Left seems as out of touch with
the majority of Americans as ever. Some labor leaders seem more interested in helping to destroy Third World leftist movements than in
challenging the power of corporate America. Some peace and environmental activists propose sweeping reforms, such as demilitarization or
closing toxic industries, without proposing alternatives for workers who
they would displace. And the national Democratic elite continues to
march to the Right in an effort to look like an elephant instead of a don-
key.

To get back in touch with its core constituency, Kuttner suggests
that the Democratic party take a lesson from the 1988 Jesse Jackson
Rainbow Coalition Campaign:

> It was Jackson who demonstrated the latent power of economic pop-
> ulism. . . . [Jackson] also had a very clear message. And it was a mes-
> sage directed squarely at the Party's long-ignored working-class
> base. . . . In state after state, white working class voters declared that
> of all the candidates, only Jackson seemed to be speaking to
> them. . . . He became the first candidate since Robert Kennedy to win
> the hearts of both black and white working people.

Jackson's message, a theme that garnered him more than seven million votes in the 1988 Democratic presidential primaries, was simple. He
advocated broad-based social justice. Social justice means fairer distribution of the nation's assets and income via progressive taxation. It means
meaningful economic assistance for the working poor, the disabled, the
elderly, the unemployed. It means that corporations, in return for
countless governmental favors, owe it to the American people to invest
in domestic job creation and job security. It means good schools, streets
safe from crime, national health care, and a right to clean air and water.
It means equality and fairness, not only for all Americans, but for the
people of the Third World as well.

No, formerly Democratic working-class voters did not become

Reaganites. They were protesting having the full cost of affirmative action placed on their backs instead of sharing it with business and the affluent. They were searching for someone to do something about ever-increasing plant closings, declining wages, and rising payroll taxes. In retrospect, most can see that Reagan was not the answer. But neither are the conservative Democrats.

CHAPTER THREE

America: The World's Leading Capitalist

THE UNITED STATES OF AMERICA IS THE MOST capitalistic of the major industrialized nations. This is not because America is a leader in per-capita gross domestic product, per-capita income, or productivity growth, for it is not. America does, however, have one of the most pro-business, inequitable, and inhumane socioeconomic systems in the industrialized world.

When America's socioeconomic system is compared to the systems of the other major industrialized nations—Britain, Germany, France, Italy, Sweden, Japan, and Canada—America consistently ranks near the bottom in fairness and equality. In almost all categories that measure economic equity—progressive taxation and income distribution; concern for social welfare, such as government spending on health and education; and worker rights, such as union influence and vacation and maternity leave—citizens of most other industrialized countries fare far better than Americans.

America has long ranked last among major industrialized nations in spending on entitlement programs. In his 1984 book *The New American Poverty*, Michael Harrington cites a study that compares America's social-welfare spending—Social Security, unemployment insurance, welfare, Medicaid, Medicare, and food stamps—with that of other countries. If one looks at the percentage of gross national product (GNP) spent on social programs, Harrington says, "there is a marked contrast between this country and all the other (relatively) rich nations."

In Sweden, which has a strong welfare-state, a 1970s study by the Organization for Economic Cooperation and Development found that only 3.5 percent of Swedes had incomes below the poverty line, compared to 13 percent of Americans. Correspondingly, Sweden's infant mortality rate was almost half that of the United States. Harrington also cites a study showing that, in the 1970s, the former West Germany spent more than twice as much of its GNP on social programs as did the United States. Even Japan, another very capitalistic society, spent more of its GNP on domestic programs than the United States. The American welfare state, Harrington concluded, "is the cheapest in the advanced capitalist world."

Numerous other international comparisons support Harrington's conclusion. America and South Africa are the only two industrialized nations without national health insurance. In addition, Marian Wright Edelman, of the Children's Defense Fund, points out that while seventy nations assist pregnant women financially and offer medical care, and sixty-three nations provide a family allowance, the United States provides neither. Nor does the United States provide or require employers to provide paid—or even unpaid—maternal or parental leave. Most other industrialized countries do, ranging from twelve weeks at 80 percent of pay in Japan and fifteen weeks at 60 percent in Canada to thirty-five weeks at 100 percent in Finland and thirty-eight at 90 percent in Sweden.

An international comparison by the Brookings Institution also shows that the United States spends less on the needs of its citizens than any major industrialized nation. Using 1986 data, the study found that in America, the ratio of nondefense-related state, local, and federal government spending to GNP is one of the lowest in the major industrialized world: while the American government spent 31 percent of the country's GNP on health, education, welfare, and the public infrastructure, Japan spent 32 percent; Britain 41 percent, West Germany 45 percent, France 50 percent, and Sweden double the U.S. level at 62 percent.

Another international study found that the United States spends far less on its public infrastructure than other major industrialized nations. The study showed that the U.S. government's net investment in roads, airports, public buildings, sewers, subways, parks, and bridges from 1980 to 1989 amounted to a meager three-tenths of one percent of its gross domestic product during the period. In contrast, Canada spent 1.8 percent, Britain 2 percent, Germany 3.7 percent, Italy 4.8 percent, and Japan 5.7 percent of gross domestic product on building and maintaining their infrastructures.

As befits the world's leading capitalist, the income gap between rich and poor is wider in America than in other major industrialized nations. In *The Politics of Rich and Poor*, political analyst Kevin Phillips cites a 1984 *Los Angeles Times* study on worldwide income distribution. The study showed that the ratio of income received by the richest 20 percent versus the income received by the poorest 20 percent was more than twice as large in America as in Japan, Sweden, and the former West Germany, and significantly larger than in France, Great Britain, and Canada. A more recent United Nations study of income equality found the same result. Using income data from 1980 to 1988, the U.N. study found that, with the lone exception of Australia, the United States had the highest rate of income inequality among the top twenty-one industrialized nations. Another study of income equality, the Atkinson Inequality Index, rated America's income distribution the most unequal among the major industrial nations.

Not surprisingly, America also has one of the widest gaps between executive and worker pay. Despite declining corporate profitability, a 1988 *Business Week* survey found that the average CEO at America's largest companies made ninety-three times as much as the average factory worker. When CEOs of small and medium companies are included, the gap between the average worker and the average CEO drops to 17.5 times. This is in contrast, reports Michael Wolff in *Where We Stand*, to multiples of 11.6 in Japan, 6.5 in Germany, 8.9 in France, and 9.6 in Canada. Even worse, while *Business Week* reports that average annual compensation for CEOs rose to $1.9 million in 1990, the U.S. Census Bureau reports that during the same period, almost one in five year-round, full-time workers earned an income below the poverty level.

America also has one of the most pro-business, regressive tax structures in the industrialized world. In 1988 American corporations' share of the federal tax burden was only 13 percent, down from 32 percent in 1952. In addition, a maximum tax rate of 31 percent for individuals means that billionaires pay taxes at the same rate as much of the middle class. "The U.S. tax burden on the wealthy," says Wolff, "is among the lightest in the developed world." At the same time, payroll taxes eat up almost 10 percent of the income of the average worker but take a much smaller proportion of income from the rich, since they are a flat-rate tax and only apply to the first $53,400 in income. "No other democratic country," exclaims New York senator Daniel Patrick Moynihan, "takes as large a portion of its revenue from working people at the lower end of the spectrum and as little from persons who have property or high incomes."

As one would expect in an overwhelmingly pro-business society, American businesses wield virtually uncontested control of the country's labor force. The United States has the lowest rate of unionization in the industrialized world. By 1991, the percentage of the American work force that was unionized had dropped to 16.4 percent versus 26.8 percent in Japan, 34.6 percent in Canada, 33.8 percent in Germany, and 41.5 percent in the United Kingdom. This low rate of unionization, combined with anti-labor government policies, gives American workers little protection against declining wages, job exportation, mass layoffs, and unsafe corporate production practices.

The United States has the highest occupational fatality rate in the industrialized world. Calling occupational accidents "a silent epidemic," health and safety activist Nancy Lessin reports that "people are being maimed, mangled, killed, and poisoned in the workplace." During a single year, according to the National Safe Workplace Institute, approximately 11,000 American workers are killed on the job. Nine million more are injured, and 70,000 of these injuries lead to permanent disability.

According to Barbara Brandt, of the Shorter Work-Time Group of Boston, "almost every other industrialized nation (except Japan) has fewer annual working hours and longer vacations than the United States." In contrast to the United States, she reports, many European unions were successful in reducing work-weeks during the 1980s: for example, one very large West German union won a 37.5-hour work-week in 1987; some British workers won a 37-hour work week in 1990; and in the early 1980s, France passed legislation declaring a 39-hour work week. Meanwhile, Harvard economist Juliet Schor reports, Americans are working an average of 160 hours a year more than they did some twenty years ago—the equivalent of almost a whole extra month of work. Americans also work more than workers elsewhere: Schor points out that "[Americans] work about 320 hours more per year than workers in such countries as Germany and France." In addition, America is one of the few industrialized countries without mandated vacation leave. German law mandates a minimum of three vacation weeks, while Sweden, Spain, and France require businesses to give employees a minimum of five weeks' vacation.

The United States is one of the few industrialized countries that relies on the free market—in other words, the whims of business—to meet the economic needs of the country. The majority of industrialized nations use national economic planning and full-employment policies to promote national economic priorities. "Indeed, when we look across the spectrum of paternalistic, conservative, or socialist-minded capitalisms," write economists Lester Thurow and Robert Heilbroner, "we see that virtually all of them rely heavily on government-private cooperation to attain desired micro and macro goals, and to minimize the problems of capitalism's own workings. In this spectrum, the United States and Britain are almost alone in their declared intention of rolling back the influence of government and allowing the spontaneous forces of the market to become the main guides for the system."

In Japan, the government plots and coordinates labor strategies and national economic goals with big business, banks, and labor. In France, there is an elaborate goal-setting process involving industry, labor, and government. In Germany, banks and big business work closely with the government—with input from trade unions, who by law maintain seats on corporate boards. And in Sweden, a partnership between business, labor, and government maintains full employment through a nationwide job-listing service, subsidized job training and retraining, and subsidies for locating industries in underemployed communities.

But in America, the economy and the work force are largely at the mercy of big business. And while the government can give to big business in an attempt to influence economic policy, it cannot guarantee what it will receive in return. For example, in 1979 Congress voted to guarantee $1.2 billion in loans to save Chrysler from bankruptcy. The rationale behind this act of corporate socialism was that it would save American jobs. By 1985, however, Chrysler employed one-third fewer workers than it did in 1979, since more and more of its cars and parts were manufactured outside the United States.

In 1981 the government gave multinational corporations huge tax cuts to stimulate job production in America. Instead, many corporations invested their tax savings in job-reducing corporate buy-outs and in low-labor-cost countries such as Korea, Hong Kong, Taiwan, Singapore, and Mexico. In Mexico's free-trade zone alone, U.S. corporations built almost 1,800 manufacturing plants, where they transferred approximately 500,000 U.S. jobs during the 1980s. Accordingly, by the late 1980s a full 29 percent of America's "foreign imports" came from plants owned by American corporations. Overall, according to liberal economists such as Robert Kuttner and Benjamin Friedman, net business investment in job-producing plants and machinery stagnated or actually declined after the 1981 tax cut.

The United States has also fallen behind much of the industrialized world in energy conservation. The United States, with 5 percent of the world's population, consumes 27 percent of the world's oil and produces almost 32 percent of the world's industrial waste. It spends a full 10 percent of GNP—twice the level of Japan and significantly higher than Germany—on energy. But instead of following the lead of other nations and developing a conservation policy, the Bush administration recently offered a new *energy* policy, a policy that calls for expanded offshore drilling, opening the pristine Alaska National Wildlife Refuge to oil exploration, and the inauguration of a new generation of nuclear power plants.

THE COST OF CAPITALISM

In an overwhelmingly pro-business society, grave social costs are to be expected, since the country's assets are used predominately to seek economic growth and profit, not social well-being. And indeed, America suffers from widespread environmental degradation and urban decay, and rates of illiteracy comparable to some Third World countries. In addition, our children suffer: the child poverty rate in America averages four times the rate in other major industrialized nations, and America ranks a lowly twenty-fourth in infant mortality.

But one would also assume that America has obtained some benefit in return—at a minimum, capitalistic gains such as dominance in world trade, increased industrial productivity, and rapid economic growth. The fact is, however, that being the leading capitalistic nation has yielded America little.

The average American's standard of living, as measured by the 1990 United Nations Human Development Index, ranked seventh when compared to standards of living worldwide. The nation's per-capita GDP has fallen below that of Sweden, Norway, Germany, Finland, Japan, and

Switzerland. The nation's rate of productivity growth—increase in goods or services produced per worker—and real average worker earnings have been declining for twenty years. Since 1973 average real weekly earnings have fallen 14.3 percent, and since 1978 the number of working poor—employed persons earning below the poverty level—has risen by 66 percent.

In 1980 the United States had a surplus in foreign trade—exports over imports—of $32.1 billion. By 1988, that surplus had turned into a $111 billion deficit. In addition, America's debt burden and budget deficit have also soared. In 1980, total debt stood at $914 billion and the budget deficit stood at $74 billion. By 1991, however, the nation's debt had reached $3.7 trillion dollars while the budget gap was over $350 billion.

In sum, America's preoccupation with unrestrained free-market capitalism has cost our society dearly. Other countries are not only faring better than the United States economically, but they are doing so with far more socially equitable economic systems. In fact, there appears to be some correlation—unseen by America's elite—between a stronger welfare state and economic progress.

In a study of national economic growth from 1930 through 1984, historian Robert S. McElvaine compared growth under Democratic presidents to growth under Republican, and presumably more conservative, presidents. What he found was startling. During Democratic administrations, GNP growth averaged a whopping 5.11 percent: more than six times faster than GNP growth under Republican administrations, which averaged only eight-tenths of 1 percent.

An interesting historical phenomenon called "Fordism" also challenges the wisdom of America's current economic direction. Early in this century, when Henry Ford wanted to create a mass market for his Model T, he realized that working Americans would have to earn higher wages in order to afford cars. Therefore, he dramatically raised his workers' wages—earning prompt attacks from his fellow industrialists for being a "socialist."

Ford argued that "in underpaying men, we are preparing a generation of underfed children who will be physically and morally undernourished; we will have a generation of workers weak in body and spirit." Other capitalists grudgingly followed Ford's lead, and, according to Michael Harrington, began to support what has been called "welfare capitalism." These Ford-inspired "trickle-up" economic policies led to one of the strongest periods of real income growth in history.

Harvard economist Robert Reich points out that countries with strong unions and higher wages produce higher-quality products, have faster-increasing worker productivity, and suffer fewer costly labor disputes. "In the mid-1980s," he reports, "the average number of days per year lost to industrial disputes for every one thousand employees was over 1,000 in the United States and over 800 in Britain, compared to 45 in Sweden, 250 in Japan, and 85 in West Germany." The anti-union environment of the United States during Reagan's term, and of Britain under Thatcher, carried substantial costs.

In addition to the correlation between stronger unions and stabilized production, Reich argues that because countries like Germany, Sweden, and Japan have full-employment policies and encourage worker participation, the workers in these countries are not resistant to automation or to innovations that lead to increased productivity. "Workers in these countries understand that their fates are tied to the profitability and competitiveness of their industries. They [the workers] are the ultimate beneficiaries of productivity improvements." In contrast, "American (and British) workers," writes Reich, are "notoriously suspicious of automation, mechanization, or other innovations to improve productivity—and for good reason, since their jobs may be jeopardized as a result." Accordingly, not only is productivity increasing at a faster rate in heavily unionized countries than in the United States, but "the quality of products made in America or Britain is widely considered to be inferior to those of West Germany or Japan."

Environmentalists also point out the negative impact of free markets on prosperity. They note that the during the 1980s, the most energy-efficient countries, notably the former West Germany and Japan, were the biggest economic successes. And author Craig Canine points out that if the United States pursued energy conservation to the extent that Japan has, it could save up to $2.2 trillion over the next twenty years. Oil imports alone, he estimates, could be reduced by as much as 3.5 million barrels a day.

Except for a fortunate few, America's position as one of the most capitalistic countries in the world offers few benefits. It certainly does not benefit the average citizen, nor does it benefit the country as a whole. America desperately needs fundamental changes in how it conducts business. It needs an economic strategy that addresses the distribution of wealth, social welfare, and environmental health. It needs an economic system that measures success not just by the growth of GNP and corporate profits, but also by the improvement of living standards for average Americans.

REAGANOMICS

Over the past hundred years, America's economy has tended to lean toward the free-market end of what economists call the "welfare state" or "mixed economy." Although the term "mixed economy" is used to describe the economies of virtually all of the industrialized nations, the degree of government intervention versus private capitalism varies widely from nation to nation. Scandinavian countries such as Sweden and Finland, and France under the leadership of Socialist President François Mitterrand, all lean, as Britain did before the election of Margaret Thatcher, toward the socialist end of the spectrum. These countries have or had heavy government involvement in the economy, including government ownership of crucial industries, full-employment policies, and socialized medicine. Conversely, the United States tends to rely heavily on private capital—the free market—to meet the needs of its population.

Under the Reagan and Bush administrations, however, the American economy was pushed toward a free-market extreme. Essential industries that were once regulated to protect their and the public's interests, such as airlines, trucking, banking, and savings and loan institutions, were decimated by deregulation. The health and safety protection afforded the public through government agencies such as the Environmental Protection Agency and the Occupational Safety and Health Administration were dangerously eroded. And government involvement in the health, education, and income maintenance of the American public was severely curtailed.

Indeed, in 1980 presidential candidate Ronald Reagan's proposed economic agenda was a godsend for free-market economists, libertarians, and traditional conservatives. It was also extremely attractive to the average American, who was unable to read between the lines. Reagan promised lower taxes, more jobs, lower inflation, less government regulation, and a stronger defense. After his election, armed with a "new" economic theory called supply-side economics and a Heritage Foundation plan titled *Mandate for Leadership* (which essentially recommended the elimination of Franklin Roosevelt's New Deal and Lyndon Johnson's Great Society programs), Reagan began to impose his free-market experiment on America.

Unfortunately for America, free-market theory had already been proved wrong in the 1920s, and it would be proved wrong again, just as George Bush predicted when he called Reagan's proposed policies "voo-doo economics" in the 1980 campaign. What Bush and many others knew all too well was that despite a new name—supply-side econo-mics—there was really nothing new about Reagan's economic agenda. It was a recycled version of the Calvin Coolidge-style economics that had been so soundly discredited during the Great Depression. Even Re-publican political analyst Kevin Phillips had to admit that "most of the Reagan era's legislative and regulatory approaches were familiar from prior conservative periods: taxes were eliminated or reduced; discretion-ary federal domestic outlays for low-income and Democratic constitu-encies were reduced; federal regulatory agencies were restrained; federal merger law enforcement was relaxed; money was intermittently tight and real interest high, reflecting a preference for creditors over debt-ors."

Reservations about Reaganomics were widespread among the eco-nomically astute. Nobel Laureate and economist James Tobin predicted that supply-side economics would "redistribute wealth, power, and op-portunity to the wealthy and powerful and their heirs." Supply-side economics was "an economic theory based on alchemy," according to investment banker Peter Solomon; a scheme to reduce the size of the federal government by producing "horrendous deficits," claimed *The New York Times*; a giveaway to the rich that would not encourage "productive" investment, wrote economist Lester Thurow; "social secu-rity for the disabled large corporation," said economic historian Emma Rothschild; and "class warfare," according to historian Arthur Schlesinger.

The proposed tax cuts and regulatory cutbacks were extremely at-tractive to big business, however. Hence, business lobbied hard for their passage, leading to what journalist William Greider described as a "bid-ding war" between Republicans and Democrats as to who could be "more generous" to big business. *Congressional Quarterly* described the phenomenon as "an amazing spectacle . . . Democrats trying to out-bid Republicans for the affections of the business community." Indeed, without the support of powerful pro-business Democratic congressmen and senators, many Reaganomics giveaways to big business would not have been possible.

In July 1981 Reagan's Economic Recovery Tax Act was passed. This act, which cut taxes by $749 billion over five years, heavily favored corporations and the affluent. In 1983, the percentage of federal tax receipts paid by corporations fell to a meager 6.2 percent, down from 21 percent in 1980 and 39 percent in the 1950s. More than a third of all profitable corporations were able to avoid paying any taxes at all.

Corporations were not the only beneficiaries of Reagan's generosity. The 1981 tax bill also provided substantial benefits to high-income taxpayers by cutting their tax rates 25 percent and decreasing both capital gains and inheritance taxes. By 1989 taxes paid by individuals and families earning between $500,000 and $1 million, according to *Philadelphia Inquirer* reporters Donald L. Barlett and James B. Steele, had fallen 45 percent from 1970 levels.

For working-poor and middle-class wage earners, the effects of the so-called tax cuts were altogether different. To restore much of the revenue lost to tax breaks for the wealthy, the White House and Congress created the Social Security funding crisis—a looming future deficit in the mythical Social Security Trust Fund if workers did not cough up higher payroll taxes. In fact, there is no Social Security Trust Fund. Current payroll deductions go directly to current Social Security recipients. Today's excess payroll taxes are used to fund the federal government's general operating expenses; Social Security could just as easily, and much more equitably, be paid from income tax revenues. "Most economists agree," say Neil Howe and Phillip Longman in *The Atlantic Monthly*, "that Social Security will not offer large categories of younger participants anything approaching a fair market return on what they paid into the system." (In contrast, they report that today's retirees will receive between two and ten times the amount they have paid in, assuming they invested in Treasury bonds.) Nonetheless, in 1983, the governing elite soaked workers with a $200 billion increase in payroll taxes.

Since approximately three-quarters of all wage earners pay more in payroll taxes than they do in federal income taxes, the result of this tax increase was obvious and swift. By 1985 total federal taxes paid by the bottom 20 percent of all households had increased by a whopping 26 percent from 1980 levels.

Reaganomics did not stop with shifting tax burdens from the rich to the poor. It went on to attack all impediments to corporate growth and profits, including unions, decent wages, environmental protection, consumer-safety regulations, and regulations that restrict industry practices. Reagan himself led the assault on unions. He instituted what Michael Harrington called "the largest mass firings in labor history" when he destroyed the air traffic controllers' union during its illegal 1981 strike—a union that, ironically enough, had gone against labor at large and supported Reagan's candidacy in 1980. This event, however, was only the beginning. According to economists Charles Wilber and Kenneth Jameson, "[Reagan let] business know that the federal government would not interfere with union-busting tactics used to control wage costs. . . . In the ensuing years business adopted a policy of wage reductions, plant relocations, strategic bankruptcy filings, and replacement of union labor with non-union labor."

The assault on unions went beyond the law. Harvard Law School professor Paul Weiler has estimated that "by 1985, one in ten pro-union workers was illegally discharged." He also reported that the number of charges of unfair labor practices soared during the 1980s, resulting in an average two-year delay before the National Labor Relations Board (NLRB) could even process charges.

Corporations had the Reagan-packed federal courts and the NLRB on their side. With their blessing, corporations resorted to bankruptcy, worker lockouts, hiring scabs as permanent replacements, plant relocations, and industrial spies and anti-union consultants. As a result, union membership declined dramatically during the decade. With it went workers' wages. By 1986, according to the National Committee on Pay Equity, the inflation-adjusted annual earnings of male high school graduates aged twenty-five to thirty-four had dropped 16 percent since 1973.

Although there was a net increase in jobs during the Reagan era, this increase was concentrated in part-time jobs without benefits and in the lower-paying service sectors of the economy. In fact, "among the fastest-growing of all careers," according to Robert Reich, "[are] custodians and security guards." Wilber and Jameson cite evidence that suggests that as many as 60 percent of the estimated 12 million new jobs paid less than $7,000 a year. The number of full-time workers whose 1990 earnings fell below poverty-level income for a family of four—$12,195—rose from 12.1 percent of the work force in 1979 to 18 percent in 1990. The young fared even worse: the percentage of full-time workers aged eighteen to twenty-four whose earnings were below poverty levels rose from 22.9 percent in 1979 to 43.4 percent in 1990. As a result of the decline in wages, nearly 60 percent of Americans whose incomes fall below the poverty line, says Reich, come from a household where at least one member is in the workplace.

Reagan also set his sights on environmental, worker-safety, and consumer-protection regulations. The administration's initial attempts to reduce regulation were crude, consisting of obviously pro-business appointments to regulatory agencies. The most blatant of Reagan's appointments were Anne Burford as head of the Environmental Protection Agency (EPA) and James Watt as Secretary of the Interior. Under Burford, a former consultant for Dow Chemical headed up the EPA's regulatory reform effort, and an Exxon lawyer became general counsel. Meanwhile, Watt appointed the former general counsel of the Louisiana-Pacific Corporation, one of the nation's leading cutters of timber on public lands, to be assistant secretary of agriculture in control of the Forest Service. According to *The Chicago Tribune*, both Watt and Burford had "close personal associations" with right-wing financier Joseph Coors. Before coming to Washington, Watt was president of the Mountain States Legal Foundation, a group founded by Coors to fight environmental regulation.

In Washington, however, Watt became a public-relations nightmare. He insulted women, people of color, and the disabled. He bragged of his desire to sell off public lands to corporate interests and openly downplayed concerns about the future health of the environment by suggesting that the future might never come. "I don't know how many future generations," Watt told the House Interior Committee, "we can count on before the Lord returns." Watt so infuriated the public that a Sierra Club petition seeking his removal gathered more signatures than any other petition ever submitted to Congress. Shortly thereafter, Watt was summarily dumped.

Congressional investigations into allegations that Burford's EPA illegally favored industry over the public interest found that top EPA officials had indeed cooperated with major industrial polluters to reduce contamination standards and to lower the cost to industry of cleaning up toxic waste dumps. Burford resigned under pressure from Congress after Rita Lavelle, who Burford had put in charge of the EPA's Superfund toxic-waste clean-up effort, was fired for misconduct. Lavelle eventually was sentenced to a six-month jail term for perjury. After completing its investigation of the EPA, the House Energy and Commerce Oversight Subcommittee concluded: "During 1981, 1982, and

1983, top-level officials of the Environmental Protection Agency violated their public trust by disregarding the public health and the environment, manipulating the Superfund program for political purposes, engaging in unethical conduct, and participating in other abuses."

But pro-business appointments were only one method Reagan used to reduce the regulation of industry. He also slashed the operating budgets of regulatory agencies, thereby severely limiting their ability to enforce regulations. During Reagan's first term, says William Greider, the EPA's staff was cut by 20 percent. The number of Occupational Safety and Health Administration (OSHA) inspectors was cut by 400, and correspondingly, the number of citations issued declined by one-half. The enforcement of strip-mine regulations by the Interior Department was reduced by some 60 percent. The National Highway Traffic Safety Commission budget was reduced by 22 percent, and its investigations into potential car defects dropped from eleven to four a year.

IS FREE TRADE REALLY FREE?

The town of Nogales, Mexico, sits barely two miles south of the U.S. border, in a U.S.-Mexican free-trade zone. There, Mexican workers toil long hours in U.S.-owned plants for less than a dollar an hour. To survive, the workers and their families live in shacks, many made from discarded wooden shipping pallets and cardboard boxes. On cold nights, they burn rubber tires to stay warm. Outside the shacks, fifty-five-gallon drums that once contained toxic chemicals store drinking water.

Down the road from the workers' shacks sit the plants of companies such as IBM, Kodak, ITT, Rockwell, United Technologies, Memorex, Unisys, and Kimberly-Clark. In the state of Sonoma, there are at least several dozen plants that are likely producers of some type of hazardous waste, but only a handful have notified the EPA or Mexican authorities, as required, that they are doing so. The rest, it is assumed, dump their waste in illegal landfills or the river.

Back across the U.S. border, an estimated 2 million American workers suffer from jobs lost to Mexico and other Third World countries during the 1980s. In other words, neither the environment, Third World workers, nor American workers have received

Even more sinister was the cynical new regulatory review procedure implemented by the White House's Office of Management and Budget (OMB). OMB applied a "cost-benefit" analysis to regulations proposed by government agencies to insure that the cost of complying with the regulation did not exceed the savings in human lives or other social goods. OMB found few regulations cost-efficient, since it used industry-supplied estimates of the economic cost—and because the cost-benefit analysis, according to Congressman John Dingell of Michigan, valued a human life at $22,500.

In a *Newsweek* article, OMB was described by critics as the "National Security Council of regulatory policy—immensely powerful, but largely unaccountable." They charged that OMB, by overruling or "sitting on" agency regulations, "weakened or delayed protections on everything from drugs in the home to chemicals at the workplace." "Regulations," exclaimed Public Citizen lawyer David Vladeck, "some-

---

or are likely to receive in the future any benefit from George Bush's highly touted Free Trade agreements.

But labor, human rights activists, and environmentalists are not the only ones that should be concerned about Bush's free trade agreements: all Americans should. The goal of free trade is the "harmonization" of regulation—the creation of uniform minimum standards that governments, by international law, would be prohibited from exceeding. What this means, according to the consumer advocacy group Public Citizen, is that "the administration could achieve through trade agreements what it has been unable to accomplish in other ways—rolling back protection in areas such as pesticides, asbestos, clean air, clean water, worker safety, meat inspection, and species conservation."

Bush's free trade is not free. It will be costly to American citizens' health and income. Free trade will give multinationals further license to exploit the countries with the lowest wages and fewest environmental regulations. Even more, it will take from the American people their sovereign right to determine their own standards of health, consumer, and environmental protection and replace the public's desires with the decisions of a tribunal of international business leaders.

times go into the black hole of OMB and never emerge again."

OMB weakened and delayed for almost seven years legislation to eliminate explosive grain dust from grain elevators. It weakened an OSHA mandate restricting health-care workers' exposure to cancer-causing chemicals used to sterilize medical equipment. It tried to block an OSHA regulation requiring companies to notify workers of the risk of toxic chemicals used in their jobs. And it also attempted to block the EPA's ban on asbestos.

When Bush assumed office, he continued to use OMB to squash regulations. "During [Bush's] first year in office," writes Greider, "OMB changed, returned, or scuttled 24 percent of all new regulations." In addition, Bush established another anti-regulatory office, the Council on Competitiveness, which conducts much of its business in secret. The council, under the leadership of Vice President Dan Quayle, also works to protect the interests of business. In 1992 the Bush administration blocked an OSHA effort to limit the exposure of six million workers to toxic chemicals, nixed a proposal to require auto manufacturers to install fuel filters, forced the EPA to halve the number of protected "wetlands" acres, and weakened an EPA proposal to reduce emissions from utility plants. Arthur E. Rowse, writing in *The Progressive,* says "[Bush's] message to business is clear: Bring us your saddest cases of overregulation and we will cure them—even if it proves fatal to some people."

Industry deregulation was another important part of Reaganomics. Deregulation actually started during the Carter administration: Carter had signed legislation to deregulate the airlines and the trucking industry before he was voted out of office. Reagan accelerated the process. His administration eased antitrust regulations and corporate merger laws, and added telecommunications, insurance, pension funds, savings and loan institutions, and banks to the list of deregulated industries.

The fallout from deregulation was swift. Airline service to as many as 130 smaller communities was dropped. By the end of the decade, the average age of the airlines' planes had almost doubled, an estimated 50,000 airline employees had lost their jobs, and many others had taken pay cuts. In addition, a number of airlines went belly up. The carnage of deregulation was also evident in the trucking industry. Of the top thirty trucking companies operating in 1979, seventeen have folded. In 1990, 1,581 trucking companies failed, as opposed to only 186 in the year before deregulation.

The greatest impact of deregulation, however, occurred in the financial markets. Corporate assets that could have been invested in creating jobs and boosting productivity were used to purchase stocks, junk bonds, or even whole companies. Healthy corporations such as R.J. Reynolds, Beatrice, and Simplicity Pattern were laden with heavy debt or broken up and sold for their parts. Others, such as Macy's, Eastern Airlines, Revco Drugs, Circle K, and Florsheim Shoes, wound up in bankruptcy court. Firms that did survive often had to close plants, fire employees, raid employee pension funds, and reduce investment in research and development in order to pay off mountains of debt.

With investment restrictions removed, savings and loans, banks, and insurance companies rushed to add high-risk commercial real estate, commodity futures contracts, and overpriced junk bonds to their investment portfolios. While Wall Street, creator and purveyor of these high-risk investments, watched its profits soar, investors' fortunes disappeared. Billion-dollar insurance companies, such as Baldwin-United and First Executive, went bankrupt. In 1989 the number of bank failures reached a record 524—twice that of any year of the Great Depression. As a result, Congress was forced to appropriate $30 billion dollars to *begin* the bailout of the depleted Federal Deposit Insurance Corp (FDIC)—there were still $613 billion worth of troubled bank assets in January of 1992.

If the savings and loan bailout, which may eventually cost $500 billion, is the forerunner of the things to come in the banking and insurance industries, the American taxpayer is in deep, deep trouble. For taxpayers not only had to replace the squandered billions, but they also had to pay for an army of lawyers, Wall Street consultants, and real-estate experts feeding off the trough of the bailout agency. According to Stephen Pizzo in *Mother Jones,* a congressional inquiry found that the FDIC spent $733 million for private lawyers to sue former thrift executives, but only recovered $373 million dollars—51 cents for every taxpayer dollar spent. It seems that the same Wall Street firms who earned billions helping to run the saving and loan industry into the ground will now earn billions more cleaning it up.

CORPORATE WELFARE

While Reaganomics cleared the decks so that corporations could generate unlimited profits in the free market, it also found ways to give business opportunities directly—corporate socialism, if you will. The cornerstone of the corporate welfare program was a trillion-dollar increase in military spending during the decade. From refitting obsolete battleships to building the troubled B-2 bomber to the billions spent on Star Wars, the Reagan administration freely doled out weapons contracts. These, by the way, according to Harvard economist Benjamin Friedman, included contracts for $435 claw hammers, $792 for doormats, and a $7,622 coffee pot.

Welfare payments—called farm subsidies—to tobacco growers and other large agribusinesses were also raised. The maritime-marine industry continued to receive $400 million a year in welfare payments called "operating subsidies." Ranchers and loggers continued to pay considerably less than the market rate to use public lands for commercial purposes. And multinationals such as Boeing and General Electric continued to receive welfare payments called "export allowances."

In order to pay for his corporate welfare program and huge tax cut for the affluent, Reagan called for a massive cut in spending on social programs. In 1981 the Reagan administration changed the eligibility rules for Aid to Families with Dependent Children (AFDC) and Social Security disability insurance. As a result, 50 percent of working-poor families lost AFDC benefits, another 40 percent saw their benefits reduced, and 40 percent lost medical benefits. Almost half a million mentally and physically disabled people were illegally thrown off Social Security disability roles. (Those who were able to appeal—approximately half—eventually had their benefits restored.) In total, between 1981 and 1984 four million people lost their welfare, Social Security, and food stamp benefits.

In addition, the Reagan administration's cut in federal grants to state governments has contributed to massive state deficits and deepening cuts in state funding for welfare. By the late 1980s, many cities and states were flat broke. By 1992, the states of California and Connecticut had budgeted expenditures that exceeded revenues by more than 30 percent. California resorted to paying state employees with IOUs; Bridgeport, Connecticut, located in one of the richest counties in the country, declared bankruptcy. Across the country, state and local funding for schools, health care, libraries, and police protection have been severely curtailed. And according to a 1992 Center for the Study of the States report, forty states have reduced already meager AFDC benefits, twenty-seven states have frozen or eliminated general assistance benefits to adults without children, and thirteen states have cut payments designed to avert homelessness.

After almost ten years of Reaganomics, according to the Congressional Budget Office, the nation's wealthiest 450,000 families had seen their net worth almost double, to $4.4 trillion. The number of millionaires more than doubled between 1980 and 1988, according to conservative political analyst Kevin Phillips, to 1.3 million, while *Forbes* reported in 1988 that the number of billionaires had hit 52, up from only a handful in 1981. Phillips exclaimed: *"No parallel upsurge of riches had been seen since the late nineteenth century, the era of the Vanderbilts, Morgans and Rockefellers."*

In contrast, the real income of the bottom tenth of Americans dropped 14.8 percent. In fact, all but the wealthiest 20 percent suffered an income loss during Reagan's reign. With the exception of defense contractors, Wall Street, and the newly created millionaires and billionaires, it is hard to find anyone who is now better off.

Susan Demarco and Jim Hightower, the populist former Texas commissioner of agriculture, described the gravity of the situation best when they wrote:

> It had taken more than 50 years of historic struggle by citizens'
> groups—pushing the New Deal, Fair Deal, New Frontier and Great
> Society—to reduce the total wealth owned by the top families from
> the estimated 36 percent share they clutched before the Depression
> to the 'more democratic' share inherited by Mr. Reagan. But, in a
> historic blink, Washington wiped out the struggles of half a century,
> altering the rules governing taxes, spending and interest rates to
> move an unprecedented share of America's money up the economic
> ladder. Today, the top 1 percent of Americans possess more net
> wealth than the bottom 90 percent.

PROGRESSIVE ECONOMICS

The objective of progressive economics is to achieve environmentally sustainable economic growth and a broad and equitable distribution of income and wealth. In America, where the economic system is diametrically opposed to the goals of sustainability and fairness, nothing short of a fundamental restructuring will suffice. We need a transformation away from unrestrained capitalism toward an economic system more in concert with the rest of the industrialized world. Below are some suggestions for a new economic order.

ECONOMIC PLANNING

For decades, prominent economists have argued that America can no longer depend on corporate self-interest to decide the fate of America's economy, environment, and social well-being. They, along with social justice and environmental activists, have long advocated economic planning to create an environmentally and socially sustainable economy. Economic planning, write Thurow and Heilbroner in *Economics Explained*, "springs up under capitalism to provide public objectives the market cannot formulate by itself, or to repair damages to which the market itself may have given rise."

Those who have advocated economic planning include Nobel laureate Wassily Leontief, author and former Harvard economist John Kenneth Galbraith, MIT economist Lester Thurow, economist Robert Heilbroner of the New School for Social Research, University of Chicago sociologist William Julius Wilson, author Michael Harrington, and Harvard economists Robert Kuttner and Robert Reich. They have been joined by a new breed of "environmental" economists and activists who advocate economic planning as the best way to achieve sustainable growth and development in concert with environmental constraints.

Wilson calls for a progressive "macroeconomic policy" that includes a labor-market strategy and fiscal and monetary policy to stimulate "balanced growth." The late Harrington also called for economic planning, with its primary goal the "creation of a full employment economy." Robert Reich calls for a "high-technology" industrial policy that emphasizes government investment in "education, training, retraining, research and development."

Under the new progressive economic order, national macroeconomic planning must be used to achieve environmentally sustainable and balanced economic growth; adequate profits for private industry; productivity enhancement; government/industry research and development priorities; and full employment. The planning apparatus should include a national economic planning board drawn from business, labor, and government as well as advocates for the environment, the poor, women, and minorities. This board would evaluate America's economic priorities and then guide all of its constituent groups in cooperating to meet these priorities.

TAXATION

A new tax policy is needed to eliminate the gross injustices in the current tax system, to raise funds for domestic needs, and to reduce the deficit. This can be done by (1) eliminating payroll taxes; (2) fully taxing entitlement benefits such as Social Security received by high-income individuals; and (3) raising income taxes on corporations and high-income individuals. In fact, "a federal income tax as progressive as it was in 1978," estimates Reich, "would require the top 10 percent of income earners to pay $950 billion more [over the next decade] than they are supposed to now."

Taxation should also be used to meet the priorities established by the economic planning board. For example, fertilizers and fossil fuels should be taxed at a higher rate in order to reduce pollution, while alternative energy sources and mass-transit systems should be given tax breaks. To stimulate private job-training programs, low-income housing development, and job creation in targeted communities, tax credits for industry could be established.

BUDGET CONSIDERATIONS

The peace dividend must be realized immediately by sharply curtailing military spending. According to Robert L. Borosage, director of the Wolfson Center for National Affairs, "former defense secretaries and planners also now agree that $150 billion could be cut from the military budget annually, largely by eliminating weapons that have no current mission and reducing our assistance to allies against a threat that doesn't exist."

Borosage, whose organization is a joint project of the Institute for Policy Studies and the New School for Social Research, suggests using the peace savings in the following way: $20 billion to reduce poverty and child neglect, $22 billion for housing, $8 billion for education and training, $35 billion for national health insurance, and $41 billion to clean up military nuclear-waste and private hazardous-waste sites and rebuild the nation's decaying infrastructure. This would still leave $20 billion for deficit reduction.

Indeed, the peace dividend, along with higher taxes, would not only reduce the budget deficit, but would provide American citizens with benefits long enjoyed by citizens of other industrialized nations. These include national health insurance, subsidized child care and maternal leave, job-training programs, adequate mass-transit systems, safe roads and bridges, an adequate and well-trained police force, and decent schools and housing for all. In addition, there would be more funds to invest in nonmilitary research and development. This, says Robert Reich, would help America regain ground in "the high-technology race," leading to increased employment opportunities for workers.

LABOR MARKET POLICIES

A full-employment policy must become a government priority. A guaranteed jobs initiative designed along the lines of Illinois senator Paul Simon's Guaranteed Job Opportunity Program would provide employment for those who are unsuccessful in finding work in the private sector. Simon's program would provide skilled jobs building and repairing schools and hospitals, sewage systems, harbors and ports, and highways and city streets, and for curing the nation's ailing environment.

Job-skills training must be provided to those who are unqualified for the jobs available through the full-employment program. The current Job Training Partnership program could be expanded to include those who do not currently qualify as well as the workers who will be displaced as the economy is demilitarized and restructured for environmental sustainability. In addition, tax credits should be available to corporations who invest in improving the skills of their work force. Government assistance should also be available to workers who want to enhance their skills or move to faster-growing industries. Transitional assistance for workers seeking employment or involved in job-training programs should replace the current program of unemployment insurance.

Labor unions must be strengthened. At a minimum, we must pass legislation outlawing the permanent replacement of striking workers and levying tougher penalties, including criminal sanctions and denial of government contracts, on employers for violations of labor laws. In addition, the National Labor Relations Board must be overhauled so that it cannot be stacked with anti-labor appointees, as it was during the Reagan administration.

ENTITLEMENT PROGRAMS

The endless series of entitlement programs—Social Security, disability insurance, food stamps, unemployment insurance, and AFDC—should be rolled into one universal income-maintenance program. Incentives and supports, such as child care, job-skills training, and tax credits should be designed to encourage those who can work to do so. In addition, to discourage dependency, we should establish some mechanism to reduce entitlement payments over time to able-bodied adults without small children.

FREE TRADE

Bush's free-trade policy should be scrapped. A new tariff structure should be implemented to insure reciprocal fair trade and to prevent multinational corporations from profiting by exploiting the Third World's environment and labor. One interesting approach is Oklahoma senator David Boren's proposal to impose additional duties on imports from countries that fail to impose adequate environmental regulations on producers. Even better would be to include additional duties on countries with abusively low wage rates. Although proposals such as these would increase the cost to consumers for some imported products, it would go a long way toward ending the exportation of jobs and decreasing the differentials in wages and environmental regulation between America and the Third World.

GRASS-ROOTS BUSINESS DEVELOPMENT

Seed grants and loan programs that enable workers and farmers to start or acquire businesses should be encouraged. This is especially important for small businesses or farms in regions of high unemployment and for firms operating in industries encouraged or recommended by the economic planning board. Tax policy should also provide incentives to encourage employee or union buyouts of existing private enterprises.

CORPORATE RESPONSIBILITY

Corporations that violate federal and state laws or invest overseas to avoid paying fair wages or meeting environmental standards should be financially penalized. The government procurement process should differentiate between corporations that are socially responsible and those that are not. Preference in the awarding of government contracts should go to enterprises that are cooperating with the agenda of the economic planning board, that are working to improve the communities in which they are located, that have good relationships with their labor force, and that are working to preserve the environment. Companies that are found guilty of crimes or of violating OSHA, EPA, or other government agency's regulations should be banned from receiving government contracts for a significant period of time.

CONCLUSION

To capitalists and many mainstream economists, these proposals may seem radical. Many of these policies, however, are currently at work in countries whose economic fortunes far exceed our own.

In fact, a progressive economic order will not only be beneficial to average citizens, but to industry as well. By using the peace dividend and higher taxes to eliminate the budget deficit, the government will be largely removed from the long-term debt market, which would reduce long-term interest rates and the cost of capital. The elimination of the payroll tax and the implementation of a single-payer national health insurance program would reduce payroll costs. These measures would also remove two of the biggest impediments—payroll taxes and health insurance benefits—to the hiring of full-time employees.

Putting more people to work would increase the nation's total disposable income. This would lead to increased corporate revenues that could be invested in more job-producing machinery and equipment. Placing import restrictions on goods from countries that allow exploitation of their labor force or environment would put socially responsible companies on a equal cost basis with their competitors.

Progressive economics would also boost the rate of productivity growth. International studies show that countries that invest in nonmilitary technology as opposed to military spending have sharply higher rates of growth in manufacturing productivity. Research cited by Charles Schultze of the Brookings Institution suggests that investments in public infrastructure add more to the nation's productivity growth and output than do investments in private business. Research cited by

Thomas Bodenheimer and Robert Gould suggests that $1 billion spent on education employs 62,000 people, while "$1 billion for the MX missile employs only 14,000." In addition, according to Nobel laureate Lawrence Klein, a 10 percent increase in military expenditures would lead to an additional $12 billion increase in the trade deficit.

Accordingly, by diverting government spending from military purposes to rebuilding the nation's infrastructure and investing in nonmilitary, high-technology research and development, America can not only increase employment and its share of world trade, but also begin to reverse the decades-old decline in productivity growth. This, according to Leftist and mainstream economists alike, is the key to reversing the declining American standard of living.

A new progressive economic order could do a lot for America. It could put people to work earning living wages; it could train the untrained, rebuild the nation's cities, and lead industry to a competitive position in world trade; and it could reverse the decline in productivity growth. It is not only the key to a new social justice in America, but to national prosperity as well.

SWEDEN'S SOCIAL DEMOCRATIC ECONOMY

While the United States is the most capitalistic of the industrialized nations, Sweden is the most socialized. For over fifty years, the leading political party in Sweden, the Social Democratic Party (SDP), has worked to develop Sweden into a model for democratic socialism. It has worked to establish a political and economic system that promotes free enterprise, moderates the harsh side effects of capitalism, provides a strong welfare state, and offers high levels of democracy and equality to its citizens.

Sweden's citizens enjoy, according to reporter Eric Black of the Minneapolis *Star Tribune*, "socialized medicine, socialized day care, socialized education through university, socialized pensions, unemployment benefits of 90 percent of working wages—even subsidized newspapers and a mandatory minimum paid vacation of five weeks for full-time workers." "Compared with the United States," writes Black, "Sweden has a longer life expectancy, a lower unemployment rate, higher voter participation, less crime, fewer pupils per teacher, a lower infant-mortality rate and a higher literacy rate."

Sweden also has a thriving democracy. The United Nation's Development Program Human Freedom Index—a measure of citizens' rights to assemble, speak, and choose religious and sexual practices; freedom for political opposition, trade unions, and the press; and gender equality, privacy, and legal rights—rated Sweden the most democratic and free country in the world. Thirty-one percent of elected officials in Sweden are women, compared with 13 percent in the United States. Average voter turnout for a national election is 86 percent; fewer than half of eligible American citizens vote. And like other European countries, Swedish voters can choose from a host of political parties, ranging from the far left to the far right.

Sweden also has a strong economy and one of the highest standards of living in the world. Sweden's per-capita gross domestic product is higher than America's and is among the five highest in the world. Seventeen of Sweden's major corporations, including automakers Volvo and Saab, are among the world's five hundred largest corporations. Sweden exports half of its industrial output, and the government has a balanced national budget. And in addition to being third in patents produced per capita and fourth in Nobel Prizes awarded since 1950, Swedish students' test scores in math, physics, and chemistry rank among the highest in the world.

The average Swedish household has more than twice the savings of an average American household. Fifty-five percent of households own their own home, while renters pay average monthly rents that are one-quarter the average paid by American renters. Sweden suffered only nineteen murders by handgun in 1988; the nation's overall murder rate is less than a fourth the rate in the United States. Sweden is also very environmentally conscious. It is a leading recycling country; it has reduced the use of agricultural pesticides by half over the past five years; and its air is almost twice as clean as America's. In addition, Swedish city dwellers enjoy almost twice as much park and urban green space as their American counterparts.

Although Sweden, as Jay Walljasper puts it in *Utne Reader*, "serves as the political Promised Land" for American progressives, it does have its problems. In Sweden's September 1991 election, the Social Democratic Party's share of the vote fell to 37.6 percent, turning control over to a coalition of nonsocialist parties and a conservative prime minister. This shift in electoral support is largely a result of concern over record unemployment (3.4 percent), anxiety about Sweden's impending entry into the European Community, and a desire for greater choice in the day-care and health-care systems. There was also growing discontent with the SDP. Regressive tax legislation initiated by the SDP, according to Joanne Barkan in *Dissent,* "alienated...supporters who want equality and strong government." In addition, in the 1988 election the SDP promised longer parental leaves and vacations but failed to deliver. "The party," says Barkan, "made one-hundred-eighty-degree turns on lots of issues."

While some outside observers claim that the conservative gains in recent elections and Sweden's entry into the European Community signal an end to fifty years of successful socialist democracy, they are dead wrong. As political scientist Henry Milner, author of *Sweden: Social Democracy in Practice,* points out, Swedish *conservatives* are well to the Left of American *liberals.* Even Stellan Artin, the head of the powerful Swedish Employers' Federation—the Swedish business lobby—supports social democracy. "The collectivist part of the welfare state," says Artin, "will continue to be high by world standards."

To those who believe that Sweden should move to the right as it becomes part of the European community, the Swedes respond with a better idea."Many Swedes—in and out of the Social Democratic Party—" writes Walljasper, "feel they've created a society worth preserving. They believe that Sweden's impending entry in the European Community should be an occasion to elevate EC social and environmental standards to Sweden's level....And they think the Swedish model...will still hold inspiration for people around the world."

CHAPTER FOUR

Class, Race, and Gender Bias

Cᴌᴀss ᴡᴀʀꜰᴀʀᴇ ᴀɴᴅ ᴛʜᴇ sᴛᴜʙʙᴏʀɴ ᴘᴇʀsɪsᴛᴇɴᴄᴇ of racism and sexism have long been the predominate obstacles to the creation of an equitable and just society in America. Together, these three social sins account for much of the decline in the economic fortunes of the working class, the feminization of poverty, and the development of an urban underclass. In addition, class, race, and gender bigotry have severely hampered the ability of groups with similar economic and social needs to work together in their own political best interests. Equally damaging, bigotry has blinded society to the common weave among class, race, and gender issues and has hampered the nation's ability to develop workable solutions to social problems.

The civil uprisings in the aftermath of the Rodney King verdict, for instance, were characterized by many political leaders as a race riot. But this is a misguided analysis which not only obscures the broader economic realities underlying the violent outbreaks, but will also, no doubt, lead to a faulty government response. Troy Segal, writing in *Business Week,* warned that ignoring the underlying causes of the riots will only lead to more domestic turmoil in the future. "To see the verdict and the riots as just more evidence of the racial divide in America," warns Segal, "is to ignore a potentially more dangerous split: The growing gulf between the haves and the have-nots." Segal quotes a white Seattle resident who, when caught looting by television news cameras, shouted "It's not black vs. white. It's rich vs. poor. And we're poor."

This rioter was not alone. According to *Newsweek*, "Looters of all races owned the streets. . . . Blond kids loaded their Volkswagens with stereo gear; . . . Filipinos in a banged-up old clunker stocked up on baseball mitts and sneakers. . . . A few Asians were spotted as well." So many whites and Hispanics were arrested during the uprising that *U.S. News & World Report* called the riots a "class rebellion" and an "equal opportunity feeding frenzy."

Despite the riots' egalitarian nature, the official "spin" from Washington was that the riots were an uprising by the African-American underclass, led and fueled by violence-prone street gangs. What was needed, Bush claimed, was more law and order. But, as Northwestern University sociologist Christopher Winship explains, "making poverty a black issue obscures the chasm between rich and poor." It is a great divide, suggests Segal, "that many politicians would just as soon keep under wraps." To view poverty and injustice as an issue of economic bias against the working-class would be to remove the camouflage of racism from the reality of widespread economic decline, worker exploitation, and failed government policy.

The camouflage of racism is at work in another highly publicized social issue: welfare reform. Again, it is camouflaging the bias in government and corporate policy against the working-class behind the cloak of bigotry. The failure of welfare reform should have highlighted the worsening economic plight of members of the working class of all races, by focusing attention on why single mothers can't get off welfare or what happens to single mothers who do. It should have brought increased attention to the gender pay gap and to discrimination against women in the job market. It should have generated a national debate on the increasing feminization of poverty and increasing poverty among American children of all races. And it should have generated social outrage at the increasing brutality of the government assault on the poor. In this assault, says Yale professor Theodore Marmor, "America has moved from a war on poverty to a war on the poor."

A sincere analysis of welfare reform would have quickly yielded the following conclusion: the economic predicament of low-skilled workers in America is so bad that single mothers who receive AFDC are better off staying on welfare than joining the work force. They are better off not because the benefits that they receive are adequate, but because wages for low- and semi-skilled workers are vastly inadequate. According to *Time,* for far too many Americans, work does not pay: "The problem is that the American economy no longer provides enough decent jobs for low-skilled workers. . . . Even two-parent working families have a hard time making it at the low end of the pay scale."

According to 1990 Census Bureau statistics, 14.4 million full-time workers earn less than poverty-level wages—less than $6.10 an hour. For women, who are subject to both discriminatory hiring practices and pay inequality, the situation is even worse. Twenty-five percent of women earn below poverty-level wages, and women represent 67 percent of the labor force earning the minimum wage—a paltry $4.25 an hour, or $8,840 a year.

In addition to the problems of low wages and gender bias in the workplace, many working single mothers have to either pay for or survive without health insurance. Most low-paying jobs don't provide insurance, and these women are not "poor enough" to qualify for Medicaid. Working mothers also have to pay child care expenses, transportation costs, and payroll taxes. When all work-related expenses are tallied, Harvard public policy professor David Ellwood estimated that a single mother has to earn more than 125 percent of the minimum wage to equal her disposable income on welfare.

This, of course, assumes that after completing her employment training the single mother can find a job. In many low-income urban areas, the unemployment rate exceeds 30 percent. "People will get training for employment," says University of Chicago sociologist William Julius Wilson, "but if there aren't jobs out there, in the long term, it is just going to be self-defeating." This was exactly the case with Wisconsin's welfare reform program. According to Ruth Conniff, associate editor of *The Progressive,* not only did that state's program fail to help participants find jobs, but "welfare recipients who did not participate in the program were *more successful* in finding work than were people who went through the job-training program." Such poor results, however, did not prevent Wisconsin from increasing funding for the failed training program from $7 million in 1987 to almost $50 million in 1990.

Welfare reform, like many politically motivated government initiatives before it, has, in Conniff's words, led to "some unbelievably stupid results." "States are spending millions of dollars on job training in areas where there are no available jobs," she writes, "and experiments that punish poor people for missing school or having babies are plunging thousands of families into economic ruin."

Unfortunately, welfare reform was never rational. In their book *Chain Reaction*, Thomas and Mary Edsall write: "A significant segment, a 'swing' sector, of the white public [has] come to make a distinction between what Republican pollsters called 'good welfare'—Social Security, education, health, police—and 'bad' welfare—food stamps, Aid to Families with Dependent Children, and other means-tested programs favoring poor or near poor heavily black and Hispanic constituencies." This perception has come about despite the fact that 60 percent of those who receive AFDC benefits are white. *Time* notes that "the reluctance of taxpayers to foot that bill [for 'bad' welfare] is hardly eased by the stereotype of inner-city welfare mothers having baby after illegitimate baby while their boyfriends sell crack on street corners," even though the average AFDC family actually has *fewer* children than the average American family.

This welfare hysteria, of course, is not accidental. It was intentionally inflamed, if not provoked, by conservatives to generate political support for their policies. It has also served as a convenient excuse for the damage that conservative policies have inflicted on the middle class. Indeed, Reagan's Chicago "welfare queen," a fictional woman who he claimed earned over $150,000 a year from entitlements, was "one of Reagan's favorite and most often-repeated anecdotes," according to the Edsalls.

The lack of rational analysis due to the racial rhetoric surrounding welfare reform is unfortunate, for it prevents the working class from seeing the true causes of its own economic decline. If work does not pay for a mother on welfare, it does not pay for others as well. And if the cost of health insurance and child care makes it prohibitive for a welfare mother to work, these factors are also draining the budgets of dual-earner couples and single working mothers.

What welfare reform should have led to was not further racial divisiveness but a call to end the economic warfare against low-skilled wage earners. It should have led to a call for a full-employment program, restrictions on job exportation and plant closings, legislation to strengthen unions, a higher minimum wage, and an end to regressive taxation, including the repeal of the payroll tax. It should have led to pressure on the government to do something about the pay gap between men and women and the lack of equal opportunity for women in employment. It should have produced greater government support for the working family, including national health insurance, subsidized child care, and a national parental-leave policy. Instead, welfare reform only widened the already gaping racial divide.

The "unbelievably stupid results" of welfare reform are just one example of how the three social sins—class, race, and gender bias—have served to stymie social progress. In spite of what white working-class males have been led to believe, they have more in common with the average working woman, the average African-American or Hispanic worker, even the average welfare mother, than they do with affluent conservatives. The best goal for all Americans, writes journalist Danny Collum in the Christian magazine *Sojourners*, is to seek "democracy, equality, and self-respect":

> These ideas should unite a vast majority of Americans of all colors
> on the basis of self-interest—from the angry whites of Bensonhurst
> to Pittston coal miners' families to the angry blacks of Watts. That
> is especially true if you consider, as I do, job security, a family
> wage, and free health care to be among the minimum requirements
> for the maintenance of self-respect. A coalition formed around such
> notions could unite everyone except those very few whose pursuit of
> unlimited profit seems to require an American population torn and
> deluded by racial alienation and inequality.

People of all stripes must learn to look beyond conservative rhetoric and see divisiveness for what it is: working-class economic suicide. Racism and sexism, as former presidential candidate Jesse Jackson has often suggested, are devices used by the ruling elite to divide the natural coalition of the members of the working class. As a result, working-class whites are, in effect, as much victims of bigotry as are people of color. What average Americans need, no matter what their race or color, is what affluent conservatives are working hard to deny them: a decent income, a fair tax system, a government support system in concert with the rest of the industrialized world, and an end to corporate exploitation of workers and the environment.

As long as the majority allows itself to be divided, the current ruling class, which is described by eighty-two-year-old socialist economist Paul Sweezy as "the smartest ever," will continue to accumulate virtually all of America's wealth, while the economic fortunes of the majority will continue to decline indefinitely.

CLASS WARFARE: FROM HAYMARKET
SQUARE TO REAGANOMICS

In America, class polarization is better characterized, in the words of
Berkeley sociologist David Barash, as "class warfare." Barash neatly
summarized class aggression when he wrote:

> While they pursue policies that benefit the wealthy at the expense
> of the poor and the middle, conservatives proclaim the myth of a
> classless society so dear to almost every American's heart. . . . With-
> out a hint of embarrassment, conservatives have even argued that
> the poor need their poverty (or at least, the threat of it) to keep
> them industrious, while at the same time, the rich need their wealth,
> and the prospect of adding to it . . . for the same reason!

Despite the common myth of America as a classless society, class
polarization has long been a part of the American landscape. Before the
New Deal, American workers toiled long hours in hazardous factories
and were paid extremely low wages. Attempts to improve worker conditions, usually though unionization or strikes, were met with propaganda characterizing organized workers as communists; with pro-business court rulings; with anti-labor legislation; and, all too often, with violence. Capitalists, using private armies or the forces of the state, sometimes even attacked militant workers, as they did in the infamous 1886
massacre in Chicago's Haymarket Square.

These and other overt attempts to squash working-class demands
for social justice made class polarization easy to observe during the first
decades of this century. After World War II, however, things changed.
America was virtually the only industrialized nation whose economy
had not been destroyed by the war. From 1945 to the late 1960s, America enjoyed unprecedented industrial growth, and with it, great prosperity. It was a time when trickle-down economics actually worked for
most Americans. Standards of living rose for virtually everyone. Indeed, according to the leading intellectuals of the day, America had become one universal middle class.

It was during this period of widespread prosperity, which was accompanied by the fervent anti-communism of the 1950s, that, according
to Barbara Ehrenreich, "classlessness [became] part of America's official
ideology." "The full-blooded, old-fashioned notion of class—as in *class
struggle*—was now suspect and un-American, part of a left-wing heri-

tage that mainstream intellectuals were fast repudiating." Accordingly, new sociology texts supported the myth of classlessness, and teachers and writers who thought otherwise found themselves without a job or a publisher.   .

But as the rebuilt economies of the industrialized world began to assert themselves, America's economic fortunes begin to decline. America's business leaders, many of whom had become complacent due to the lack of international competition during the postwar period, were unprepared for the reemergence of Japanese and European industries in the world market. Instead of resorting to improved technology, superior management, or other tactics to boost sagging profits, American business turned to Reaganomics, and with it, to overt class warfare.

Corporate America was determined to restore its declining fortunes on the backs of working men and women. "The Reagan administration," write Thomas and Mary Edsall, "—acting to secure profits and success for American business, as well as to keep American labor competitive in low-wage world markets—pressed policies that kept wages down for those in the bottom half of the income distribution." The attack on labor included union busting; the illegal firing of pro-union workers, with the tacit approval of the Reagan-packed National Labor Relations Board; widespread plant closings; and the exportation of plants and jobs to the Third World. Meanwhile, the Reagan White House steadfastly refused to raise the minimum wage, the first administration ever to do so.

Throughout the decade, writes Thane Peterson in *Business Week,* "corporate America whacked away at labor costs. It tamed unions, exacted givebacks, and laid off millions of hourly workers. Yet, multitudes of U.S. companies [still] can't compete with their international rivals." Thane argues, however, that labor, which averages less than 15 percent of total product cost, is not the problem: management is. Thane points out that corporate overhead, "chiefly plump white-collar bureaucracies," runs at 26 percent of sales for American manufacturers, versus only 21 percent for Western Europe and 18 percent for Japan. Undoubtedly, much of this cost has to do with the excessive salaries and other benefits received by upper-level management. But it also has to do with class polarization. Upper-class executives seem ready to throw blue-collar workers out on the street at the toss of a hat, but they lay off their class counterparts, middle- and upper-level white-collar employees, only as a last resort.

Harvard economist Robert Reich also sees class bias in the way that corporate America treats its work force. Despite claims that industry is spending more than $30 billion a year to improve the skills of the American work force, "the truth is," claims Reich, "that American business has spent very little on educating its workers." According to Reich, "employees with college degrees are 50 percent more likely to receive corporate training than non-college graduates, and executives with postgraduate degrees are twice as likely to get training as those with college degrees." In addition, Reich cites a survey showing that only 8 percent of firms provide training to improve workers' writing and verbal skills. "In short," says Reich, "training is typically provided to employees who need it least."

One of the reasons corporate America ignores its low- and semi-skilled work force, according to Reich, "is that American corporations are increasingly finding the skilled workers they need outside the United States and hiring them at a fraction of what they would pay in America." In addition, service industries such as health care and retail have also found a way around training their workers, through changes in the immigration laws. In the early 1980s, faced with a shortage of nurses, the Reagan administration began granting temporary work visas to foreign nurses; in 1989, more than 10,000 of these nurses were granted citizenship. Today, facing a shortage of skilled workers, the Bush administration has pushed through an amendment to the immigration laws allowing an influx of up to 54,000 skilled foreign workers a year. Instead of investing in the training of the American labor force, says Reich, "when American workers don't measure up, American business simply turns elsewhere."

The tax and spending policies of the Reagan era were also a direct assault on the American worker. Reaganomics socked wage earners with a $200 billion payroll-tax increase. While the tax deductibility of consumer interest was repealed, the deductibility of mortgage interest—even for second homes—was retained. Writing in *Dissent*, National Housing Institute board members Peter Dreier and John Atlas point out that "about one-third of this year's $47 billion homeowner subsidy goes to the 3.8 percent of taxpayers with incomes over $100,000"; more than 81 percent of this tax break goes "to the 20 percent of taxpayers who earn over $50,000." While the Donald Trumps of the world can write off $2 million mortgages on their homes, there are no tax breaks for renters, who are usually lower-income individuals, or for the poor, who saw funding for federal housing assistance slashed from $33 billion in 1980 to $9 billion in 1991.

In addition to tax breaks, Neil Howe and Phillip Longman write in *The Atlantic,* households earning more than $50,000 also receive a quarter of all federal benefits, totaling at least $200 billion. The authors show that in 1991, households earning more than $100,000 collected $9,280 in federal tax breaks and direct benefits, while those earning less than $10,000 received, on average, only $5,690.

Federal cuts in scholarship programs have made it exceedingly difficult for working-class youths to attend college. At the same time, overall funding cuts to public schools have also had a disproportionate impact on the working class. Journalist Holly Sklar, writing in *Z Magazine,* cites statistics showing that funding per pupil in schools in lower-income communities can be as much as nine times lower than funding to schools in upper-class communities. The education bias also extends to private colleges; Sklar cites a recent *Boston Globe* article on "legacy admissions" that noted that at Harvard, the acceptance rate for children of alumni was more than twice the overall rate of acceptance, despite the fact that "the average admitted legacy at Harvard between 1981 and 1988 was significantly *less* qualified than the average nonlegacy."

Class bias is also evident in the Federal Reserve's administration of foreign exchange and interest policy. These policies, while advantageous to bankers, were a disaster for the working class. Author Philip Mattera argues that the Federal Reserve's use of high interest rates to engineer a recession was as much for the purpose of generating unemployment that would temper the demands of labor as it was to curb inflation. "What was to workers an economic disaster," writes Mattera, "was to business a chance to regain its control of the system." David Cantor and Juliet Schor argue in *Tunnel Vision* that "economic policy was being shaped to satisfy the demands of big banks, who wanted a high dollar. The consequences for the trade deficit, unemployment, and social hardship were met with indifference." They cite a study that estimated that, as a result of the high dollar, as many as 1.3 million jobs in manufacturing were lost from 1981 to 1985.

Workers were not the only group hurt by the Federal Reserve-induced recession of the early 1980s. The nation's farmers were devastated. The value of farm land in many areas was cut in half, foreclosures rose, and by 1985 the number of farms had declined by more than 20 percent. According to William Greider, when Federal Reserve chairman Paul Volcker spoke to a group of farmers who were pleading for an end to high interest rates, Volcker replied: "Look, your constituents are unhappy, mine aren't."

Reagan's attack on the working class made an impact not only on its income, but also on its health. The White House appointed pro-business regulators to the Occupational Safety and Health Administration (OSHA) and at the same time slashed its budget. As a result, the number of citations issued to corporations for worker-safety violations during the Reagan administration declined by half. Not surprisingly, the United States has the highest occupational fatality rate in the industrialized world.

Given this disregard for the health of workers, it should not be surprising that the average life span for members of the working class is significantly shorter than it is for those in the professional classes. John Hopkins professor of health policy and sociology Vicente Navarro reports that class differentials in mortality rates are even higher than race differentials. Writing in *The Nation*, Navarro cites a 1986 study that showed that unskilled blue-collar workers died of heart disease at a rate 2.3 times that of managers and professionals, while the heart-disease mortality rate for African-Americans was only 1.3 times higher than whites. Navarro also cites a study on Americans suffering from chronic medical conditions. From 1983 to 1988, debilitating chronic illness among people with incomes over $60,000 declined, while it rose for those earning less than $10,000. Navarro also reports that in other industrialized nations that keep class-based health statistics, not only are mortality rates for the working class higher than the upper classes, but the differentials are widening. In summary, Navarro writes:

> We as a nation need to do more to eliminate racism, but we also need to eliminate the fatal consequences of classism. . . . The publication of health statistics in racial terms assumes that white unskilled workers have more in common with white lawyers, for example, than with black unskilled workers. They do not. White workers have far more in common, in the way they live, get sick and die, with black workers than with white lawyers. . . . Yet the way in which statistics are kept does not help to make white and black workers aware of the commonality of their predicament.

By the end of the decade, it was clear that Reaganomics was the victor in the class war. High-paying jobs in manufacturing had been replaced by jobs paying wages below poverty level. The wealthiest 450,000 families—the top one-half of a percent—had seen their net worth soar from approximately $2.5 trillion in 1983 to $4.4 trillion by the end of the decade, while the incomes of the middle and working classes had declined precipitously. Economist Lester Thurow was prompted to exclaim that the middle class "is becoming an endangered species."

AMERICA'S CLASS MAKEUP

As Barbara Ehrenreich has pointed out, America has considered itself a classless society since the 1950s. By that decade, the concept of class division had been all but eliminated from textbooks and the mainstream media, and the perception that "what is good for business is good for America" and "a rising tide lifts all boats" had been adopted by most Americans. Although it was obvious that there were rich and poor, Americans believed in equality of opportunity, or, as Robert Reich defines it, the myth of "The Triumphant Individual." "It's the parable of the self-made man," writes Reich, the belief that "with enough guts and gumption, anyone can make it on their own in America."

New Horatio Algers do appear now and then, but the reality is that the odds of going from rags to riches are about as good as winning a million-dollar lottery jackpot. According to a number of research studies, the best predictor of where one's children will wind up is where they start: in their parents' income class. Even worse, the poor and the lower and middle classes have been in a fifteen-year downward economic spiral that some economists warn could produce the first generation of young families to fare worse than their parents. If this trend is not arrested, downward mobility in future middle-class generations may become the norm.

This lack of upward mobility is due to the fact that the avenues of economic progress have been cut off, partially as a result of increasing international industrial competition, but largely because of government and corporate policy. Underfunded and ineffective schools, along with cutbacks in government college loans and scholarships, make it increasingly unlikely that a working-class youth will be able to use education as a vehicle for upward mobility. Poverty-level wages, job exportation, plant closings, employment discrimination against women and minorities, and lack of skill-providing job-training programs make employment an unlikely vehicle for upward mobility. And entrepreneurship, without access to sources of capital, is also an unlikely path upward.

Without a decent education, real employment opportunities, or capital to start one's own business, upward mobility is just a dream. This is the lesson we all must learn, so we can begin to fight back. "Trickle-down" theory and the myth that "a rising tide lifts all boats" are lies. We must also realize that government policy is not classless. Reaganomics was a boon to the rich and a curse on the working class. In America, while we may all be created equal, corporate interests and the affluent get all the breaks.

These lessons must be used by the working and middle income classes so that they may discard the myth of classlessness and learn to think in terms of their own class interests. The concept of class must again become an object of discussion and debate. For, as Barbara Ehrenreich explains, "the point of discussing class is ultimately to abolish it. Tax the rich and enrich the poor until both groups are absorbed into some broad and truly universal middle class."

MIDDLE-CLASS ECONOMIC SUICIDE

What is most perplexing about the issue of class is why so many Americans support policies that are contrary to their own class interests. Without broad-based political support, the powerful few in what C. Wright Mills once described as the predominately white, male, and affluent world of the "power elite" would not be very powerful. While they would still have their wealth, they would no longer have the political muscle to promote government policies that injure virtually everyone but themselves.

So far, there are no signs of mass resistance to the class warfare being waged by the elite. John Kenneth Galbraith's *The Culture of Contentment* is an attempt to explain this perplexing phenomenon. He postulates that many Americans, including professionals, corporate and government bureaucrats, educators, and even some "dual paycheck" blue-collar workers, find life quite comfortable and reasonably secure—for them, the status quo is quite satisfactory. This group, which Galbraith calls "the contented," contains the majority of the middle class. And since their main preoccupation is protecting their own standard of living, they typically support the status quo. Barbara Ehrenreich, in *The Fear of Falling*, makes similar observations about upper-class professionals, although to Ehrenreich, it is not professionals' contentment, but their fear of losing their incomes and status, that makes them so resistant to change.

Whatever the cause, the system provides this professional, or "contented," class with income, personal status, and a sense of security. It also leads to a high degree of self-absorption. As Galbraith notes, the contented will tolerate social injustice as long as it does not infringe on their own fortunes. In explaining their tolerance of America's wide disparity in wealth, he writes: "The price of prevention of any aggression against one's own income is tolerance of the greater amount for others. Indignation at, and advocacy of, redistribution of income from the very rich, inevitably by taxes, opens the door for consideration of higher taxes for the comfortable but less endowed."

Galbraith makes another interesting point about the mind-set of the contented. "The fortunate and the favored," he writes, "do not contemplate and respond to their own longer-run well-being. Rather, they respond, powerfully, to immediate comfort and contentment." In other words, while many of the contented profess to be concerned about the environment or poverty, for example, they are not willing to make personal sacrifices, or, even more, to risk the personal uncertainty that may arise if fundamental changes in America's economic and political system are implemented in order to address these problems.

Here lies the paradox of American society: a ruling minority elite, historically notorious for their lack of foresight, manipulates policy for their own short-term self-interest, while a contented majority passively supports that elite *against* their own long-run self-interest. The poor, the unemployed, the underemployed, and the morally indignant watch helplessly as the contented passively help the elite place a financial noose around all our necks.

GENDER BIAS

In China, where births are largely restricted to one per family, female babies are sometimes killed so that the family can attempt to conceive a son. In some Muslim countries, women who "disgrace" their families are killed at the hands of their own family members. In India, where cows are sacred, women are burned to death by dissatisfied husbands, who are rarely prosecuted for their crimes.

WHY HETEROSEXUALS SHOULD SUPPORT GAY RIGHTS

Gay men and lesbian women are the most discriminated against group in America. This is not only because they, like minorities, are subjected to hate crimes and housing discrimination, or because they, like women, experience sexual discrimination. It is not because gay couples, like unmarried heterosexual couples, cannot take advantage of their mates' health coverage or other family benefits. It is not even because they are the most prominent victims of the government's failed AIDS policy. Gays and lesbians are the most discriminated against precisely because they suffer *all* of these prejudices.

To tolerate discrimination against homosexuality is to endorse such abuses not only against gays and lesbians, but also against women and people of color. Discrimination against a lifestyle is akin to discrimination based on skin color or gender. They are all prejudices founded on ignorance, and they must be purged if our society is ever to become morally just.

Despite this, many organizations on the Left turn a cold shoulder to the gay and lesbian movement. As *Village Voice* writer Donna Minkowitz points out, groups like the NAACP and Amnesty International refuse to take a stand on gay and lesbian rights, and "mainstream feminism is still noticeably cool to gay and lesbian liberation."

America's gay and lesbian community is an effective and essential part of the Left. Their battle against the Religious Right and the ruling elite is the same battle fought by people of color, women, and the working class. It is a battle for individual freedom, equality, and social justice. Gay and lesbian rights is very much part of the Left's agenda, and needs and deserves the support of all progressives.

If you believe American culture puts a much higher value on female life, consider this: "Some states quasi-officially condone the 'passion shooting' by a husband of a wife caught in an act of infidelity," according to sociologists Joseph Julian and William Kornblum. "The reverse . . . is known as homicide."

In a 1988 study of the plight of women worldwide, the Population Crisis Committee surveyed ninety-nine countries—covering 92 percent of the female population—in the areas of health, marriage and children, education, employment, and social equality. None of the countries surveyed received an excellent score; Sweden, with its strong welfare state, ranked the highest, scoring eighty-seven out of one hundred possible points. Fifty-one of the ninety-nine countries surveyed ranked poor, very poor, or extremely poor. In the study, the United States ranked first in educational opportunities for women, but fell to twelfth in employment, sixteenth in health, eighteenth in marriage and children, and twentieth in social equality.

Despite the gains in women's rights that were made in the 1960s and 1970s, women are still treated as second-class citizens in political, economic, and social affairs. While women have made strides in obtaining equal educations, they graduate into a workplace where their pay still averages just 64 cents for every dollar that a man earns doing similar work. According to Julian and Kornblum, in 1984 the average male high school dropout earned more than the average female college graduate. Women, despite their educational achievements, are still shuffled into lower-status, lower-paying jobs. They make up 70 percent of all retail clerks, 97 percent of all typists, and 99 percent of all secretaries. As a result, 67 percent of all minimum-wage earners are women, and two-thirds of all poor adults are women.

Even when women gain entry into traditionally male careers such as business, law, and engineering, they find that access to top-tier positions is limited by a "glass ceiling," a mysterious point which few women pass. Correspondingly, women make up less than half a percent of top corporate managers and less than 8 percent of federal and state judges. In a 1992 *Business Week* survey of four hundred women executives at major corporations, 52 percent said that the "rate of progress" for women in corporations had slowed, 56 percent believed a glass ceiling for women existed, and 63 percent said that women are likely to be paid a lower salary than men for the same job. As for the number of women who rise to the position of president or CEO of a public company, Marion Sandler, president of Golden West Financial Corporation, says "you can count them on one hand—with fingers missing."

With the ascent of the New Right and the Religious Right in the 1980s, the attack on women and their rights took on a new intellectual and religious justification. Right-wing think tanks like the Heritage Foundation and the Council for National Policy, along with the Moral Majority and a host of highly visible television evangelists, began an all-out assault on women's rights. The Right blamed women's drive for equality for the increasing rate of divorce and violence against women, for welfare dependency, for the decline of the traditional family, for increased drug abuse, and even for "America's rapid decline as a world power."

Susan Faludi, in *Backlash*, and Russ Bellant, in *The Coors Connection*, document the Right's vicious assault on women's rights. The Right labeled feminists "moral perverts," "enemies of every decent society," "blasphemers," and "satanic." An anti-ERA brochure produced by Phyllis Schlafly called the "ERA mentality . . . the source of today's social evils—hostility toward women, preborn babies, men, family, church, state, and God." Council for National Policy founder Tim LaHaye called day-care a "secular humanist plot to steal the hearts and minds of millions of little children." Howard Phillips, founder of the Conservative Caucus, claimed that feminists were behind "the conscious policy of government to liberate the wife from the leadership of the husband."

Despite the nasty and often ridiculous tone of the Right's rhetoric, with Reagan and Bush in the White House the Right was able to block movement toward gender equality in the 1980s. Reagan and Bush appointees to the Supreme Court and other federal judgeships, along with conservative appointees at the Equal Employment Opportunity Commission (EEOC), made it extremely difficult for women to pursue remedies against job discrimination and sexual harassment in the workplace successfully. Even though the number of sex-discrimination complaints filed with the EEOC rose dramatically during the 1980s, in the first half of the decade, the number of victims who received financial compensation dropped two-thirds. From the Supreme Court's *Webster* and *Casey* rulings to Bush's "gag order" forbidding family-planning clinics that receive federal funds from even mentioning the word "abortion," abortion rights were severely restricted. And as Faludi points out, "one-third of the Reagan budget cuts . . . came out of programs that predominately serve women," while much-needed family initiatives, such as family-leave policies and subsidized child care, were thwarted by the Right.

The inequality and brutality toward women in America is troubling. But equally disturbing is the loss that our whole society suffers from restricting the feminine voice in politics, business, and culture. Sociologist James Garbarino, in *Toward a Sustainable Society*, writes:

> One key to making the transition to a sustainable society is to replace masculine forms and themes that dominate public life with feminine concepts of power, value and social interaction. . . . If the feminine perspective is not in the driver's seat, we are headed down the wrong road. . . . If we are to move toward a sustainable society, we must alter our ideologies and institutions so that they will hear the feminine voice and resonate with it.

Ann Lewis, the former political director of the Democratic National Committee, cites poll results that support Garbarino's call for a greater feminine voice in public life. Writing in *Ms.*, Lewis says women are "more likely to support gun control legislation and less likely to advocate increased military spending or shipping arms to regional conflicts in Central America." In addition, "on issues like health care, child care, education, and the elderly, women are more likely than men to believe that government should take an active role." A *Life* poll found the same results: 50 percent more women than men feel that poverty and homelessness are extremely important social problems; half again as many women as men also want the government to help develop child-care programs and provide greater support to working parents; and more women than men "believe that addressing social problems is a better way to reduce crime than beefed-up law enforcement." Sociologist Elise Boulding describes the value of the feminine voice best: "the ingenuity of women may be the most precious resource the human race has left."

Fortunately, 1992 is shaping up to be the year of the woman in American politics. Women are expected to turn out in record numbers to vote for women candidates, eighteen of whom are running for national congressional seats. Electing more women, such as 1992 primary winners Carol Moseley Braun, Barbara Boxer, Dianne Feinstein, and Lynn Yeakel, would not only help squash the Right's attack on abortion rights and women's equality but would also go a long way toward creating a more humane America and a future for the country's children.

RACISM

Many of the problems that face minority communities could be reduced by addressing the concerns of the working class as a whole. This includes remedies such as a full-employment program, job-training initiatives, a higher minimum wage, equal funding for public schools, and national health insurance. But the scourge of institutionalized racism will also have to be eliminated to achieve any semblance of equality and justice for people of color in America.

Racism transcends class barriers. While the African-American middle class has grown substantially since affirmative action was implemented—from one in seventeen African-American families in 1967 to one in seven in 1989, according to the Population Reference Bureau—it is still afflicted by institutionalized racism. In some areas of the country, upper-income African-Americans—families earning between $50,000 and $75,000 a year—are refused mortgage loans at a rate almost three times greater than whites earning the same income. The rejection rate for affluent African-Americans is almost as great as that of lower-income whites. Furthermore, as former tennis champion Arthur Ashe points out, while minorities are over-represented as the stars of major-league sports, they are rarely given the opportunity to serve in management-level positions. "The crazy theories of black intellectual inferiority are alive and well—especially in baseball and football," claims Ashe. "African-Americans like myself can't help but conclude that there's a conspiracy of sorts that limits our access to management-level positions." And while minorities have been granted entry to corporate America, like women, they rarely break that glass ceiling to reach the top management ranks.

When racism is combined with class warfare, the combination can be horrifying. The infant mortality rate in some low-income minority neighborhoods exceeds that of many Third World Countries. In New York City the unemployment rate for African-Americans aged sixteen to nineteen is more than 91 percent. A full 41 percent of the country's Puerto Rican population lives in poverty, while 50 percent of African-American children under six years of age are impoverished.

For lower-income people of color, the failure of the nation's educational system has all but trapped them in poverty. As *Business Week* notes, "many [inner city] schools can't teach children the basics that potential employers require, and some public schools are more noted for their hallway gunfights and drug sales than for their graduation rate."

As a result, in Boston, for example, 40 percent of the students will not finish high school, while half of the students who do manage to graduate will be functionally illiterate. Jonathan Kozol reports in *Savage Inequalities* that the public schools with the most horrendous conditions are all predominately minority, while the public schools that resemble Ivy League college campuses are all predominately white. Without the opportunity to obtain a decent education, people of color slip deeper into poverty: from 1973 to 1989, the earnings of African-American high school dropouts fell an incredible 50 percent.

And, as if poverty and declining wages are not enough, minority communities have long been the dumping grounds for the poisons produced by American industry. Three out of five African-Americans and Latinos, and approximately half of all Asian/Pacific Islanders and Native Americans, live in areas with uncontrolled toxic-waste sites. Studies by sociologist Robert D. Bullard and the Commission for Racial Justice found that a community's racial makeup was a more significant factor than neighborhood income in how corporate polluters select sites for their dumps. "It's not a poverty thing. It's not a class thing," says Dr. Bullard. "It is racism, pure and simple."

As the Rodney King videotape showed, violence and brutality are also realities of life for people of color. Minorities face much higher rates of violence than whites, not only from the police, but also from among their own. Almost half of America's murder victims are African-American. In the United States, according to Steve Whitman in Z *Magazine*, "a Black person . . . is 7.4 times more likely to be imprisoned than a white person, [and] one out of every two Black men will be arrested in his lifetime." The incarceration rate for African-Americans is more than *four times* higher than the incarceration rate for blacks in South Africa.

The large number of African-American men imprisoned, unemployed, or dead has had an impact on the African-American family. Conservatives claim that the reason 62 percent of poor African-Americans live in female-headed families is a loss of "traditional values." Raw statistics point to another explanation: there are not enough "marriageable" poor and working-class African-American men to go around. Between homicide, imprisonment, and unemployment, arguably less than half of inner-city African-American men are in a position to raise and support a family. Combine this with a lack of access to sex education, birth control, and abortion services, along with welfare programs that deny benefits to a mother and her children if a man is in the home, and you produce a large number of families without husbands.

It may be true that there is a values and morals crisis in minority communities, but that crisis is no greater than the crisis facing the whole country. To expend so much political rhetoric on the morals of the African-American underclass, however, while not addressing the morals of a government, a defense industry, a savings and loan industry, and other industries that are rife with thieves, swindlers, and influence peddlers, is racism. To fail to address the morals of corporate leaders who knowingly and illegally dump poison in the nation's rivers or knowingly sell harmful, even deadly, products to the public, is racism. To focus on rising African-American crime rates, while not addressing the rise in white crime, is racism.

Indeed, America spends so much political and media energy pondering the plight and pathology of people of color that, African-American journalist Jake Lamar suggests, it may be time for white America to look in the mirror. Writing in *Esquire,* Lamar declares:

> I'm concerned about the state of white America. It's not just the major problems plaguing the white community that worry me—the breakdown of the white family, the growing white underclass, the rampant social pathology—but also the more subtle convolutions of white consciousness. . . .
>
> I've witnessed the poignant efforts of young whites striving to conform to the vague tenets of the mainstream, taking crushingly dull jobs, settling down with the least challenging of spouses, dreaming of the perfect family, groping for an illusory sense of security. . . .
>
> Your tribes seem unable to keep the peace among yourselves— the Yugoslavians are killing each others like animals, the Soviet republics are reverting to atavistic loyalties, and radical nationalists are popping up all over the place. Given your bloody past, one can't help but wonder: Can you be trusted to run a country in a civilized manner?

Like many others, Lamar suggests that solutions to the problems that face minority communities will come when the broader society begins to address its own problems and stops using race as a scapegoat, like an alcoholic uses another drink, to escape from its own bleak predicament.

ELIMINATING CLASS, RACE, AND GENDER BIAS

Much of what needs to be done to cure social discrimination, from a legislative point of view, is covered in other chapters. It includes a higher minimum wage; union-strengthening legislation; a full-employment program with skill-providing job training and transitional income assistance; and progressive taxation, including the repeal of the payroll tax. We also need amendments to the Equal Pay Act and the Civil Rights Act that promote the concept of equal pay for comparable work, eliminate the government's exemption (the federal government is arguably the largest gender discriminator), close other existing loopholes, and make it easier for claimants to pursue their cases. Other necessary remedies include equal funding for public schools, rebuilding the nation's cities and infrastructure, reforming the court system to reduce racial and gender bias, subsidizing child care, permanently legalizing abortion by amending the Constitution, and establishing national health care.

While these legislative changes would go a long way toward promoting employment and economic equality, however, they do not address the underlying current in American society that perpetuates bigotry. Indeed, some critics suggest, the women's and civil rights movements need to step back from their primary focus on legislative reform and return to their roots. They need to create a movement to restructure America's social and economic system, not just to find a place for the more fortunate women and people of color in the status quo. "Surely the aim of the [feminist] struggle," writes Barbara Ehrenreich, "was not to propel a few women to the top of a fundamentally unjust hierarchy, in which most women counted for little more than cheap labor."

To achieve a broader goal, the Left must change the institutions that preserve outdated sexist and racist norms. These include the educational system, the church, the media, and the family. Bigotry is learned behavior. According to sociologists Joseph Julian and William Kornblum, "most children are socialized about the prevailing norms of the society into which they are born. If the society is prejudiced against certain minorities and engages in discriminatory behavior, the children will generally learn those prejudices and behaviors and think they are correct and natural." At an early age, male and female children are raised differently, from the type of attention they receive from their parents to the type of toys they are given. In most two-parent households, they observe that their mother is the primary caregiver and homemaker—even if she is employed—and that their father is frequently absent. And when they mimic the sexually or racially discriminatory behavior exhibited by one or more of their parents, they often receive parental approval.

At school, social norms are reinforced. A number of studies have suggested that, for the most part, "schools reinforce traditional role stereotypes and socialize children into traditional sex roles." This was found to be true of class assignments—girls take typing, boys take shop; of textbooks, which underrepresent females and frequently cast them in old-fashioned, traditional roles; and of teachers, both male and female, who often share traditional stereotypes about the roles of men and women and consciously or unconsciously teach, discipline, and interact accordingly.

Racial stereotypes are also reinforced in the schools. Children can adopt racist attitudes when they meet other children who reflect the racism of their parents. Textbooks, though much improved over the last decade, are still generally written from a white male Eurocentric point of view, and promote the achievements and ingenuity of the white race while relegating other cultures to sidebars, at best. This not only confirms for children the superiority of the white race, but also adds to the feelings of inferiority felt by many nonwhite students. Finally, many teachers and counselors, who rarely receive training in racial sensitivity, tend to treat nonwhite and white students differently.

The racial and sexual socialization that children receive at home and in school is reinforced by what they view in the media. In cartoons, helpless females are saved by heroic white males. In advertising, women are usually portrayed as either homemakers or decorative sex objects. The working class is often portrayed as rednecked, unsophisticated, and crass. And if youngsters dare to watch the news, they will see African-Americans, for the most part, as violent criminals, athletes, or welfare dependents, and upper-class white males as leaders of government, the church, and the business community.

In organized religion, young people stare at pulpits filled, generally, by male priests, rabbis, or pastors. If a child's parents belong to a fundamentalist denomination, it is likely that he or she will hear Ephesians 5:23 recited a thousand times before reaching the age of eighteen: "For the husband is the head of the wife as Christ is head of the church."

Not surprisingly, it is rare that a child reaches young adulthood with an open mind about the role of men and women in society. It is also rare that a young person grows up with a genuine appreciation for people of other races and cultures. But gender and race neutrality are essential to creating a society where laws are no longer necessary to achieve equality.

The best place to achieve a social transformation is the schools. It can start with multicultural and nonsexist education. This would require further revision to school textbooks: the achievements of minorities must be presented, women must be portrayed in a variety of occupational roles, and men must be portrayed as caregivers as well as in occupational roles. In addition, teachers and school counselors need to be taught how to promote racial sensitivity and sexual equality. One current project, developed by Morris Dees of the Southern Poverty Law Center, is *Teaching Tolerance,* a semiannual magazine for teachers on fostering racial harmony among school children. Another program, Facing History and Ourselves, provides teachers' workshops on racism and prejudice through a study of historical events such as the Holocaust. Norman Siegal, head of the New York ACLU, has designed an ethics course that teaches personal responsibility, value judgments, and racial tolerance to New York City students. But these and similar programs need to be drastically expanded if they are to have a national impact on bigotry.

There are other cultural steps that could be taken as well. Women could leave sexually oppressive places of worship and find (or found) more-progressive churches or synagogues. Magazines that influence parenting behavior, such as *Parents* and *Redbook,* need to be persuaded to run educational articles offering parents advice on how to promote progressive attitudes among their children. And the organizations of the Left need to take a look in the mirror. Many of their hierarchies resemble the white, male boardrooms of corporate America.

Finally, the country must come to grips with the reality that bigotry starts at the top. It is not really an issue of dislike between working-class whites and people of color, or men battling women. It is the institutionalized nature of bigotry that is so destructive to society. Bigotry begins with political leaders, corporate leaders, union leaders, and the heads of the country's educational institutions—leaders who tolerate, if not promote, racist and sexist policies in their institutions and among their employees. If the back of bigotry in America is ever to be broken, it will have to start at the top. This, no doubt, will require a whole new breed of national leadership.

CHAPTER FIVE

Environment and Poverty

When president bush attended the united nations Conference on Environment and Development in June 1992, he may have been surprised to find that so much of the discussion focused on eradicating poverty and restraining economic growth. For the Earth Summit included the root causes of environmental degradation in its agenda: unsustainable economic development and the burgeoning gap between the rich and the poor.

Despite Bush's rejection of many of the summit's initiatives, the fact that the U.N. agenda challenged conventional economic wisdom is certainly significant. "The draft Rio Declaration on Environment and Development," writes *New York Times* journalist Paul Lewis, "commits the world's nations to a number of principles that have not been universally accepted before. At its heart is an agreement that eradicating poverty is an 'indispensable requirement for sustainable development.' "

By including a call for nations to "eliminate unsustainable patterns of production and consumption" in order to "cooperate in the essential task of eradicating poverty," the Earth Summit challenged the deeply ingrained belief that unlimited economic growth is a social good. It suggested instead that only economic growth coupled with production and consumption patterns that do not contribute to environmental degradation are desirable. In addition, it acknowledged that poverty, paradoxically, leads not only to higher mortality rates but also to over-population, as well as to deforestation, species extinction, and world instability.

In fact, the U.N. agenda contained a lesson for many of America's environmentalists as well. Environmentalists routinely interpret the concept of a sustainable society in the strictest sense: reducing the use of nonrenewable resources, pollution, and waste production. But as sociologist James Garbarino points out in *Toward A Sustainable Society*, the concept of a sustainable society encompasses much more than just environmental concerns. "A sustainable society," he writes, "supports a way of life organized around ethical and operational principles. It implies the existence of a culture and a social network within an economic system." For Garbarino, sustainable implies preserving a decent way of life for the world's future, its children. To achieve this goal, he argues, it is necessary to provide our children with a decent education, good health care, the prospect of a sufficient income, and family and institutional support systems.

Developing a sustainable society in America will require sweeping changes. We will have to redefine our economic priorities, develop a conservation program, and build a humane social welfare system. We will also have to make individual changes, such as reducing our consumption of beef, our reliance on automobiles, and our purchases of frivolous consumer items. We will have to change the way that society measures wealth and income by including the cost of environmental degradation and social dislocation in economic computations.

Changes of this magnitude are undoubtedly intimidating to politicians and corporate leaders, especially those who, like Bush, have trouble with the "vision thing." As a result, they will be extremely resistant to change. But change we must if we expect to preserve anything for our children to inherit.

POVERTY IN AMERICA

The United States has one of the industrialized world's highest rates of poverty among children. Journalist Holly Sklar reports in *Z Magazine* that according to the Luxembourg Income Study, an international survey of income and poverty in Great Britain, Australia, Canada, Germany, Israel, the Netherlands, Norway, Sweden, Switzerland, and the United States, the poverty rate for children in America is *four* times higher than the average of the other nations.

Sklar also reports that "nearly one out of four [American] children is born into poverty—the highest official rate of any industrialized nation. Poverty kills. The Maine Health Bureau found that poor children were more than three times as likely as other children to die during childhood. . . . The U.S has the world's number 1 military and economy, but ranks only 24th in infant mortality. Black America has a higher infant mortality rate than Nigeria, Jamaica, and Bulgaria."

In addition to high mortality rates, poor children suffer from malnutrition, higher rates of child abuse, inferior schools, rampant crime, toxic poisoning, violent gangs and drug traffickers, and obscene housing conditions. Many children living in ghetto neighborhoods face conditions similar to those of children growing up in the war zones of the Third World.

America's children, of course, do not suffer alone in their poverty. One in ten Americans survives on food stamps, and one in seven receives cash relief. The total number of Americans living below the poverty line reached an estimated thirty-six million people, or 14.7 percent of the population, in 1991. While the Census Bureau's official poverty line is $13,359 for a family of four, Sklar points out that "the average poor family with children" had an annual income of only $7,380 in 1990.

As a result, "many poor families," says the Children's Defense Fund, "manage by cutting back on food, jeopardizing their health and the development of their children, or by living in substandard and sometimes dangerous housing. Some do without heat, electricity, telephone service, or plumbing for months or years. Many do without health insurance, health care, safe child care, or reliable transportation to take them to or from work. Some borrow money if they can. Some beg. Some have small amounts of unreported income or feel compelled to engage in illegal activities."

The plight of the poor described by the Children's Defense Fund is not confined to the widely stereotyped welfare family, but includes people from all segments of American society: indeed, two-thirds of the poor are white. Most impoverished adults are employed; 60 percent of the poor live in a household with at least one full-time worker. The ranks of the poor include single and divorced women with children, two-parent families, high school dropouts, college graduates, veterans of the Vietnam and Persian Gulf wars, elderly retirees, and people with disabilities. The majority of the poor live in small towns or rural communities, others reside in middle-income city or suburban communities, and the remainder survive in the nation's urban ghettos.

The so-called underclass, the stereotype of all poor Americans, makes up only a small fraction of the total poor population. According to Harvard public policy professor David Ellwood, less than 10 percent of the poor are African-American or Hispanic, unemployed, high school dropouts, long-term welfare dependents, or live in concentrated areas of poverty such as South Central Los Angeles. "These [low] figures are surprising to many," writes Ellwood. "The image of the ghetto poor person has been emphasized so heavily in the media and in recent books that even those who study poverty are surprised by what they have found . . . poor Americans are more often among us than isolated from us."

Time also points out that "much of the popular thinking about welfare is contradicted by the facts":

> Welfare is not primarily a problem of the urban black underclass. Ninety percent of America's poor live in suburban and rural areas, and 60% of all AFDC recipients are white.
>
> The average AFDC family has only 1.9 children, fewer than the average U.S. family.
>
> No one is getting rich off the dole: the average monthly grant in 1990 was $377 for a family of three—less than half the poverty level.
>
> Far from spinning out of control, AFDC payments have declined 42% in real terms over the past two decades. [AFDC accounts for 1 percent of total federal spending and 3.4 percent of state spending on average.]
>
> Half of all aid recipients get off the rolls within two years. Only 2% remain for more than a decade.

Indeed, the problem of poverty is not an urban or race issue, but a much broader social problem. And it should not be of concern only to the poor or the compassionate: much of middle-class America is only one major illness, job loss, death, or divorce away from poverty.

THE STATE OF THE ENVIRONMENT

"Time is running out," warns Mustafa K. Tolba, head of the U.N. Environment Program. "The environment is now worse than 20 years ago. Critical thresholds may already have been breached."

Tolba's somber assessment accompanied the release of a U.N. report that said that one billion people breathe unhealthy air, skin cancer and malnutrition are rising, and our air, water, and farmland are growing increasingly polluted.

ATMOSPHERIC DISASTER

The worldwide increase in skin cancer documented in the U.N. report is attributed to the continuing deterioration of the ozone layer. Since a hole was discovered in the ozone layer over Antarctica more than ten years ago, scientists have been monitoring its spread. In February 1992, U.N. scientists predicted that if the ozone layer is depleted another 5 percent by the year 2000 (roughly the current rate of depletion), the result would be an increase in HIV infections due to the harmful effect of ultraviolet radiation on the body's immune system, 300,000 additional cases of skin cancer worldwide, over 1.6 million more cases of cataracts, and a dramatic decrease in worldwide food production.

Ozone depletion isn't the only looming disaster: there is also global warming. A number of scientists project that in the next fifty years alone, the "greenhouse effect"—the trapping of solar heat in the lower atmosphere because of industrial pollution—will lead to a rise in the earth's temperature of between four and nine degrees Fahrenheit.

Global warming on this scale would be catastrophic. Island nations and low-lying countries would be severely flooded, if not submerged, as the warming oceans expanded and rose—the Environmental Protection Agency estimates a seven-foot rise in sea levels by the year 2100. Already, the Alliance of Small Island States reports that a number of low-lying islands have been evacuated due to rising sea levels caused by global warming. Once-fertile food-producing areas like the Midwest would become virtual dustbowls, while forests, plants, fish, and other animals that do not adjust quickly enough to the rapidly changing ecosystem would become extinct.

DEFORESTATION

Along with global warming and ozone depletion, we also need to find a solution to deforestation. According to the World Resource Institute, the world's forests are being destroyed at a rate of eighty acres per minute. In the past century alone, over half of the world's tropical rain forest has been cut down.

One does not have to be a nature lover to be concerned by the destruction of the world's forests. As Dr. Helen Caldicott, co-founder of Physicians for Social Responsibility, puts it, trees are "the lungs of the earth." Trees, along with other plant life, absorb carbon dioxide—a major contributor to global warming—and in return release life-sustaining oxygen. Burning trees, however, does just the opposite. In 1987, according to authors Jeremy and Carol Grunewald Rifkin, "more than 1.2 billion tons of [long-stored] carbon dioxide were released into the atmosphere from clearing and burning the forests of Amazonia . . . [contributing] 9 percent of the total worldwide additions to global warming from all sources."

Deforestation is also one of the chief causes of soil erosion, which is a serious threat to the world's food supply. In the Amazon, Caldicott tells us, "every day, each tree transpires into the air hundreds of gallons of water, which evaporates and creates the afternoon rain. When the forest is destroyed, the transpiration of water ceases, the rain stops, the soil dries out, and the region becomes a desert." And indeed, as Caldicott reminds us, "humid tropical rain forest" once stood in what is now the desert of the Middle East. In Panama, where deforestation destroyed trees necessary for the prevention of topsoil runoff, once-fertile land now threatens to clog and even to close the Panama Canal. And in Ethiopia, according to the 1992 Earth Journal, "where over 90 percent of the forest in the once rich and fertile highlands have been cut down," more than a billion tons of topsoil wash away each year. The result: 8,000 square miles of desert where fertile land once lay, and mass starvation.

In the United States, timber companies are depleting America's ancient forest at an alarming rate. Not only does this occur on private land, but it also occurs on federally owned lands. Even worse, our government sells its valuable timber to loggers at bargain-basement prices. By some estimates, the federal government has lost $5.6 billion selling foresting rights over the last decade. "Publicly owned lands are cut," says

New York Times writer Donald G. McNeil, Jr., "because the Forest Service sells them so cheaply that loggers would be foolish to say no. [The Forest Service] builds roads, pays rangers, absorbs the risk of fires and insects, then sells at a loss." The same practice is extended to cattle ranchers: many of the nation's public rangelands, wildlife refuges, and even national parks are leased at a loss to ranchers for grazing cattle.

BIODIVERSITY

The clearing of forests for cattle grazing, timber, and mining and oil exploration, in addition to driftnetting (dragging fishing nets that stretch as far as thirty miles behind a boat, snagging everything they encounter), and hunting and trapping, have led to an alarming rise in the rate of species extinction—perhaps as many as one species per hour. Some scientists, say the Rifkins, "predict that one quarter to one half of all species on earth will become extinct within the next thirty years."

By destroying natural habitats, humans make it impossible for many species of plants and animals to survive. In the United States, the shrinking of wetlands threatens hundreds of species of birds, fish, and other animals. It is also destroying one of nature's most efficient ecosystems: wetlands are an enormous aid in flood control, since they absorb excess rains and purify water flowing from the land into rivers and bays.

TOXIC POISONING

While global warming and ozone depletion threaten the Earth's future, the poisoning of our air, food, and water and the proliferation of nuclear and chemical toxins are killing people in America today. According to Helen Caldicott, "in 1987, some 10.5 billion pounds of toxic chemicals were released into the air, water, and soil of the United States." Two and a half million tons of these poisons came from the country's single largest polluter, the U.S. government, while another 1.6 billion tons of reported toxic releases came from just ten corporate polluters.

Much of the nation's drinking water is contaminated. In 1988 the EPA found pesticides in the groundwater—the source of drinking water for 50 percent of the population—of 39 states. Author Nancy Green, in *Poisoning Our Children*, reports that scientists have found the cancer-causing agent MX "in every chlorinated drinking water tested for it."

MX and another cancer-causing agent, DCA, are widely considered the most hazardous substances found in drinking water today. What is ironic is that these two agents are in the water as a result of attempting to purify it: both MX and DCA form as a result of adding the widely used disinfectant, chlorine, to water.

In Los Angeles alone, writes Caldicott, "about 125 million pounds of toxins are discharged into the . . . air each year." Not surprisingly, a recent study of the lungs of a hundred Los Angeles youths who had died accidental deaths showed that 80 percent had "notable abnormalities in lung tissue, and 27 percent had severe pathology."

While Los Angeles may be the smog capital of the United States, its plight does not even compare to the thousands of small communities that stand in the shadows of chemical refineries. In the Mississippi River town of St. Gabriel, "twenty-six petrochemical factories belch 400 million pounds of chemicals, including the carcinogens benzene, carbon tetrachloride, chloroform, toluene, and ethylene oxide into the air each year." In Louisiana, there is an eighty-mile stretch of the Mississippi River known as "cancer alley" that contains more than a hundred petrochemical plants and oil refineries. And in Chicago, an impoverished public housing project called Altgeld Gardens, which is surrounded by chemical plants, a paint factory, and seven waste dumps, has one of the highest rates of cancer in the nation.

In addition to chemical plants, many communities are home to toxic or nuclear waste dumps. Here, radioactive materials and cancer-causing chemicals seep into the drinking water, fill the air with thick, foul-smelling, poisonous fumes, and in some cases, such as Love Canal, ooze into the neighborhood's basements. Davis, California's drinking water was contaminated by university researchers who buried hundreds of dogs that had been used for radiation research on campus property. In Oak Ridge, Tennessee, home to a nuclear bomb factory, the U.S. government, according to *Time*, admits to having "littered the surrounding countryside with everything from asbestos and mercury to enriched uranium." At the 560-square-mile Hanford Nuclear Site, near Richland, Washington, "a third of the ground water is contaminated and about ten square miles of soil are polluted with toxics, heavy metals and uranium." All together, the cost of cleaning up the nation's nuclear and hazardous waste sites could be as high as $750 billion.

CONSUMER POISONING

As Nancy Green points out, you don't have to live near a petrochemical plant or a hazardous waste dump to receive a substantial dose of toxic poisoning. There are hazardous chemicals in the food we eat, the common consumer products we use in our homes, and in our workplaces and our children's schools.

Today, according to Helen Caldicott, there are more than 80,000 different pesticides in use, and "no information is available on the human toxicity of 63,200 of these commonly used chemicals." These toxins, designed to kill insects and weeds, are routinely sprayed over grains, vegetables, and fruits. Pesticide residues are present not only in agricultural products, but also in the beef and milk of cows that eat that grain and in the fish whose lakes are polluted by runoff from farmlands.

Green reports that more than thirty different pesticide residues have been found in carrots alone. Amazingly, a recent study showed that 17 percent of domestic carrots had traces of cancer-causing DDT, banned by the EPA in 1972. Dieldrin residues were also found; this chemical was banned in 1974 because it was shown to produce birth defects. Indeed, one of the indirect findings of this study was that pesticide residues can remain in the soil for decades.

Nonorganic carrots and other vegetables are not our only problem. Green also reports that, according to the U.S. General Accounting Office, 143 drugs and pesticides, 68 of which are known or suspected to cause cancer, birth defects, or mutations, are likely to leave toxic residues in raw meat. To kill the parasites that thrive in the appalling conditions in which most livestock live, livestock are routinely treated with toxaphene, a member of the DDT family. Green also estimates that 80 percent of all pigs slaughtered for market have pneumonia as a result of inhaling the ammonia used to control the overwhelming stench of modern-day pig pens. In addition, livestock consume over twelve million pounds of antibiotics annually. They are also given growth and other types of hormones. One of these hormones, DES, has been linked to cancer, sterility, atrophied testicles, voice changes, and leukemia. Although DES was eventually banned by the Food and Drug Administration (FDA), according to John Robbins in *Diet for a New America*, DES, along with a number of similarly toxic but legal hormones, is still widely used today.

In addition to food products, toxins are also found in common household products. Pest-control and lawn-care chemicals for home use contain toxic chemicals similar to those used by farmers. Common products like detergents, cosmetics, disposable diapers, and baby oils can contain numerous harmful toxins. These toxins include naphtha, a central nervous system depressant (in dishwashing detergent); cancer-causing butylate hydroxytoluene (in lipstick, baby oil, eyeliner, and soap); and dioxin (in chlorine-bleached disposable diapers, sanitary napkins, coffee filters, and milk cartons). This proliferation of toxins in the household can make housework deadly. Green cites a fifteen-year study that showed that "women who stayed at home all day had a 54 percent higher death rate from cancer than women who had jobs away from the home." The study attributed the higher death rates to increased exposure to the chemicals in household products.

So what are the FDA and the EPA doing to protect Americans from these poisons? The answer is, frankly, very little. The EPA and FDA rely heavily on industry research and testing to determine potential health risks. The FDA itself only inspects about 1 percent of the food sold in the United States. In addition, half of the pesticides currently available cannot be detected by standard testing procedures, and all pesticides introduced before 1977 are exempt from testing for health risks. Even when a chemical or product is found to pose a health risk, bureaucracy and politics can keep it on the market for as much as a decade, as was the case with cancer-causing asbestos products. Indeed, instead of having to be proven safe before they can be sold, products in America are often considered safe until they maim or kill someone.

ERADICATING POVERTY

So far the widespread misperceptions about the poor and welfare in America have blocked any meaningful debate about eradicating poverty. Instead, politicians and policy experts argue about ways of curbing the cost of welfare (which totals less than 1 percent of the federal budget); curing welfare dependency, which afflicts a tiny minority of welfare recipients; or providing workfare programs that teach few, if any, real job skills. When a broader discussion of poverty does occur, it usually focuses on providing breaks to businesses to create new jobs. Notably absent in these debates, on both the conservative and the liberal sides, is any discussion of meaningful wealth-distribution policies, increased welfare payments, restrictions or penalties for plant closings and job exportation, a full-employment program, or a higher minimum wage.

INCREASE THE MINIMUM WAGE

The majority of poor adults have jobs. The working poor simply need higher wages. According to the Census Bureau, 18 percent of American workers earn incomes that are below poverty level. One solution to low wages, recommended by leading poverty experts such as David Ellwood and Harvard public policy professor Mary Jo Bane, is to raise the minimum wage. As President Franklin D. Roosevelt declared when he established the minimum wage decades ago, "no business which depends for its existence on paying less than living wages to its workers has any right to continue in this country."

Full-time employment at the current minimum wage level totals a meager $8,840 a year. Coretta Scott King, co-chair of the National Committee for Full Employment, suggests that the proper level for the minimum wage should be 50 percent of the average hourly wage in private industry. An increase to this level would go a long way toward bringing the working poor to solvency.

Two other federal policy changes could be extremely helpful to the working poor. The regressive Social Security payroll tax, as discussed in chapter 3, should be eliminated. Instead, Social Security should be funded more equitably through a progressive increase in the federal income tax. This policy change alone would increase the disposable income of the working poor by approximately 7 percent. Second, the earned income credit—an actual tax rebate to low-income families— could be increased. This would raise the incomes of many working families above the poverty level.

FIGHTING THE FEMINIZATION OF POVERTY

While increasing the minimum wage would be of great benefit to all workers, it would be especially helpful to women. Sixty-seven percent of workers who earn the minimum wage are women. And as David Ellwood points out in *Poor Support*, the poverty rate for families headed by working women is even worse than the statistics indicate. "The poverty line," writes Ellwood, "does not take account of work expenses like day care or transportation. Thus, some women who are not officially poor undoubtedly have disposable incomes below the poverty line."

Low wage levels coupled with the cost of child care and medical expenses force many single mothers to seek welfare instead of employment. "For a very large proportion of single mothers," says Northwestern University sociologist Christopher Jencks, "it's impossible to find a job that pays as well as being on welfare." David Ellwood conservatively estimates that a single mother working full-time would have to earn more than 125 percent of the minimum wage before her disposable income—still well short of the poverty line—equaled her disposable income on welfare. For most mothers, however, the break-even level may be far higher than Ellwood projects: his calculations assume that child care can be found for $1 an hour.

Much of what has come to be termed the "feminization of poverty" could also be eradicated by providing equal pay for women. In 1986, women who worked full time earned an average of only 64 cents to every dollar earned by men. This, exclaims Susan Faludi, was "exactly the same gap that working women had faced in 1955." Indeed, journalist Holly Sklar cites a 1977 government study that showed that equalizing pay for women would halve the number of poor families.

To be able to participate in the work force, single mothers need national health insurance and subsidized child care, along with higher wages. Government-supported preschool for all three and four year olds would also help, as would keeping elementary schools open until 6:00 p.m. to provide a place for school-age children to remain until their parents returned home from work. Other family assistance initiatives include a bill proposed by Democrat Thomas Downey and Republican Henry Hyde in the House that would guarantee the payment of a minimum level of child support and allow increased use of the Internal Revenue Service to collect payments from absent fathers. In addition, employers should be required to adopt humane paid family-leave policies to prevent working parents from being economically penalized for having and nurturing children. These federally mandated leave policies should allow fathers as well as mothers to take time off to nurture their children.

URBAN DEVELOPMENT

The public-works projects performed under the full-employment program discussed in chapter 3 would help bring jobs and capital investment back into low-income neighborhoods. But this alone will not be enough. In addition, the residents of low-income communities need seed grants; long-term, low-interest loans; and technical assistance so they can start small businesses and co-ops in their own neighborhoods. Many of these communities are in dire need of basic commercial services: grocery stores, hardware stores, laundromats, repair shops, automotive services, and beauty salons. Seed grants will not only allow new community businesses to meet these needs, but will also revitalize long-abandoned business districts. In addition, special tax credits could be given to new businesses that hire welfare recipients on a full-time basis.

We need programs to promote the rehabilitation and construction of new low-income housing for the homeless as well as lower-income families. Slumlords who refuse to bring their properties up to building-code standards must be fined and, if necessary, have their properties confiscated.

FULL EMPLOYMENT, TRAINING, AND EDUCATION

There has been a recent national uproar because American students rank below Japanese, Korean, and European students in math and science tests. This "crisis," however, pales in comparison with the fact that an estimated twenty-seven million Americans—predominately poor—cannot even read and write, while one in four students—again disproportionately poor—drops out of high school. Although many reforms have been proposed to improve American students' test scores, little has been said about the impact of the gross inequality of public-school funding on poor and minority youths.

Conservatives, many of whose children attend the very best public or most expensive private schools, will tell you that funding does not matter in education. They will cite examples of an impoverished school here or there whose students are performing close to the national average. But these examples are exceedingly rare. In the main, students from impoverished school districts perform and graduate from high school at rates substantially below the national average.

Benjamin DeMott reported that in 1988, Princeton, New Jersey, spent $7,015 per public school student while Camden, New Jersey, spent only $4,500. "Only 7 percent of Princeton pupils failed standard proficiency tests," writes Demott, "whereas a percentage eleven times greater failed in Camden." In Texas, before that state's Supreme Court outlawed school financing based on local property tax receipts in 1989, the inequality of school financing was even worse. According to Holly Sklar, "per-pupil spending [ranged] from $2,000 in the poorest districts to $19,000 in the richest."

In reality, it is exceedingly difficult for even the most motivated students to learn adequately without the proper tools or in grossly over-crowded classrooms. It is also very difficult for students to maintain an interest in school when their curriculum is limited to only math, science, and English.

Jonathan Kozol, in *Savage Inequalities*, paints a vivid and disturbing picture of America's almost entirely segregated schools, in which poor, black students suffer from constant shortages: of paper and chalk, of basic equipment from playgrounds to science labs, and, more than anything, of staff. Many of the school buildings have leaking roofs, broken windows, and broken heating systems. Kozol describes one school in the North Bronx, formerly a roller-skating rink, that had no windows. Another, in East St. Louis, Illinois, had sewage backing up into the school's kitchen and bathrooms. Meanwhile, upper-income, primarily white schools often enjoy an embarrassment of riches.

Lower-income children start their education with "faith and optimism," writes Kozol, "and they often seem to thrive during the first few years." But by third grade, the average low-income student begins to fall behind, and by sixth grade, widespread truancy has set in. The route from truancy to dropping out, Kozol points out, is "direct and swift."

All of the nation's children need a well-financed, quality education. Students in Camden deserve no less than students in Princeton. In fact, they need more: they need additional resources that address the special needs of children living in poverty, such as security, nutrition, and counseling. To accomplish this, more school systems could be decoupled from real estate taxes and funded equally out of general state revenues. The federal government could achieve a similar result by requiring states to fund schools equally.

Studies by J. S. Fuerst, of the Loyola University School of Social Work in Chicago, show that poor children who attended Head Start and also received six to nine years of additional intensive educational assistance graduated from high school at a rate almost equal to the national average of 80 percent. In contrast, only 62 percent of the children who attended Head Start alone graduated, while just 49 percent of poor children who didn't attend Head Start graduated. In explaining these findings, Barbara Willer, of the National Association for the Education of Young Children, said: "The best program in the world for a very short time at age four is not going to help children" when they must cope with the conditions of today's inner city neighborhoods.

Fuerst's findings strongly suggest not only that Head Start needs to be fully funded, to reach *every* poor child, but also that we need to incorporate special programs to provide extra help for poor students into public school curriculums.

A UNIVERSAL SOLUTION

The key to eliminating poverty is not more welfare programs, according to William Julius Wilson, but "a comprehensive program of economic and social reform" that includes "policies to promote balanced economic growth . . . a nationally oriented labor-market strategy, a child support assurance program, a child care strategy." David Ellwood agrees that welfare is not the answer. He suggests instead a transitional support system, a higher minimum wage, child care assistance, and national health insurance.

America's citizens, both impoverished and middle class, need a new and humane contract between the government and its citizens. We need a universal, comprehensive package of social policies that addresses not only the root causes of poverty—low wages, unemployment, a flawed income-transfer system, and an ineffective education and training system—but also the draining economic constraints on the working and middle classes as well: lack of affordable health care, child care, and housing; racial and gender discrimination; drugs and crime; unenforced child-support laws; and lack of access to birth-control options.

RESTORING OUR ENVIRONMENT

Scientists, environmentalists, and our political leaders have known what must be done to repair the environment for some time. But because environmental restoration has significant short-run costs for industries such as utilities, timber, mining, oil, and petrochemicals, the preferred tactic of the pro-business Reagan and Bush administrations has been to conduct more research, convene more meetings, and otherwise stall.

Even worse, in recent years industry and its paid politicians and "experts" have gone on the offensive, offering free-market solutions to help the environment. Hence we now have a market for "pollution credits" which allows corporate America to buy and sell the right to pollute our environment. Another tactic is litigation. Detroit's Big Three automakers, when hit with a $40 million bill for the cleanup of a Superfund toxic waste site, decided to sue everyone who had ever used the site, including a Girl Scout troop. All told, billions of dollars earmarked for environmental cleanup have been spent on litigation. In addition, the Bush administration's Council on Competitiveness, headed by Vice President Dan Quayle, has been working behind the scenes on behalf of polluters to block EPA regulations.

And recently, a grass-roots anti-environmental movement has developed on the Right. Called "Wise Use," it is headed by veteran right-wingers Ron Arnold and Alan Gottlieb. To garner support, Wise Use employs the standard New Right tactic of sending out millions of direct-mail pieces that denounce environmentalists for creating the country's economic woes and calls them "nature fascists" and "evil incarnate." Their growing membership, according to *Outside* journalist Jon Krakauer, is "an unlikely mélange of disgruntled ranchers, farmers, loggers, miners, trappers, millworkers, hunters, off-road-vehicle owners, oil workers, labor unions, large corporations, and sundry other entities." And their mission is clear. "The environmental movement is a rich, powerful menace to society," says Ron Arnold, "and we intend to destroy it."

With pro-business politicians in Washington and an environmental backlash at the grass-roots level, environmentalists face a difficult task. Much change is needed to achieve an environmentally sustainable society, but these changes will be resisted fiercely by corporate polluters, their paid political lackeys, and their financially supported groups like Wise Use.

COMBATING ATMOSPHERIC POLLUTION

The burning of fossil fuels (coal, oil, and wood) and industrial and consumer chemical emissions are the primary causes of the destruction of the Earth's atmosphere through ozone depletion and the greenhouse effect. Ozone depletion is primarily caused by a group of chemicals called chlorofluorocarbons, or CFCs. CFCs are gases used in refrigeration, air-conditioning, aerosol cans, and the manufacture of styrofoam. Solid-fuel rocket launches also release ozone-depleting chemicals into the atmosphere: the space shuttle releases 240 tons of hydrochloric acid into the atmosphere at each launch. Although world leaders signed an international treaty in June of 1990 agreeing to phaseout CFCs by the year 2000, environmental scientists argue that the timetable needs to be accelerated. At the least, President Bush and Congress must be persuaded to join Germany, which has vowed to phase out the use of CFCs by 1993.

The greenhouse effect, which is leading to global warming, is caused by the release of certain gases into the atmosphere. Carbon dioxide is the primary culprit; it is produced by the burning of fossil fuels in utilities, plants, and automobiles, or during the burning of forests. Three other chemical emissions also contribute to global warming: nitrous oxide, a by-product of auto, airplane, and power plant exhaust; methane, primarily emitted by cows during digestion; and CFCs.

The United States is the world's leading carbon dioxide producer: with only 5 percent of the world's population, it emits 27 percent of the world's carbon dioxide. Ten percent of America's GNP (roughly $500 billion) is spent on energy; this includes, for instance, the cost of oil and of producing electricity. In contrast, Japan, which is much more energy-efficient, spends only 5 percent of its GNP on energy.

Greater energy conservation in the United States would certainly help slow global warming. But it is less widely known that it would also save industry, consumers, and taxpayers billions of dollars. Indeed, if the United States attained Japan's level of energy efficiency, the nation would save approximately $250 billion a year. For example, an increase in average automobile fuel economy to forty miles per gallon could save the nation 2.4 million barrels of oil a day. And, according to *Time,* a switch from incandescent to compact fluorescent light bulbs could cut $11 billion a year from utility bills.

Conservation would also lead to increased employment. While the cost of building and operating a wind farm is a fraction of the cost of building and running a nuclear power plant that generates the same amount of electricity, a wind farm requires five times the number of staff members to operate. Many new jobs would be created by programs to make buildings more energy efficient and the development of light train systems in urban areas and high-speed train systems nationwide. The development of new technologies like recyclable, high-efficiency batteries for electric cars, efficient solar electric cells, and state-of-the-art industrial plant scrubbers could lead to an increase in export-related jobs as other nations become increasingly conservation-oriented. In total, estimates *Time*, "the global market for environmentally friendly products is worth an estimated $200 billion a year, and has just begun to take off."

All of this, however, would require a strong national conservation policy. This policy would have to include taxes on the burning of fossil fuels and the emission of polluting chemicals. It would require a national program to increase the energy efficiency of buildings and to provide incentives to industry for the development of alternative energy sources such as wind, biofuels, and solar and geothermal power. In addition, the conservation program needs to provide incentives to expand the country's mass-transit system, including the introduction of high-speed passenger trains. Other necessary policies include higher taxes on gasoline and on inefficient automobiles and higher fuel economy requirements for auto manufacturers.

PROTECTING NATURE

Congress must designate the Arctic National Wildlife Refuge, in Alaska, off-limits to oil and gas exploration. It also needs to establish a no-net-loss policy for the nation's forests and wetlands. Commercial logging in the old-growth forests of the Pacific Northwest should be, if not banned, then at least discouraged, by raising fees to loggers. Ranchers who graze cattle on public lands should also pay fees high enough to discourage unwise use.

We also need a national policy to promote biodiversity, including removing loopholes in the Endangered Species Acts. Stronger sanctions against countries that violate international endangered species, conservation, and fishing agreements also need to be imposed.

WASTE REDUCTION AND CLEANUP

We must conduct a national public relations campaign to encourage recycling and discourage the use of nonrecyclable products. We need to impose "green taxes" on environmentally threatening industrial activities: air, ground, and water pollution; waste generation; the depletion of nonrenewable resources; and the manufacture of disposable or nonrecyclable items. And Congress must allocate the funds to clean up the nation's toxic waste sites.

CONSUMER POISONING

Consumers must become more conscious of the ingredients in the products they purchase. Even if we made desperately needed revisions to FDA and EPA policies for the approval of chemicals and drugs, it would be unwise to depend on these agencies to protect our health. We need stronger enforcement and the possibility of jail sentences to prevent manufacturers from rushing untested products to market or, even worse, hiding evidence of health risks. But the best consumer protection is information: seek information on toxic-free products such as organic foods and nontoxic cleaning products and cosmetics and buy these instead of common, toxic products.

ACT LOCALLY

Although we must address the health of the environment on a national level—and from a global perspective—much can still be done locally. Communities can introduce measures to encourage the use of mass-transit systems, to ban products such as styrofoam packaging, or to prevent the construction of toxic-waste dumps. They can also push public officials to make local government buildings more energy efficient and to assure that vehicles purchased by their local governments are fuel efficient.

In addition, there is a lot that you can do on your own. You can participate in or help set up recycling programs at home, at school, or on the job. You can boycott companies that pollute the environment. You can purchase energy-efficient or water-saving appliances and devices. And you can use mass transit, a bicycle, or walk whenever possible. At the least, you can read one of the many books that outline the hundreds of individual actions we all can take to help preserve the environment.

CHAPTER SIX

Foreign Policy and the Third World

IN A FITTING END TO THE COLD WAR, THE BERLIN wall, a symbol of humanity divided, was torn down not by NATO tanks or Soviet rockets but by unarmed human hands. Communism in the Soviet Union also collapsed, pulled down by the will of everyday people seeking freedom and social justice.

The cold war was waged at grave cost to America. Forty years of bloated military spending—totaling over ten trillion dollars—drained much-needed investment money from industry, public infrastructure, and human development. Hundreds of thousands of America's young were maimed in Korea, Vietnam, and other cold war conflicts. And, as author Christopher Lasch explained in a 1990 *New York Times* article, there were other costs as well:

> Preoccupation with external affairs led to the neglect of domestic reforms, even of basic services. The development of secret police organizations, the erosion of civil liberties, the stifling of political debate in the interest of bipartisan consensus, the concentration of decision-making in the executive branch, the secrecy surrounding executive actions, the lying that has come to be accepted as routine in American politics—all these things derive either directly or indirectly from the cold war.

But while the cold war inflicted enormous costs on America, and the Soviet Union as well, no one suffered more than the people of the Third World. For it was on their land—Vietnam, Nicaragua, Korea, El Salvador, Afghanistan, Ethiopia, Indonesia, Angola—that the cold war was actually fought. It was also under the pretext of the cold war that America's elite supported apartheid in South Africa and funded an assortment of right-wing, murderous dictatorships from the Shah of Iran to Jonas Savimbi's UNITA death squads in Angola.

Now the cold war is over, and the people of the former Soviet Union have sent the world a message. It is a message that serves as a warning, writes *The Nation* editor Marcus Rakin, "to modern governments, of whatever ideological stripe, that do not meet the needs of their people." The Soviet people, who disbanded a government that was woefully inadequate to their needs, are the true winners of the cold war.

While the people of the former Soviet Union are now free of the cold war, Americans are not. For America, the war will go on. Most likely it will have a new name, a new pretext, and new bogeymen—Cuba, Iraq, Libya, and North Korea are leading contenders. For as we will see, America was waging war on the Third World long before the Soviet Union came into existence. It was not a war to defend against an "evil empire," but a war to guarantee access to cheap labor, foreign land, and natural resources. It was a war fought in behalf of worldwide capitalism and the fruits it bears for America's elite.

For many liberals, the end of the "official" cold war offers hope for a new U.S. foreign policy. "The world is changing and so also must U.S. foreign policy," writes the Brookings Institution's John Steinbruner. But the elite must still protect their interests, such as access to Middle Eastern oil and other Third World natural resources. As a result, George Bush went to war against his former ally, Saddam Hussein, and invaded Panama to bring his former CIA employee, Manuel Noriega, to justice. And instead of bringing in new leadership to chart a post-cold war course for the CIA, Bush chose thirty-year veteran Robert Gates, despite his connection to the Iran-contra scandal and his inaccurate and (as some suggested during his confirmation hearings) possibly falsified reports on the economic and military health of the Soviet Union.

These recent post-cold war events show that it is business as usual in Washington. And indeed, America's Third World policy will not change unless progressives force it to. The end of the cold war has not brought an end to the movements for peace, nuclear disarmament, or human rights. Instead, it has brought a new beginning. It is an opportunity, now that we are out from under the cloud of the Red Menace, for activists to educate the public about the true cost of militarism; to show that American imperialism has led to death, hunger, oppression, and massacres around the world; and to show the American public that its country's foreign policy, like its domestic policy, is designed to benefit business. It is an opportunity to show America that there is a better way.

THIRD WORLD POLICY: IN WHOSE INTEREST?

Despite decades of rhetoric using the threat of Soviet expansion as an excuse for U.S. intervention in the Third World, the fall of the Soviet Union will not bring an end to U.S. aggression. In fact, the "communist threat," the "domino theory," and the "global rollback" doctrines were all developed after a long history of capitalism-inspired Third World intervention. Almost a century ago, Major General Smedley D. Butler (a two-time winner of the Congressional Medal of Honor) described the impact of capitalism on America's Third World policy like this:

> War is a racket. . . . I spent 33 years and 4 months in active service. . . . And during the period I spent most of my time being a high-class muscle man for Big Business, for Wall Street and the bankers. In short, I was a racketeer for capitalism. . . .
>
> Thus I helped make Mexico and especially Tampico safe for American oil interests in 1914. I helped make Haiti and Cuba a decent place for the National City Bank boys to collect revenues in. I helped in the raping of a half a dozen Central American republics for the benefit of Wall Street. . . . I helped purify Nicaragua for the international banking house of Brown Brothers in 1909-1912. I brought light to the Dominican Republic for American sugar interests in 1916. I helped make Honduras "right" for American fruit companies in 1903.

A study of America's foreign-policy practices by Northwestern University history professor Laurence Shoup and author William Minter came to a similar conclusion. In their book, *Imperial Brain Trust*, they write:

There is a large body of evidence, conveniently ignored by [foreign policy] theorists, that the actual result of multinational corporate capitalism in the Third World is poverty and repressive governments. That poverty is the main product of multinational corporate power has been convincingly argued by numerous scholars. . . . Evidence of multinational corporations requiring and scheming, directly or indirectly, to achieve repressive, reactionary governments is also substantial. The influence of Anaconda, Kennecott, and ITT in Chile in 1970-1973, and the United Fruit Company in Central America are but two examples. Instances of bribery and corruption of government officials are numerous. The actions of the CIA in various parts of the world have frequently directly served the interest of multinational corporations.

America's Third World policies maintain access to cheap raw materials and labor, protect American assets overseas, and support Third World governments whose policies are amenable to the maximization of profits by U.S. companies. Accordingly, Third World countries whose governments reject U.S.-styled free-market capitalism and opt instead for land reform, fairer wealth distribution, or pro-labor legislation, or who are suspected of being soft on communism, are subjected to severe retribution from the United States.

ECONOMIC WEAPONS

America's position as a superpower emanates not only from its military superiority, but also from its willingness to use its economic might as a weapon. Following a carrot-and-stick philosophy, America gives foreign aid, bank loans, and access to its domestic markets to those Third World nations it favors and withholds these important assets from those of whom it disapproves. America's economic weapons include $9 billion in foreign aid a year, $300 billion in outstanding Third World bank loans, American influence at the World Bank and International Monetary Fund, and an intelligence network with a $30 billion annual budget.

Under the Reagan administration, for example, Jamaica implemented supply-side economic policies recommended by the United States, and received a 1,000-percent increase in foreign aid. As a result, its foreign debt more than doubled. Largely as a result of the debt burden, the Jamaican dollar has plummeted and inflation and interest rates have soared, while, at the behest of the IMF, the Jamaican government has ended food subsidies and cut spending on social services. Reaganomics was also forced on Grenada after its 1983 "rescue." In 1990, the North American Congress on Latin America reported that Grenada's foreign debt had reached record levels and unemployment hovered somewhere between 25 and 30 percent. In addition, "agricultural productivity [had] declined following a 'reverse land reform.' "

FOREIGN AID

Military aid is the largest single component of the foreign-aid budget. The bulk of this money goes to Israel, Egypt, and Turkey, to protect America's perceived interests in the Middle East. More than a third of the nations which receive the remainder of the money are militarily controlled governments, many of which are documented users of torture and other forms of violent political repression against their citizens.

A second component of the U.S. foreign-aid program, Economic Support Funds (ESF), are funds provided to build roads, schools, sewer systems, and other major nonmilitary projects. These funds serve the same purpose as military aid, however. According to a State Department presentation to Congress, ESF are "to support U.S. economic, political and security interests and the advancement of U.S. foreign policy objectives." A U.S. Army public affairs officer, explaining the army's increased "nation-building" activities (road-building and other infrastructure projects) in Panama after the 1989 U.S. invasion, put it more bluntly: "We have a difficult battle on this continent shaking off, let's say, our historical experience of years ago which labeled us the Ugly American. . . . It is in our best interest . . . to improve our image."

The smallest component of U.S. foreign aid is the food aid program. With the exception of a modest program called Title II food aid, the term "aid" itself is somewhat misleading. Most of the food provided under these programs is not given or donated, but actually sold to the Third World. Food aid serves as much as a way for U.S. farmers to dispose of surplus corn, rice, and wheat as it does as a program to prevent hunger. Because of its dual objectives, its ability to help the poor is severely limited. As Frances Moore Lappé, co-founder of the Institute for Food and Development Policy, puts it, "most of our food aid cannot reach hungry people; they simply are too poor to buy it."

DEBT AND TRADE

America also uses import and export trade policies and its influence on lending institutions, both domestic and multilateral (e.g. the World Bank and the International Monetary Fund) to promote its interests in the Third World. According to Susan George, associate director of the Transnational Institute—the international arm of the Institute for Foreign Policy Studies—the politicized use of debt has replaced colonialism as the preferred method of acquiring access to Third World assets and enforcing compliance with Western goals.

Ironically, the large net outflows from the Third World to Western banks—$130 billion from Latin America alone between 1982 and 1987—has a negative impact not only on debtor nations, but on U.S. industry as well. According to a study by the Joint Economic Committee of the U.S. Congress, nearly 90 percent of the drop in U.S. exports from 1981 to 1985 was due to a drastic decline in exports to the Third World: funds these countries would normally have used to purchase goods and services were being used to make interest payments to U.S. banks.

Debt payments have also severely limited undeveloped countries' ability to meet basic domestic needs. This, according to Peruvian economist Denis Sulmont, has led to "anti-austerity" riots in twenty-two countries. When countries attempt to delay debt payments so that they can address citizens' demands, the response from the United States and other lender nations often makes matters worse. When Peru, for instance, attempted to limit debt service to 10 percent of export revenues, the West retaliated with a trade embargo. "By 1988," Susan George writes, Peru's economy "was in shreds."

Throughout the Third World, Washington has used loans and trade policy to punish disobedience and reward compliance. In 1987, when former Costa Rican president Oscar Arias developed a Nicaraguan peace plan that was supported by virtually all of Latin America's leaders, Washington was furious. The United States immediately inflicted on Costa Rica the same economic punishment it had previously inflicted on Nicaragua: it denied Costa Rica access to new American bank loans and placed bans on Costa Rican imports. In contrast, Egypt won forgiveness for $1.3 billion in American debt (at American taxpayers' expense) in return for its support in the Persian Gulf War. And in 1991, after the United States had blocked efforts by Europe and Japan to end the sixteen-year trade embargo against Vietnam, MIT linguistics professor and political activist Noam Chomsky wrote: "the U.S. . . . . intends to exploit the opportunity to teach valuable lessons to others who might have odd ideas about disobeying U.S. orders. . . . Those who do not follow the rules must be severely punished, indefinitely."

THE CIA

The final component of U.S. Third World policy is the use of the CIA and military force to support or put in place government leaders who support U.S. objectives. Since it was founded in 1947, the CIA has successfully overthrown a number of communist, socialist, or nonaligned democratically elected governments in Third World countries. These include Iran in 1953, Guatemala in 1954, the Belgian Congo (now Zaire) in 1960, Brazil in 1964, the Dominican Republic in 1965, Greece in 1967, and Chile in 1973.

Under the Reagan and Bush administrations, the use of the CIA as a proxy for foreign diplomacy increased dramatically. By the mid-1980s, Reagan had nearly tripled the budget for intelligence operations, to an estimated $30 billion in 1991. By 1986, the number of covert operations, according to *The New York Times,* had doubled from the Carter years, reaching more than forty operations a year.

The CIA has used a number of tactics to undermine unwanted Third World leaders. Its most frequent strategy is to provide weapons, intelligence information, money, and military training to opposition groups. A second strategy, used in Indonesia and Brazil, is to provide weapons to or bribe the military while denying aid to the U.S.-opposed government. A third strategy is intimidation, usually accomplished by financing terrorist groups or death squads such as the Nicaraguan contras. A fourth strategy, used in the former Belgian Congo and attempted in Cuba, is the outright assassination of political leaders.

Drug trafficking has played an integral role in financing CIA-sponsored, right-wing guerrilla groups. "In Afghanistan, as in Indochina and . . . Central America," write Peter Dale Scott and Jonathan Marshall in *Cocaine Politics,* "the White House and CIA chose to look the other way while their allies sold vast quantities of drugs to the U.S. market." Thomas Bodenheimer and Robert Gould also cite CIA involvement in drug trafficking in Southeast Asia and Central America, including the use of CIA planes to carry drugs. In 1988 *The New York Times* quoted a Reagan administration official in reference to drug trafficking by the U.S.-backed Afghan guerrillas: "We're not going to let a little thing like drugs get in the way of the political situation."

The list of CIA-backed Third World leaders reads like a *Who's Who* of sleaze. According to activist and author Roger Peace, "the U.S. [has] supported some of the most detested dictatorial regimes in the world," including the Shah of Iran, Ferdinand Marcos in the Philippines, François Duvalier in Haiti, Anastasio Somoza García in Nicaragua, Augusto Pinochet in Chile, Mobutu Sese Seko in Zaire, Ngo Dinh Diem in Vietnam, and Mohammad Zia in Pakistan. Not only did these dictators resort to torture and murder in an attempt to maintain power, but many of them looted their countries' treasuries of millions—in several cases, billions—of dollars. But none of these sordid associations is more revolting than the CIA connection to right-wing death squads. During the past forty years, the CIA has supported death squads in Nicaragua, El Salvador, Guatemala, Angola, and, worst of all, in Indonesia.

In its efforts to overthrow Indonesia's democratically elected president, Sukarno, during the 1960s, the CIA provided funding and weapons to military death squads under the leadership of Indonesian general Suharto. According to Kathy Kadane, of the States News Service in Washington, D. C., statements by several CIA officials, including former director William Colby, confirmed that the CIA provided a "shooting list" of four to five thousand communist party members to the Indonesian Army. The army's slaughter of as many as 500,000 people, which the CIA itself called "one of the worst mass murders of the 20th century," was described in 1990 by Randolph Ryan in *The Boston Globe*: "As firing squads commenced, the US Embassy fed in the names and provided communications gear to facilitate the army's sweeps across the country. Security agency eavesdroppers monitored the progress of the liquidation. As persons listed were killed, US officials checked off their names, and added new ones."

TO WHAT END?

Death squads, terrorism, civil war, poverty, hunger, and freedom denied: this is the legacy of America's Third World policy. And to what end? After studying the results of the aid component of U.S. foreign policy, Frances Moore Lappé wrote:

Despite the generosity and goodwill of most Americans, U.S. foreign aid isn't working. If its goal is to alleviate poverty abroad, we search in vain for evidence of its success. . . . If, on the other hand, the goal of U.S. aid is to heighten national security by stabilizing foreign governments and tying them more closely to us, then it is also failing.

A 1973 study of seventy-four developing countries by Irma Adelman and Cynthia Morris determined that economic growth in the Third World not only did not trickle down, but actually worsened the plight of the poor. A more recent study by the United Nations Children's Fund (UNICEF) confirmed that conditions were worsening for the poor. It showed that during the 1980s, average income declined between 10 and 25 percent in most of Africa and Latin America, while spending on health dropped 50 percent and on education 25 percent in the thirty-seven poorest countries.

The Reagan and Bush administrations' attempts to export supply-side economics—their misguided desire to turn all Third World countries into world traders like South Korea and Taiwan—have left dozens of countries across Africa, Asia, and Latin America in economic ruins. Economists Robin Broad, John Cavanagh, and Walden Bello document the destruction of the environment, the increase in poverty, and the increase in economic inequality that resulted from the application of Reaganomics to the Third World. "In the frenzy to increase exports," they write,

> countries often resort to the easiest short-term approach: unsustainable exploitation of their natural-resource base. . . . Timber exports have denuded mountains, causing soil erosion and drying critical watersheds. Cotton, soybeans and other cash crop exports have typically depended on polluting pesticides and fertilizers. . . . Tailings from mines have polluted rivers and bays.

They also cite a 1989 World Bank report that concludes that a "byproduct" of Third World Reaganomics, which prescribes sharp decreases in domestic government spending, is that "people below the poverty line will probably suffer irreparable damage in health, nutrition, and education."

In Venezuela, for instance, where GNP is growing at the incredible rate of 9.2 percent, real wages for workers have fallen 44 percent, to almost half of 1987 levels. The country's program of privatizing government programs and reducing import restrictions has led to high unemployment, increased crime, and increased civil unrest. In 1991, Venezuelan congressman and leading presidential contender Eduardo Fernandez spoke to a *New York Times* reporter about the results of exported Reaganomics: "Our economic model has caused a scandalous concentration of wealth. . . . We are suffering through the paradox of great economic growth and great growth of poverty."

After concluding that the Reagan/Bush economic model has failed, "even in the very narrow goal of pulling economies forward," Broad, Cavanagh, and Bello turn their attention to the two countries that President Bush presents as success stories: Taiwan and South Korea. They point out that "decades of uncontrolled industrial development have left large parts of Taiwan's landscape with poisoned soil and toxic water," while in South Korea, "after decades of systematic exploitation . . . the labor force erupted in thousands of strikes during the late 1980s."

America's interventionist policies have failed as well. Cuba, China, South Vietnam, Angola, Iran, and Nicaragua were once led by U.S.-supported dictators. But despite massive U.S. military aid and assistance, all of these leaders were overthrown and "Americanization" was rejected. A study of U.S. intervention in Central America also shows the ineptitude of American foreign policy. According to Richard Fagen, co-chair of Policy Alternatives for the Caribbean and Central America, CIA intervention in Central America has led to an estimated 140,000 deaths since 1980. Fagen adds:

> [Intervention] also produced 3 million Central American refugees, a prolonged civil war in El Salvador, a brutal but ineffectual contra army fighting against the Sandinista government in Nicaragua, physical damage and lost production running to billions of dollars; and still there is no end in sight to regional tensions, poverty, or violence. Allies have been alienated, billions of U.S. tax dollars wasted, and immense amounts of human and material resources diverted from other problems at home, in Latin America, and elsewhere.

America's foreign policy has not been kind to our Third World neighbors. But as former senator and presidential candidate George Mc-

Govern explains, America's social values and its democratic process suffer from our foreign policy as well:

> When a president habitually misleads the American people and Congress and pursues a foreign policy contrary to this country's values, our constitutional system of checks and balances is subverted and our democratic principles are undermined. . . . Just as it did in the 1960s, such irresponsibility at the highest levels threatens to tear apart the social fabric of this country.

BUILDING A NEW THIRD WORLD POLICY

America *can* chart a new course in its relationships with the Third World, a course that will not only contribute to peace and the alleviation of Third World poverty, but also bring a host of benefits to America.

The American public need no longer be burdened by the cost of maintaining a bloated military. American industry would benefit from a worldwide redistribution of wealth, as more people would gain the purchasing power to buy consumer goods. The American worker would benefit as a rise in world wages, along with an American commitment to"sustainable" world economics, narrowed the wage differential between Third World labor and U.S. workers. Even more important, America could become a true world leader by promoting democracy and freedom.

RESPECT THIRD WORLD SOVEREIGNTY

The United States must abandon its centuries-old practice of colonialism and allow the countries of the Third World to develop their own styles of government, elect their own leaders, and determine which economic systems are best suited to their development. In effect, the United States should adopt the concept of common security drawn up by the U.N. Commission on Disarmament and Security Issues and the Institute for Peace and International Security: "No nation can ensure its own security at the expense of another."

The United States can use its considerable influence on the Third World's political and economic elite to urge acceptance of democracy and economic reform. The United States should support the development of "people's" democracy in the Third World through the use of the United Nations and other recognized multilateral organizations for nonviolent conflict resolution. At a minimum, the United States must stop supplying arms, military advisers, and military aid to dictatorships and militarily controlled governments.

But although the United States should promote peace as best it can, it must also be willing to accept the reality of democratic development. As George McGovern solemnly reminds us, "our country was born of a revolution against foreign tyranny and unrepresentative government. Today, revolution is still the only way for many Third World peoples to begin making their own history."

SUBJECT FOREIGN POLICY TO THE WILL OF THE WORLD COMMUNITY

The United States cannot possibly expect to maintain its stature as the leader of the free world if it continues to ignore established codes of international conduct. The United Nations and the World Court were established to provide guidelines for conduct among nations. The United States should abide by these guidelines.

Congress should pass legislation, or the people should vote on a national referendum, or cities should pass nonbinding resolutions demanding that future administrations and the State Department obey international law and U.N. mandates. These resolutions should also demand that the United States recognize the U.N. and nonviolent conflict resolution as a cornerstone of U.S. foreign policy. We must never forget that it was the U.S. violation of the 1954 Geneva Peace Accords, which called for a free election in a unified Vietnam, that led to America's involvement in the Vietnam War.

ASSIST THIRD WORLD PROSPERITY

American foreign aid should be redirected from maintaining military and elitist Third World allies to bringing prosperity to the majority of the people of the Third World. Not only should aid for military and strategic purposes be reduced, but economic assistance funds that go into the pockets of corrupt politicians and business elite should be eliminated.

Instead, foreign aid should be used to develop new worker cooperatives and further the progress of the hundreds of thousands of peasant leagues, farm co-ops, worker-owned businesses, micro-enterprise credit associations, and transportation collectives that have sprung up throughout the Third World. In addition, more funds should be allocated to programs that increase literacy, improve health, and provide housing, schools, clinics, and irrigation systems for the poor.

DEMILITARIZE

The United States should become a leader in reducing the number of nuclear as well as conventional weapons throughout the world. The United States must do more than just work with the former Soviet states to reduce the superpowers' nuclear weapons to a minimal level, but it should also use the leverage of economic aid to discourage those states—and other nuclear countries, such as China—from selling weapons of mass destruction to other countries. Perhaps the United States could give foreign credits for each weapon destroyed. In addition, the United States, currently the world's largest arms dealer, should use domestic policy to discourage the arming of the Third World by American industry.

PROMOTE SUSTAINABLE GROWTH

The United States should provide aid and expertise to assist in generating economic growth consistent with environmental constraints. This includes programs to teach sustainable farming to help alleviate soil erosion and desertification; assistance in acquiring industrial pollution-control and waste-reduction technology to help reduce air and groundwater pollution; and sewer and water-treatment facilities to reduce toxin levels in coastal waters, streams, and rivers.

SOLVE THE DEBT CRISIS

To stop the debilitating impact of the Third World debt burden and at the same time help the environment, the United States should adopt some version of the proposed debt-for-nature proposals before Congress. These proposals call for forgiveness of a percentage of Third World loans in return either for portions of those debt payments being used to improve the environment or for agreement to preserve certain natural resources. As MIT economist Paul Krugman points out in *The Age of Diminished Expectations*, debt relief could actually increase the amount of repayment banks actually receive. "Reducing debt," says Krugman, "may actually enhance a country's prospects enough to increase the total expected debt repayment."

REORGANIZE THE CIA

With a new Third World policy and the end of the cold war, a $30 billion intelligence operation will no longer be needed. The intelligence budget should be substantially reduced and the resulting savings used to fund development in the Third World. The CIA's role should be confined to monitoring world developments and protecting the United States against direct assaults on its sovereign interests. In no case should it be allowed to interfere with the sovereignty of Third World nations.

BUILD A WORLDWIDE LABOR MOVEMENT

American workers have much to gain from a rising standard of living in the Third World. Not only will the growing ability of foreign consumers to afford exported American goods generate more jobs, but it will also decrease the flight of American plants to the Third World. Labor could assist this development by helping to build viable unions in the Third World. For starters, labor leaders should send organizers and funds to help workers organize to counterbalance the economic power of the Third World elite.

EDUCATE THE PUBLIC

Foreign policy is probably the government function least understood by the American public. This is partly because much of it is done in secret, and partly because Washington has thoroughly confused the public with code words like "left-wing terrorists" (meaning freedom fighters), "freedom fighters" (meaning right-wing death squads), "communism" (meaning social democracy), and "Third World capitalism" (meaning military dictatorship). The peace and human-rights movements must continue to educate not just the Left, but all Americans on the cost of misguided U.S. foreign policy. Exposure to the truth about foreign policy, whether through schools, the national media, or community organizations, would go a long way toward building future international humanists rather than imperialists.

THE NICARAGUAN STORY

The century-long U.S. involvement in Nicaragua is a prime example of the grave costs inflicted on those who seek true, not U.S.-imposed, democracy. Between 1909 and 1926, the U.S. marines invaded Nicaragua four times. Before the United States finally pulled out of Nicaragua in 1933, it installed Anastasio Somoza García as leader of the country's National Guard. In 1934 Somoza negotiated peace with the opposition leader, Augusto Sandino; he then proceeded to kill Sandino, his followers, and their families and made himself president. It was the beginning of a long, corrupt, and repressive dictatorship under Somoza and his sons. By the time the final Somoza, Anastasio Somoza Debayle, was run out of the country in 1979, the Somoza family controlled one-third of the country's arable land.

Under a new government, the social-democratic Sandinistas, Nicaragua prospered. Between 1979 and 1983, Nicaragua had the highest rate of economic growth of any country in Latin America. Under the Sandinistas, the infant mortality rate was almost halved and illiteracy was reduced from 53 to 12 percent of the population. In addition, by 1984 substantial land redistribution programs had reduced the percentage of arable land held by wealthy landowners from 36 to 11 percent. These accomplishments won the Sandinistas the support of not only small farmers and the urban poor, but the majority of the Catholic clergy and intellectuals and professionals as well. As a result, the Sandinistas won 67 percent of the popular vote in the 1984 election.

But the Sandinistas' socialist style of government practically guaranteed U.S. intervention. Indeed, Reagan came into office determined to overthrow the Sandinistas. He began by launching a propaganda campaign to build public support for their overthrow, charging that the Sandinistas were providing arms to El Salvadorian leftists and that they were Soviet-supported communist infidels bent on fomenting revolution throughout all of South America. "Unable to prove any flow of arms whatsoever from Nicaragua into El Salvador," writes former CIA employee John Stockwell, "the Reagan team . . . developed the propaganda line that they were 'returning Nicaragua to democracy.' "

In 1981 the Reagan administration began organizing Somoza's former National Guardsmen who had fled to Honduras, into the guerrilla force known as the contras. The CIA, according to Stockwell, went as far as to have Luis Posada Carrilles—who had been convicted of killing 73 airline passengers in a terrorist bombing—released from prison to assist in the contra effort. By 1983, the contras had begun wholesale attacks on teachers and government health and agricultural workers. Some suggest that the CIA provided the instructions and training for these assassinations; it is certain that the CIA provided a manual, titled *Psychological Operations in Guerilla Warfare*, which explicitly recommends the killing of civilians, especially government workers.

The Reagan administration also cut off all U.S. trade, loans, and aid to Nicaragua. It intervened with the Inter-American Development Bank to deny loans to Nicaragua and with Mexico to prevent oil purchases. By 1985—despite increases in aid from and trade with Canada, the Soviet Union, France, Greece, Sweden, and Argentina—the U.S. embargo, together with the escalating cost of military expenditures and the destruction of property on a scale so vast that over a quarter of a million people were left homeless, had brought the Nicaraguan economic "miracle" to an end. Ultimately, the trade and loan embargo was used by Washington to sway the outcome of the 1990 Nicaraguan presidential elections. George Bush made it clear that if the U.S.-supported Violeta Chamorra won the election, the United States would lift its trade embargo. Bush's message to Nicaragua's mothers was clear, wrote *The Nation* columnist Alexander Cockburn: "Vote against the Sandinistas or watch your children starve."

The Nicaraguan story is a sad one for both Nicaragua and the United States. The Reagan administration not only violated American law by secretly selling arms to Iran to finance its attack on Nicaragua, but it flagrantly violated international law as well. The United States walked out of the World Court and refused to pay the damages ordered for its illegal mining of Nicaragua's harbors. It ignored repeated U.N. sanctions condemning its aggressions. It ignored peace proposals put forth by the leaders of virtually all of the countries of Latin America. And it ignored the protests of many Western leaders, including France and Canada, who increased their aid to Nicaragua to offset U.S. damage. America truly became an international outlaw.

CHAPTER SEVEN

Disinformation

A SOCIETY THAT RESTRICTS THE DISSEMINATION of truth to its citizens is at best only partially democratic, for a society, as Thomas Jefferson wrote centuries ago, "cannot be both ignorant and free." Real democracy is based on informed public opinion. It is dependent on the public's ability to learn the truth and to make judgments, political and otherwise, on the basis of self-interest and individual beliefs.

To Jefferson, according to Auburn University political scientist Theodore Becker, "the enlightened common person [was] the bulwark of American democracy." This belief in direct and participatory democracy put Jefferson at odds with those who believed that government should be controlled by men of wealth and supposedly superior wisdom. In response to this elitist approach, Jefferson wrote: "if we think [the people] not enlightened enough to exercise their control with a wholesome discretion, the remedy is not to take it from them, but to inform their discretion by education."

Heeding Jefferson's words, the elite did not take the power of the vote away from the people. Instead, they found a way to manipulate them. Through control of the media and other institutions that work to influence the public, the elite turned to what John Dewey called "the power of ideas and emotions" to engineer societal consensus and to "cultivate ideals of loyalty." In other words, "if ordinary people gain power in a democracy through the vote," says activist Helen Caldicott, "the rich will find another way to maintain control."

What Dewey and Caldicott allude to is not an overt, Orwellian plot to control the minds and wills of the America public. Instead, they describe the subtle attempts of powerful interests to engineer support for the status quo, to maintain social order, and to develop a widespread consensus consistent with the elite's point of view. Sociologist G. William Domhoff, after studying how the elite's efforts impact public opinion, concluded in *Who Rules America Now?* that through a "network of policy-planning and opinion shaping organizations . . . [the power elite] are only partially successful in convincing wage and salary earners that [elitist] policies are in everyone's best interest. They have, [however], been able to discourage development of a large body of experts with a more liberal point of view."

The establishment of an elite-supporting, stable social order requires a common belief, conscious or subconscious, in certain social myths and values—what Harvard economist Robert Reich terms "core cultural parables." "Political culture in America," argues Reich, "—as it always has been and will be, as it is anywhere else—is permeated by myth."

American society subscribes to a number of universal myths. Among the most important of these is a nationalism that Robert Reich calls "the mob at the gates." This myth "depicts America as a beacon light of virtue in a world of darkness. . . . We are uniquely blessed, the proper model for other peoples' aspirations, the hope of the world's poor and oppressed." "In modern times nationalism," writes Eric Hoffer in *The True Believer*, "is the most copious and durable source of mass enthusiasm." Government use of nationalism was readily apparent during the cold war, the Gulf War, and during the recent spate of Japan bashing.

Media expert Herbert Schiller argues in *The Mind Managers* that another essential myth is the belief that government and social institutions serve all Americans equally and do not predominately benefit concentrated wealth and power. John Kenneth Galbraith believes the myth of the universal American middle class is all important. And Robert Reich considers the myth of individualism—the belief that anyone can succeed in America if he works hard and "believes in himself"—a powerful part of the national consensus.

To preserve these core beliefs, the information we receive from the educational system and the media must be consistent. Accordingly, American history texts present a collage of individual accomplishments, triumphant capitalism, American victories in just wars, and all-wise founding fathers who created a fair and superior system of government. The media paint the enemies of the elite as social villains, and regularly occurring government scandals are portrayed as the result of corrupt individuals, not a more widespread lack of morality in high government.

In America, the management of myth-supporting information is remarkably simple. Establishment institutions like the White House, the State Department, think tanks, and Wall Street are simply the news media's primary sources of information. ABC reporter Sam Donaldson once admitted, "as a rule, [White House correspondents] are, if not handmaidens of the establishment, at least blood brothers. . . . We end up the day usually having some version of what the White House . . . has suggested as a story." Investigative reporter Seymour Hersh is more critical: "It's a little harder for the boys in the White House to keep the troops in line than it is for the boys in the Kremlin," said Hersh in 1987, "but it is true that *Pravda* and *The Washington Post* and *The New York Times* are alike in the sense that they don't report reality so much as what a small group of top leaders *tells* them is reality."

Social consensus is also developed by limiting debate within narrowly defined boundaries acceptable to the elite, usually within the liberal-to-conservative ideological spectrum. In American politics, observes journalist Mark Hertsgaard in *On Bended Knee*, the range of debate is defined by the two-party system. During the Reagan administration, Hertsgaard argues, "venturing beyond the boundaries of the Democrat-to-Republican spectrum was rare in the extreme."

This approach, of course, keeps political and social debate within the narrowest of margins. For unlike most other industrialized nations with recognized political parties that range from the far Right to the far Left, America's two-party system rarely strays farther than slightly left of center. And since, in Hertsgaard's words, "the news media have become the single most influential actor on the stage of American politics," without the approval of the media, progressive alternatives rarely get the attention of the general public.

But the media are not the only institutions that work to manage the social order. Core beliefs and values are also heavily influenced by a nation's school system. There, at the earliest ages, we begin to learn social, political, and cultural myths and stereotypes. We learn that government and business leaders are symbols of authority and men whom we should admire, emulate, and obey. "Courageous" explorers who invaded foreign lands and slaughtered their native inhabitants for economic gain are presented as heroes. We learn about all the "great" wars and the fearless generals who led America to victory. We also learn individualism, the value of competition, and the importance of being number-one.

We learn about the uniqueness of being American, but about other cultures, people of other races, alternative lifestyles, societies that function better than our own, or about the dangers of concentrated power and elitism, we learn little or nothing at all. By the time we have graduated from high school, most of us know the world not as it really is, but from the perspective that the elite would have us see it.

MANUFACTURING THE NEWS

The news media powerfully influence most Americans' perceptions of culture, world affairs, and government. Unfortunately, what we read and hear in the news is not necessarily reality. Information that is unflattering to favored segments of society is often overlooked, skewed, or at least deemphasized, while viewpoints contrary to the establishment are rarely presented.

This pro-establishment bias is not a result of corrupt reporters and journalists; it is simply a result of the make-up of the news media themselves. First, the media are owned by a small number of corporate elite. In addition, the media depend on corporate advertising and sponsorship for their economic survival. Also, media personnel, especially at the higher rungs, are predominately white, middle- and upper-class males who surveys show to be more conservative than the population at large. And finally, as mentioned earlier, establishment institutions are the primary source of major news.

The major media outlets are owned by a small number of corporate giants. NBC is owned by General Electric, a leading environmental polluter and nuclear-weapons manufacturer. ABC is owned by $4-billion media conglomerate Capital Cities/ABC, a company founded by late CIA director William Casey. *The Los Angeles Times* is owned by Times

Warner, a $3-billion media conglomerate, and the $2-billion Tribune Company, publisher of *The Chicago Tribune*, owns a host of other newspapers and television stations.

Although these corporations hire media professionals to run their enterprises, ultimate authority and control lie with their owners and boards of directors. And they, by and large, are the corporate elite. For instance, according to Martin A. Lee, co-founder of Fairness and Accuracy in Reporting (FAIR) and his coauthor, Norman Solomon, in *Unreliable Sources*, the board of directors of Time Warner reads like a "Who's Who of U.S. business and finance. Directors include representatives from military contractors such as General Dynamics, IBM and AT&T, as well as movers and shakers from Mobil Oil, Atlantic Richfield, Xerox and a number of major international banks." As for the networks, "the boards of directors of the Big Three are composed of lawyers, financiers, and former government officials who represent the biggest banks and corporations in the U.S., including military and nuclear contractors, oil companies, agribusiness, insurance and utility firms."

Lee and Solomon document a large number of instances of conflicts of interest, censorship, and biased reporting due to the corporate affiliations of the media. So-called independent experts from conservative think tanks, many of which receive contributions from major media companies, appear regularly on network news shows and in major newspapers. Although General Electric is America's second largest nuclear power plant manufacturer, in 1987 NBC News ran a special one-hour documentary called "Nuclear Power: In France It Works." "When GE was indicted for its role in the 1988 Pentagon procurement scandal," Lee and Solomon report, "*NBC Nightly News* gave a straightforward report—that lasted about ten seconds. There was little follow-up . . . by any of the major the networks." *The New York Times*, which Lee and Solomon describe as a "fanatical supporter of nuclear weapons and atomic power plants," has three board members with ties to the nuclear power industry.

When media tycoon Rupert Murdoch was asked how much he exerts control over his newspapers, he replied "Considerably. The buck stops on my desk. My editors have input, but I make final decisions." *Los Angeles Times* publisher Otis Chandler feels the same way. "I'm the chief executive," Chandler has said, "and I'm not going to surround myself with people who disagree with me." According to former *Wash-*

ington Post editor Ben Bagdikian, several major newspaper chains, including Cox Enterprises and Scripps Howard, "have ordered their papers to adopt a uniform editorial position on key issues," including political candidates. Columbia School of Journalism instructor Chris Welles agrees: "I daresay anyone who has been in the business for more than a few months can cite plenty of examples of editorial compromises due to pressure, real or imagined, from publishers, owners and advertisers." It should not be surprising. As A. J. Liebling quipped more than thirty years ago, "the freedom of the press is guaranteed to those who own one."

The media's dependence on corporate advertising dollars also contributes to its strong pro-business bias. Television and radio receive almost 100 percent of their revenues from corporate advertising, newspapers almost 75 percent, and magazines 50 percent. And according to Edward Herman and Noam Chomsky in *Manufacturing Consent,* advertisers select advertising mediums "on the basis of their own principles. With rare exceptions these are culturally and politically conservative."

Even the Public Broadcasting Service (PBS) and National Public Radio (NPR) are heavily subsidized by corporate money. In 1981, Lee and Solomon report, 72 percent of prime-time PBS shows were either partially or fully underwritten by oil companies. In 1989, corporate donations to PBS reached $70 million; NPR corporate donations totaled $10.6 million in 1988. This heavy corporate influence is especially visible in the funding of conservative political talk shows such as "The McLaughlin Group," "One on One," and "The MacNeil/Lehrer News Hour." Indeed, liberal or progressive talk shows are virtually nonexistent in public broadcasting.

In addition, surveys have found that media employees tend to be more conservative than the public at large. A 1985 *Los Angeles Times* survey compared 3,000 editors and reporters with 3,000 ordinary people and found the media workers to be significantly less in favor of government's working to narrow the gap between rich and poor. A Brookings Institution study found that 58 percent of Washington journalists considered themselves "conservative" or "middle of the road." This conservatism is even more prevalent among columnists, where William Buckley, Robert Novack, and others prevail. Even conservative Heritage Foundation editor Adam Meyerson had to admit that "today, op-ed pages are dominated by conservatives." Not surprisingly, media employees tend to be overwhelmingly white, middle- and upper-class males. "In 1989 men held 94 percent of the top management positions in the U.S. news media," Lee and Solomon report, while only 18 percent of news directors were women.

In addition to these factors, much of the news is derived from establishment institutions such as the White House, big business, and conservative think tanks. One study cited in *Unreliable Sources* found that in a sample of 2,850 *New York Times* and *Washington Post* articles, 78 percent were "primarily based on the words of public officials." According to *Washington Monthly* editor Christopher Georges, since 1989, almost 85 percent of the stories by so-called investigative reporters at *The New York Times*, *The Washington Post*, and *The Los Angeles Times* have been "follow-ups or advances of leaked or published government reports."

This combination of factors—corporate ownership, dependence on advertising revenues, conservative editors and writers, and reliance on establishment institutions for information—renders it highly unlikely that progressive views challenging the status quo will be heard or that in-depth reporting or strong criticism of the status quo will be found in the mainstream news.

THE IMPACT OF DISINFORMATION

Most major news organizations claim in principle to subscribe to *The New York Times*'s slogan, "All the news that's fit to print." It is a principle more honored than upheld. Are you still waiting to be told what happened to the billions of dollars lost in the savings and loan scandal? Are you still wondering what really happened in the Iran-contra scandal?

Stories blaming incompetent regulators, corrupt financial speculators, and even several senators (the Keating Five), have appeared about the savings and loan scandal. *Newsweek* columnist Jane Bryant Quinn even blamed the public, calling the failures "rough justice" for the public since "we've happily fattened our savings accounts on the high rates of interest paid by insolvent S&Ls."

But precious little was mentioned in the mainstream press about how legalized bribery—large political donations—and the less than arms-length relationship between government officials and savings and loan lobbyists that is business as usual in Washington. In the same vein, the media presented the Iran-contra scandal as an isolated case instead of accurately describing an administration that routinely ignored the law to achieve its narrow objectives. Instead of alerting the public to underlying problems in government, the media stumble from one high-level scandal to another—HUD, EPA, Iraq-gate, BCCI, defense contractors. To do otherwise would put the media in conflict with the myth of government and institutional neutrality.

In addition to dancing around the real causes of business and government scandals, the mainstream media also avoid stories embarrassing to the establishment. "The mass media," write Edward Herman and Noam Chomsky, "will allow any stories that are hurtful to large interests to peter out quickly, if they surface at all." *Utne Reader* publishes the annual list compiled by Project Censored of the year's biggest unreported or underreported stories: almost all are extremely embarrassing to big business or the administration. In recent years the list has included Costa Rica banning Oliver North after a Costa Rican congressional commission concluded that his "contra re-supply network... doubled as a drug smuggling operation"; a proposal by the Nuclear Regulatory Commission and the Environmental Protection Agency to "deregulate radioactive waste to 'below regulatory concern'" so that it could be disposed of as ordinary waste; the *Houston Post*'s evidence of links between the CIA and organized crime in the failure of twenty-two savings and loans; and information that the space shuttle is one of the ozone layer's biggest threats. Despite the sensational nature of these stories, the news wires and the major news media chose largely to ignore them.

It is true, however, that important but embarrassing news is not often completely ignored. Instead, say Lee and Solomon, the media have more subtle ways of handling bad press toward the favored. These techniques include using misleading headlines; using "politically-charged labels" such as "radical" and "extreme left" to discredit establishment critics; using unnamed and "suspicious" sources to provide so-called factual information; and using biased establishment experts to put a more favorable spin on a story.

The continuous use of establishment experts—what Lee and Solomon call the "Kissinger-Haig Disease"—not only presents an extremely narrow and often biased view, but becomes tiresome to viewers as well. "I get so annoyed," social critic Barbara Ehrenreich has said, "if

I turn on one of the public affairs talk shows on TV and see usually four white men, well dressed—I'm sure they earn close to six figures a year—pontificating on . . . the minimum wage."

But even more damaging to society than the news media's selective and sometimes distorted coverage is when the media serve to dictate public attitudes and social trends. "News organizations," according to former *Atlanta Journal-Constitution* editor Bill Kovach, "are moving on to the same ground as political institutions that mold public opinion and seek to direct it."

Journalist Susan Faludi, in *Backlash*, credits "trend reporting" for building much of the resentment toward the feminist movement. "The press first introduced the backlash [against feminism] to a national audience," she writes. The media, relying on largely false information supplied by so-called experts, vigorously heralded the beginning of several major social trends, including a marriage crunch, an infertility epidemic, and a flood of working and career women leaving the work force. The continuous repetition of these stories on the networks and in newspapers and magazines served to convince many of their truth. This, according to Faludi, "acted as a force that swept the general public, powerfully shaping the way people would think and talk about the feminist legacy."

The media's eight-year campaign to paint former president Ronald Reagan as an effective and overwhelmingly popular president will likely be recorded as one of the most blatant disinformation campaigns in American history. Reagan's presidential approval ratings averaged below those of Roosevelt, Eisenhower, Kennedy, and Johnson, and were only slightly better than those of Nixon, Ford, and Carter. Even George Bush's approval rating after only three weeks in office—76 percent—was well above Reagan's highest approval rating *ever*. Moreover, surveys consistently showed that Reagan's policy positions were well to the right of the majority of American people. In an attempt to set the record straight, media critic Noam Chomsky, in *Deterring Democracy*, described the real Reagan presidency:

> It was hardly a secret that Reagan had only the vaguest conception
> of the policies of his Administration and, if not properly pro-
> grammed by his staff, regularly produced statements that would
> have been an embarrassment, were anyone to have taken them seri-
> ously. . . .

Reagan's duty was to smile, to read from the teleprompter in a pleasant voice, tell a few jokes, and keep the audience properly bemused. His only qualification for the presidency was that he knew how to read the lines written for him by the rich folk, who pay well for the service.

Despite widespread knowledge of Reagan's deficiencies, the press crowned Reagan one of the greatest presidents of all time. CBS correspondent Leslie Stahl proclaimed: "Like his leading lady, the Statue of Liberty,... [Reagan] has himself become a symbol of pride in America." *Time* hailed Reagan as "one of the strongest leaders of the 20th century," while *Fortune* hailed Reagan as a "model executive." During the 1984 presidential election campaign, *Newsweek* ran a cover story titled "How Good a President?" The "extraordinarily positive story," according to Mark Hertsgaard, led the *Newsweek* writer to exclaim privately, "I think I just re-elected Ronald Reagan." For assurances, *Newsweek* followed up with another Reagan cover story during election week titled "Landslide?" Even after Reagan had finally left office, *The New York Times* felt compelled to remind the nation once again, falsely, that Reagan had been "one of the most popular Presidents in American history."

If Reagan was wildly popular, it was largely among the wealthy and the media elite. Reagan aide Michael Deaver has written that up to the Iran-contra scandal, "Ronald Reagan enjoyed the most generous treatment by the press of any President in the postwar era." But despite the "super" Reagan image the media drew for the public, the press was well aware of its complicity in a sham. Benjamin Bradlee, former executive editor of *The Washington Post*, confessed, "we have been kinder to President Reagan than any President that I can remember since I've been at the *Post*." "NBC Nightly News" anchor Tom Brokaw admitted that Reagan got "a more positive press than he deserves."

Many in and out of the press were aware that Reagan, in the words of Hertsgaard, had "intellectual deficiencies," and was, as former Secretary of Defense Clark Clifford once put it, "an amiable dunce." In one *New York Times* article, a quote from British Prime Minister Margaret Thatcher about Reagan read, "Poor dear, there's nothing between his ears." The *Times* editorial staff, interestingly enough, headlined the article "Thatcher Salute to the Reagan Years." In *The Washington Post*, Lou Cannon observed that "more disquieting than Reagan's performance . . . is a growing suspicion that the President has only a passing acquaintance with some of the most important decisions of his administration." "Surely, by 1984," exclaims Hertsgaard, "White House reporters did not have to see daily evidence of Reagan's simplemindedness to know it existed."

In fact, Reagan made so many blatantly false and misleading statements that authors Mark Green and Gail MacColl filled a book, *Ronald Reagan's Reign of Error*, with them. For example, Reagan mistakenly told the press that submarine-launched missiles could be recalled; that workers' real earnings were increasing; that fascism was the basis for the New Deal; that there remained as much forest land in the United States today as when George Washington was at "Valley Forge"; and that 80 percent of the nation's air pollution was caused by trees.

In defense of journalism, a number of its practitioners did try to alert the public about Reagan. But journalists' attempts to portray the real Reagan were often thwarted by misleading headlines supplied by their editors, by editorial censorship, or even, in some cases, by self-censorship. Some reporters voluntarily softened their stories, either out of fear of management disapproval or fear of appearing to attack a popular president—falling, ironically, for their own propaganda about his overwhelming popularity.

The press and the Reagan presidency is a story of a press that failed the American public. Beguiled by elitist support for the administration and by censorship, both self-imposed and from above, the press failed to warn the American people, to alert us that we had elected an illusion to the country's highest office and that for eight years, according to Noam Chomsky, "the US government functioned virtually without a chief executive."

LIBERATORY AND MULTICULTURAL EDUCATION

Like the mainstream news media, the nation's schools also tend to present information in a manner that supports the status quo. Public schools teach the young not only to read and write, but also to believe the many cultural fables that underlie American mythology. These teachings are well described by Paula Rothenberg, author of *Racism and Sexism: An Integrated Study*, in her reply to a column attacking that textbook:

The traditional curriculum teaches all of us to see the world through the eyes of privileged, white, European males and to adopt their interests and perspectives as our own. It calls books by middle-class, white, male writers "literature," . . . while treating the literature produced by everyone else as idiosyncratic and transitory. The traditional curriculum introduces the (mythical) white, middle-class, patriarchal, heterosexual family and its values and calls it "Introduction to Psychology." It teaches the values of white men of property and position and calls it "Introduction to Ethics." It reduces the true *majority* of people in this society to "women and minorities" and calls it "political science." . . .

It teaches all of us to use white male values and culture as the standard by which everyone and everything else is to be measured and found wanting.

In addition to teaching the values of white males, the school system, according to some scholars, also serves a role in maintaining support for the status quo. "By building racism, sexism, heterosexism, and class privilege into its very definition of reality,'" argues Rothenberg, the traditional curriculum "implies that the current distribution of wealth and power in the society . . . reflects the natural order of things."

University of California at Berkeley professor John Hurst blames the nation's school system for much of the lack of political empowerment among the masses. Instead of empowering and educating students about the importance of participatory citizenship and how America's democracy really works, "formal education in the US," says Hurst, "has largely served to domesticate young people, . . . [helping to] maintain the status quo by fostering and legitimizing an elite whose principal commitments are to the interests of the powerful and not to those of the common good." Bertram Gross, public policy professor at City University of New York, agrees. "Almost every component of America's mammoth school system," writes Gross, "serves as a training ground in the submission to authoritative rules and procedures."

Like Rothenberg and Hurst, other scholars argue that today's traditional curriculum is out of step with a society in which people of color will soon be the majority, in which many women work and hold positions of authority, and in which tens of millions of people have rejected marriage or heterosexuality for alternative lifestyles. Cornel West, professor of religion at Princeton, suggests that the education system's failure to address these social realities is one of the causes of today's racial, gender, and sexual-orientation polarization. University of Texas anthropologist Ted Gordon and Princeton English professor Wahneema Lubiano put it more bluntly: "Anything less [than multi-cultural learning] continues a system of education that ultimately reproduces racism and racists."

University of Southern Illinois English professor Paula Bennett has described what happened when she offered her adult students a choice between the *Heath Anthology of American Literature*, a new, multicultural collection, and the standard anthology. The students, who chose the *Heath*, began to view not only history but also modern society in a new way, and began to bring articles containing alternative viewpoints into class. One was a review of *Dances with Wolves* for the *Boston Globe* by Dianne Dumanoski, in which she quotes University of Kansas historian Donald Worster's description of the real history of America:

> "We've never had good self-understanding. . . . Our national myth is an 'imperialistic one' that celebrates conquest of the land and of other people. . . . Our history has been driven by a powerful urge to acquire wealth and power. . . . "Confronting and acknowledging the imperialistic strand in our culture "should help us mature as a people."

Seeing history from all angles, Bennett reports, provided students "a context that makes violence, economic exploitation, and racism, not innocence, central to the American experience and, therefore, to the evolution of American character and literature."

So that students can be more thoroughly educated and empowered to value and participate in democracy, the school system must provide both a multicultural and, in Hurst's words, a "liberatory education"— an education that "strives to empower individuals through authentic problem-posing and dialogue among equals."

A liberatory education can be accomplished by studying not only the histories of other peoples and cultures, but also the contradictions of history. A liberatory education means debating what Thomas Jefferson really meant when he wrote "all men are created equal" while at the same time owning slaves. It includes, as author Katha Pollitt puts it, "[thinking] of all the energy and passion [our Founding Fathers] spent debating the question of property qualifications, or direct versus legislative elections, while all along, unmentioned and unimagined, was the fact—to us so central—that women and slaves were never considered for any kind of vote."

Such debates would include discussions of morality and social justice, of conflict resolution and participatory democracy. They would provide students with factual information about the contributions and struggles of people of color, women, and the working class and, by discussing different lifestyles and other choices that individuals make, would free them from dependence on stereotypes and myths so that they could not only appreciate, but fully enjoy the rich diversity that is America. By bringing reality into the classroom, our educational system could be turned from one of domestication to one of intellectual empowerment. If young people were taught both the accomplishments and the failings of the American system, perhaps they would be motivated to work to improve it.

CENSORSHIP

Like education and the media, popular culture also has an impact on the values and direction of society. Fortunately for progressives, popular culture—books, music, movies, television, art—has remained receptive to social advancement and the infusion of new ideas.

Because of this openness, however, popular culture has come under heavy attack from the New Right and the conservative movement. The right is bent on banning books—from George Orwell's *1984* to *The Best Short Stories of Negro Writers*—that it considers un-American, anti-Christian, or immoral. The New Right has also attacked music (rap and rock and roll), network television programming, the movie industry, and the arts, blaming these forums for the increase in violence, suicide, immorality, and drug use among America's youth.

The New Right has actually been quite successful in its campaign to alter the media. As Dave Marsh points out in *50 Ways to Fight Censorship*, at some schools and libraries, cultural conservatives have successfully banned undesired books and texts. Conservatives have also successfully backed the passage of "censorship laws" and, in some cases, have seen that they are vigorously enforced. In Florida, for example, the rap group Two Live Crew and retail merchants who sold their records were arrested. Conservatives even lobbied successfully to replace the president of the National Endowment for the Arts.

The power of Christian radio and televangelism has forced some publications to censor their content due to actual or threatened boycotts. *Sassy*, for instance, a magazine for teenage girls, lost nearly all its major advertisers when a censorship group called Women Aglow and the evangelical publication and radio program *Focus on the Family* targeted it for a boycott. They disapproved of *Sassy's* articles on incest victims, gay teenagers, and birth control. Forced to give in or go out of business, *Sassy* has regained its advertisers, but lost its editorial independence.

Sassy's experience will become all too common if the Left does not put up an effective fight against censorship. The New Right is a potent political and economic force; with a host of radio and television evangelists, it can rapidly build grass-roots support for its point of view. But censors can be overcome if progressives support organizations such as the ACLU, the Freedom to Read Foundation, and the American Booksellers Association's Foundation for Free Expression. Progressives must be aware of attempts at censorship whenever and wherever they occur and rise up to combat them. For as Dave Marsh warns us, "cut off one person's voice and you risk having your own larynx removed."

DEFEATING DISINFORMATION

SUPPORT AND PROMOTE THE ALTERNATIVE PRESS

To obtain a more balanced perspective on current events, read, watch and listen to progressive media sources. These include a host of newspapers and magazines, a number of alternative radio stations and programs, and alternative cable programs (see the list of alternative media sources in chapter 10).

The alternative media, for the most part, look at current events from a progressive-liberal point of view. They treat government and corporate pronouncements with a healthy skepticism. They also provide in-depth interviews with influential Americans who are rarely heard in the mainstream press. In addition, many alternative media sources provide ideas on various ways that you can get involved in making a difference.

ENGAGE IN POLITICAL CONVERSATION

With your newfound insight, courtesy of the alternative press, help others escape the bondage of disinformation. Provide your friends and acquaintances with the other side of the day's headlines. Offer them information on important events censored out of the mainstream news.

Relish political conversation and the debate that often accompanies it. Don't let peer approval or disagreement stop you from speaking out. And be sure to correct others, albeit politely, when you hear them make misleading statements or recite misleading social myths.

LEAD A PETITION DRIVE AGAINST DISINFORMATION

Present a petition to any media outlet in your community that is biased. Make it specific, pointing out specific cases of skewed, misleading, or unrepresentative news reporting. Release your petition at a rally or news conference and give copies to the local media. The support and attendance of any local celebrities you can find will help ensure mainstream media coverage of your event.

Collecting names for a petition is not difficult, but it is a time-consuming process. Try soliciting help from volunteers at local colleges or progressive organizations. A "disinformation rally," with volunteer entertainment, could also be used to gather signatures. The more names you collect, the more impact your petition will have.

CONTACT THE PRESS DIRECTLY

Let editors and producers know that the public knows what they are up to. Clip out biased news articles and mail them, with a letter explaining precisely how the piece is misleading, to the editor. Even if your letter is not printed, you have helped let editors know that the public is aware of their practices.

Call your local television and radio stations and express your concern about specific misleading or one-sided programming. Participate in radio call-in shows. Make sure listeners hear the progressive viewpoint on important community issues. In addition, send a list of prominent alternative voices to the networks and demand that they be heard on the various news and talk shows.

SUPPORT YOUR LOCAL LIBRARY

The American Library Association is a leading force in the fight against censorship. Contact your local library and find out how you can help.

In addition, lend your voice to the fight against state and local cuts in funding for neighborhood libraries. In many poorer communities, the library is the only place where youths have access to the knowledge that books provide, but these are often the first libraries to be closed when funds are cut. Meanwhile, you could volunteer to help at a library several hours a week.

SUPPORT MULTICULTURAL EDUCATION

Join the school reform movement in your local community. If schools in your state must purchase textbooks from an approved list prepared by the state, then make sure your group is present when public hearings to compile these lists are conducted.

Support having a broader curriculum taught in your neighborhood schools. Join or start a citizen's group advocating a multicultural curriculum in your local educational system. Impress upon politicians, school officials, and the media the importance of and the widespread support for multicultural education.

In addition, speak to parents' groups about the value of multicultural education. Discuss with them the advantages their children will derive from receiving a well-rounded view of American culture and of the world.

CHAPTER EIGHT

Grass-root Politics

COMMUNITY-BASED, GRASS-ROOTS ACTIVISM IS the most effective way for progressives to bring about political and economic change. Despite the political cataclysm on the national level, locally based movements continue to push their communities forward. It is on the community level that the influence of big business and the entrenched elite is weakest and the power of the people, through shared self-interest, is strongest. By actively working through local government, whether as Democrats, independents, or through third parties, progressives can overpower corporate interests to pass laws and elect legislators that truly serve the needs of their communities.

While corporations spend billions of dollars on Washington lobbyists and campaign contributions for state and national politicians, the cost of buying clout on a community-by-community level is prohibitive. As a result, influence on the community level is determined less by money and more by grass-roots participation. This is where groups with active memberships, such as labor unions, consumer organizations, social justice groups, and grass-roots environmental groups are strongest.

In a community, the desire for a clean environment, effective educational and health systems, personal safety, and economic well-being is shared by all. These common desires, along with face-to-face contact among neighbors, serve as catalysts for community involvement. Through community activism, people begin to realize that social problems are not someone else's, but their own. They see that the answers are not in Washington, but right at home. This realization is political empowerment.

When the political process begins at home, community-based groups can educate and encourage individual participation through enlightened self-interest. And by heightening individuals' awareness of the broader issues that create local grievances, communities can connect neighborhood concerns with national and even international issues. This connection is the key to building solidarity, understanding, and support, both in America and throughout the world.

COMMUNITY GOVERNMENT

Community activism offers progressives unlimited opportunities to effect social change. It is city and county governments—not state or federal ones—that regulate waste disposal, dispense social services, and manage the natural and cultural environment such as parks, libraries, and museums. It is local officials who have the authority to develop innovative social initiatives—a multicultural curriculum in the school system, a job training program for the underemployed, or a housing program for the homeless or first-time home buyers. It is local officials who have the authority to enact legislation concerning censorship and discrimination, to provide abortion services in local hospitals, and to develop day-care programs for working parents. In addition, local governments also have significant control over corporate practices through zoning, consumer fairness and environmental regulations, tax policies, development initiatives, and purchasing and investment policies.

A number of innovative ordinances passed by large and small cities across the country illustrate the power of community government. In Berkeley, California, the city government banned styrofoam; passed a mandate to recycle 50 percent of its garbage; established sister-city relationships with towns in Nicaragua and El Salvador; developed a "Mayor's Peace Initiative" calling on Congress to fund the cities, not the contras; and banned the city's investment in or purchase of goods or services from corporations doing business in South Africa or involved in the nuclear industry.

In Boston, the city government requires developers who build commercial properties to provide quid pro quos such as construction of low-income housing. The city used the power of eminent domain to enable one community organization to take over and refurbish abandoned housing. Boston also demanded that hospitals expand their services for low-income pregnant women. And, along with the state, the city adopted an innovative plan created by the Ford Foundation to train and place welfare recipients in jobs. This plan, modeled after Sweden's full-employment system, write David Osborne and Ted Gaebler in *Reinventing Government*, "was a classic unexpected success."

In Fort Collins, Colorado, city hall declared the entire city an urban wildlife sanctuary. A number of other cities have passed ordinances promoting bicycle use, such as designating bicycle boulevards and requiring bicycle parking spaces. Others have initiated policies requiring employers to facilitate ride-sharing and the use of public transportation. Some monitor industrial pollution and waste disposal much more strictly than federal guidelines require. Minneapolis, San Francisco, and Santa Monica have initiated insulation and weatherization programs to make homes and commercial buildings more energy efficient.

In addition to environmental initiatives, a number of communities and local governments have initiated programs to fight the spread of AIDS, to reduce teen pregnancies, to eliminate gender and race discrimination, to aid the homeless, and to redevelop poor communities. These programs include dispensing needles to high-risk drug users, providing hospice care for AIDS sufferers, and providing birth control and sex education to teens. A number of communities have also passed strict ordinances against discrimination in housing and employment. Other communities have started public and private partnerships to renovate low-income neighborhoods.

Local government can have an impact on national policy as well. Boston's successful job placement program is being adopted by other cities. Berkeley's Mayor's Peace Initiative, which was signed by forty other mayors, was credited with contributing to the defeat of a bill to provide funding to the contras. Nuclear free zones, sister city programs, and Jobs with Peace resolutions have been enacted in hundreds of communities across the country, sending a powerful message to Washington that much of the country disagrees with its domestic and foreign policy agenda.

THE FLOURISHING GRASS-ROOTS MOVEMENT

During the past decade, a number of influential, community-based grass-roots groups have developed. While many of these groups formed out of concern over a single issue, many have evolved to advocate a broad progressive platform. A number of these groups, such as the Rainbow Coalition, the Industrial Areas Foundation, the National Organization for Women, the Green political party, and the Citizen's Clearinghouse for Hazardous Wastes have become pacesetters in progressive grass-roots politics.

The local Rainbow coalitions are an outgrowth of Jesse Jackson's two bids for the Democratic party's presidential nomination. Although Jackson has largely withdrawn from active participation, many of the Rainbow groups continue to grow and prosper. Driven by a coalition of peace, women's rights, social justice, gay rights, civil rights, and environmental activists, local Rainbow groups have placed many progressive legislators in office. In Seattle, writes journalist Sheila Collins, "a multiracial organization of poor and working people" called the Rainbow Institute was formed for the purpose of "providing leadership development, political education, and training for grassroots people." Since 1984, the institute has elected progressive candidates to the state legislature and to Seattle's Public Development Authority, and has initiated legislation concerning sexual assault, drug abuse, low-income housing, and discrimination. By 1986, the Rainbow Institute, says Collins, "had become the controlling core of the city's political life."

In Alabama, former Jackson supporters created the New South Coalition, a collection of civil rights, labor, farm, and environmental activists. The coalition has been successful not only in getting progressive candidates elected to office, but also in fighting the corporate polluters so prevalent in low-income southern communities. In Missouri, farmers who supported Jackson have formed the Missouri Rural Crisis Center (MRCC), whose mission is "to preserve family farms, promote stewardship of the land and environmental integrity, and strive for economic and social justice by building unity and mutual understanding among diverse groups." MRCC has joined Native Americans and the National Toxics Campaign to fight against toxic waste dumps and has joined with African-American churches in St. Louis and Kansas City in a project called "Farm-to-City Marketing Cooperative," a program to promote and sell low-cost, nontoxic farm products to low-income urban residents.

In Vermont, the Rainbow Coalition merged with the Progressive Coalition to form the Progressive Vermont Alliance. Separately, these groups worked to turn this once heavily Republican state into one of the most progressive in the country, electing a large number of progressives to local offices, including the mayor of the state's largest city. Together, they were powerful enough to send social-democrat Bernie Sanders to Congress.

Another progressive grass-roots organization, the Industrial Areas Foundation (IAF), has been extremely successful in bringing political empowerment to working-class people across the country. The IAF was founded in 1940 by University of Chicago sociologist Saul Alinsky, a community organizer and the author of *Rules for Radicals*. The IAF is currently comprised of twenty-four active grass-roots groups, such as Baltimoreans United in Leadership Development (BUILD), Communities Organized for Public Service (COPS) in San Antonio, and the Metropolitan Organization (TMO) in Houston. Together, these community groups represent over 1,200 parishes and two million politically active individuals.

Although IAF represents some of America's poorest communities, through its pursuit of shared interests, it has been able to build a powerful coalition of African-Americans, Mexican-Americans, and working-class whites. In Baltimore, mayoral candidate Kurt Schmoke adopted the IAF agenda as his own and become the city's first African-American mayor. In California, IAF community programs convinced the legislature to raise the state's minimum wage. And in San Antonio, exclaims William Greider, the local IAF group's "presence [has] fundamentally redirected the flow of political power in the city." Of the combined power of the ten IAF groups in Texas, Greider writes:

> Something is being built in Texas politics that does not respond to
> the usual alignment of money and influence. The politicians may
> not understand the theological talk about "love and power" but,
> when IAF talks, they listen respectfully. After all, those are live vot-
> ers going to all those IAF meetings.

One national group with hundreds of active local chapters, the National Organization for Women (NOW), is also making a big splash in local politics. Based on a platform of "freedom from all forms of discrimination . . . ; the right to a decent standard of living, including adequate food, housing, health care, and education; the right to clean air, clean water, safe toxic-waste disposal, and environmental protection; [and] the right to be free of violence, including the threat of nuclear war," local NOW volunteers are working to elect progressive men and women to political office throughout the country.

Another rapidly growing grass-roots political movement is a European import, the Green movement. Now comprised of four hundred local groups in forty-six states, the Greens address issues ranging from sustainable economic growth, urban development, and toxic pollution to Native American rights and wilderness preservation. With its growing political strength in smaller cities and towns, the American Green party has elected candidates to political office in California, Massachusetts, North Carolina, Missouri, Montana, Wisconsin, Connecticut, and New York.

Although many view the American Greens as a white, middle-class movement concerned exclusively with the environment, the Green philosophy goes far beyond that. The broader Green agenda, according to Green organizer and political scientist John Rensenbrink, is "to redefine the purpose of government and business from profit maximization to meeting the needs of people consistent with the environment and to relocate power away from the elites and the federal government and return it to the community level." While the Green party is currently composed primarily of environmentalists, ecofeminists, and proponents of sustainable economic growth, the party has been making efforts to broaden its base. It has a small and growing "leftist" contingent, the Left Green Network, which is trying to organize working-class support around the issue of capitalism's exploitation of labor and the environment. And in an effort to reach people of color, the Green party has initiated a number of plans to address minority concerns, such as inner city urban development and the eradication of environmental racism.

For student grass-roots activists, there is the Student Environmental Action Coalition (SEAC). Formed in 1988, SEAC already lists a thousand college groups and hundreds of high school organizations among its members. Local SEAC groups have campaigned on issues such as opposition to the Persian Gulf War, below-poverty-level wages for African-American campus employees, toxic waste dumps, AIDS prevention, and nuclear power. And through its growing collaboration with campus Greens, SEAC is becoming more involved in the political process. This greater political awareness, as Eric Odell, editor of the SEAC newsletter, sees it, is part of moving toward SEAC's goal of "broadening the definition of the environment to include everything that affects us in our daily lives."

In many cases, grass-roots single-issue advocacy can lead to a movement for broad-based political change. This has been the case with the Gulf Coast Tenants Organization (GCTO), a Louisiana organization formed primarily as an African-American tenants' rights group, and the Citizen's Clearinghouse for Hazardous Wastes (CCHW), an organization formed to fight toxic waste dumps.

Although initially concerned with the abusive practices of slumlords and farm land owners, GCTO's concerns broadened when it became aware that many of the communities it serves, which are located in areas with large concentrations of petrochemical plants, had cancer rates as high as eighteen times the national average. This, and the results of a study by the United Church of Christ that "isolated race as the most important variable that determined where poisonous wastes are placed," mobilized this small tenants' group into a powerful political force. GCTO organized an eleven-day march, joined by both black and white labor, environmental, and civil rights supporters, to highlight the deadly conditions faced by those who reside and work in "cancer alley." These and other lobbying efforts led to state and local government resolutions to clean up Louisiana's polluted air, water, and land, including passage of a state law requiring a fifty-percent reduction in chemical emissions by 1994.

But GCTO did not stop there: it went national. In 1990 it joined with other minority activists in drafting a letter to the top ten environmental organizations highlighting the practice of environmental racism and calling attention to the racist practices of these organizations. When the letter was reprinted in *The New York Times*, the Group of Ten were highly embarrassed. In 1991, GCTO joined the Latino-led Southwest Organizing Project, the United Church of Christ's Commission for Racial Justice, and a number of Native American and Asian Pacific American organizations to convene the National People of Color Environmental Summit in Washington, D.C. The purpose of the highly publicized summit, says GCTO director Pat Bryant, was "to make a clear statement of intention to build a national/international social justice movement which pivots around stopping the rape of the Earth and the poisoning of all its people, especially the disproportionate poisoning of people of color."

The Citizen's Clearinghouse for Hazardous Wastes transformed itself from a local group opposing toxic waste dumps into a national group fighting for social justice. CCHW was an outgrowth of the Love Canal residents' fight for compensation for the toxic poisoning that destroyed their community. Founded in 1981 by Love Canal community leader Lois Gibbs, CCHW has helped organize communities across the country that are threatened by incinerators, toxic dumps, and other types of corporate pollution.

The issue of neighborhood pollution has turned many previously politically inactive citizens into community activists. CCHW's membership includes more than 1,700 groups nationwide, described by CCHW as "moms and dads, farmers and factory workers, people of different race, gender and income." Neighborhood groups affiliated with CCHW have moved from fighting pollution in their own backyards to assisting next-door communities to forming statewide coalitions. CCHW groups have assisted the communities of color that have become the prime targets of corporate polluters; for example, they have joined Native Americans for a Clean Environment in that group's fight to prevent corporate efforts to use Indian lands for "mega-dumps." Some individual members have even traveled to India, Mexico, and other Third World countries to assist in establishing CCHW groups there.

In addition, CCHW groups are expanding beyond the environment to address other issues of social justice. Some groups have become extremely active in local politics. Others have formed coalitions with local labor unions to confront environmental issues in the workplace. Still others have joined church groups and social activists to address community health-care needs, sustainable job development, and community concerns of all sorts.

As these grass-roots groups clearly demonstrate, community empowerment is a dangerous thing for the ruling elite. It may start small, centering around a single issue. But in most cases, as the process heightens the political awareness of the participants, the movement's concerns will grow. Innovative community groups and local governments, fueled by progressive officials and activists, can make a difference. They can improve our environment, our schools, and our health-care system. They can put people to work and curb corporate abuse. They can counter right-wing attacks on free speech, equal opportunity, and abortion rights. And through example and leadership, they can influence progress throughout the country as well. "Act locally, think globally" is more than a slogan. It is the way for progressives to rebuild America, from the ground up.

PUTTING PROGRESSIVES IN OFFICE

One of the primary goals of progressive individuals and grass-roots groups alike is to see more progressives win public office. Working within the Democratic party or as independents, groups such as NOW and the Green party have worked to increase the number of women, environmentalists, and peace and social justice activists in positions of political power. These groups, outfinanced by supporters of the status quo, depend on committed grass-roots volunteers to achieve political success. While the progressive movement has won most of its political successes on the local level, it is beginning to make a splash on the national political scene as well.

One of the best recent examples of this is the Illinois senatorial campaign of Carol Moseley Braun. Riding the wave of women's outrage at powerful Democratic incumbent Alan Dixon's vote in favor of Clarence Thomas, Braun scored an upset victory in the Democratic primary, defeating not just Dixon but also a wealthy Chicago lawyer; together, her male challengers outspent her ten to one.

Braun, an energetic and capable state legislator who earned a best legislator award from the Independent Voters of Illinois, was best known for her work on behalf of women and the poor. With a simple but powerful message, "Let's give government back to the people," Braun energized a powerful statewide coalition that included women, social activists, gays and lesbians, people of color, people with disabilities, and students. These "Braunies," according to the *Chicago Tribune*, ranged "from North Shore socialites to hospital cooks, from barely voting age to ripe old age. They're white, black, Hispanic and Asian American."

The political forecasters called Dixon all but a shoe-in, but the pundits were as out of touch with the voters as Dixon was. Republican women from predominately white counties crossed over to vote in the Democratic primary for Braun, a liberal African-American. In Chicago, voter turnout reached new heights as many previously uninterested voters cast their ballots for Braun. In the end, Dixon the Giant lay slain while progressives were looking forward to supporting Braun in the general election.

Braun's victory, like those of California's Barbara Boxer and Dianne Feinstein and Pennsylvania's Lynn Yeakel, illustrated the strategy and the power of progressive grass-roots politics. First, progressives must run in local and national Democratic primaries against conservative

Democrats, or as independents in the general election. Second, the campaign must build a coalition of community organizations to build grass-roots support and recruit volunteers. Third, the campaign must encourage the disenfranchised to vote. And finally, the campaign must have a populist message that can energize women, working-class men, people of color, and social, environmental, and peace activists.

Community organizations and their members play a big part in getting progressives into office. They can provide funding, visibility, and much-needed volunteers. They can also educate the public about the importance of progressive issues such as the environment, economic fairness, corporate accountability, and equal rights. And by providing the manpower to address voters person to person, they can offset the financial disadvantages progressive candidates typically face.

To "take back government," each of us must become a community activist. The following section offers some ways that you can do your part to make a difference.

BECOMING A POLITICAL ACTIVIST

JOIN A GRASS-ROOTS ORGANIZATION ACTIVE IN YOUR COMMUNITY

Instead of just sending money, get involved with a group working for change in your community. There are a number of groups with broad social agendas to choose from (see chapter 10 for a list). Whichever group you choose, try to make sure of the following: that the organization is not entirely single-issue oriented; that it is involved in issues you care about; that is truly concerned with the needs of the community; and that it is involved in your community's political process, either through advocacy, legislative lobbying, protest, or the support of candidates or legislative proposals.

BECOME A CAMPAIGN VOLUNTEER

Commit yourself to working for a progressive candidate in both the primary and general elections. Volunteers can answer phones, prepare and distribute campaign literature and press releases, and canvass door-to-door to solicit support for a candidate. Volunteers can also help raise funds by telephoning or mailing letters to potential donors, or even hosting fund-raisers—small ones at their homes or larger ones else-where.

People with special skills, such as in advertising, graphic design, journalism, or public speaking, can be especially helpful. Without the money to hire high-paid political strategists, volunteers must help plan campaign strategy, design and write campaign literature, and speak on behalf of a candidate. Well-spoken volunteers can attend the meetings of community and other grass-roots organizations to encourage these groups to join in helping to elect a candidate.

RUN FOR OFFICE

If there is no progressive candidate running for a particular office, con-sider running yourself! Thousands of people with no political experi-ence—students, artists, homemakers, clergy, teachers, business people—have successfully run for public office. You can do it too.

There are many influential political offices which can be sought on relatively small budgets. These may include representing your district in a city or state legislature, or even Congress, but there are also school boards, city commissions, county boards, village trustees, and many other offices. All that is required is determination, a good message, a core of volunteers, and an effective campaign strategy.

If you do consider running for a particular public office, begin by re-alistically assessing your chance of winning. Ask yourself: Are the per-tinent voters angry, or generally satisfied with the incumbent? Are there strong concerns, such as abortion, education reform, zoning, local landfills, or city services, on which your stand separates you from the incumbent? Who are the other candidates, and will they compete for your progressive voting block or split it? To answer these questions, you might consider doing a small survey of your neighbors.

Second, ask yourself whether you can build the required campaign apparatus to win. After eliciting the support of your family and friends, discuss your proposed political platform with community and grass-roots organizations. Share your agenda with them and ask what issues they are concerned about. If you can get a group or two to support your candidacy, you have acquired the beginnings of your volunteer corps.

Next, find out about the necessary filing requirements. These in-clude filing fees (usually under $100) and the number of petition signa-tures required (if any) to get on the ballot. Finally, figure out how you are going to raise the money needed to finance your campaign. At a minimum, your expenses will include telephone charges and the cost of printing and mailing campaign literature. A more elaborate campaign might also include office space, a paid staffer, and political posters, buttons, or stickers. Fund-raising options you should consider include direct mail and door-to-door solicitations, as well as fund-raisers hosted by friends or sympathetic organizations.

Once you are firmly committed, you will need to create your campaign strategy. It should include a strongly articulated platform of beliefs and legislative goals. It should also include strategies for generating free press coverage, for recruiting and using volunteers effectively, for receiving endorsements and appearing before sympathetic community groups, and for door-to-door canvassing by you and your volunteers.

You can run either as an independent candidate or in the Democratic party primary (if you run as a Republican you may scare away many progressive voters). In most cases, running in a party primary is preferred. First, unless you are well known or have an extremely powerful message, party affiliation will add credibility to your campaign. Second, the primary will give you and your campaign the experience, and the added visibility and name recognition, needed to be successful in the general election. Finally, if you win in an upset in the primary and become the party's nominee, you will receive party funding and other support. In addition, private donations and volunteers will be much easier to come by once you have demonstrated that you have the ability to win within the party. But don't let money and the party's newfound acceptance go to your head. If it was a grass-roots, populist campaign that led you to success in the primary, then that is what will lead you to victory in the general election.

ORGANIZE A VOTER REGISTRATION DRIVE

The number-one difficulty facing liberal and progressive candidates is lack of voter participation. In the last congressional election, only one-third of those eligible to vote even bothered. Unfortunately, citizens who fail to vote are generally the ones who feel most alienated from the system: minorities and the poor. These are the people who have long supported liberal and progressive Democrats.

The answer is not, as the national Democratic elite think, to look more like Republicans to compete for upper-class, active voters. It is to energize the disenfranchised to become part of the political process again. As liberal economist Robert Kuttner explains, "if people with household incomes of $25,000 or less voted at the same rate as wealthier people, Democrats again would overwhelmingly be the majority party."

To become a voter registrar, first check to see whether your union, your church, or a grass-roots organization you belong to has a voter registration program you can join. If not, organize one yourself. Contact your state's board of elections and ask how to be deputized and what the state's registration requirements are. When you have your voter registration credentials and have been supplied with registration forms (some in Spanish, if necessary), you are ready to go.

Set up a table outside a supermarket or shopping center, a college campus, or near a busy street corner. In addition, with permission, you can register voters at a Sunday church service, a local community center, or at neighborhood block parties and picnics. But you must be creative to get people's attention. Make signs, play music, or otherwise attract attention. And remember to keep records of those you have registered, so you can contact them again near election day to make sure they get out and vote. For additional information, write or call Project Vote for the booklets *How to Develop a Voter Registration Plan* and *How to Register Voters at a Central Site* at 1424 16th Street, NW, Suite 101, Washington, D.C. 20036; (202) 328–1500.

LOBBY LEGISLATORS

Make sure your elected officials, both local and in Washington, know how you and your organization feel about upcoming legislation, or the lack of it. There are a number of ways to accomplish this: letters, faxes, and phone calls; petition drives; addressing the legislative body; or holding a well-publicized rally.

Letters, faxes and phone calls: For national issues, you can write or call your district's congressional representative and your senators, either in Washington or at their state offices. For state or local concerns, you can contact your state representative, city councilperson, mayor, and governor. No matter who you contact or how, your position will be recorded. This is way one elected officials monitor public sentiment on issues and upcoming legislation.

In your letter, fax, or phone call be courteous, specific, and brief. If you are communicating about upcoming legislation, state the title of the proposed legislation and, if possible, its assigned legislative bill number. Then briefly state the specifics of the bill and explain clearly why you are for or against it. If you are proposing action on an unaddressed community issue, strongly state why the issue concerns you and what you believe the legislator needs to do to address it.

To prepare your communications, you will have to do a little homework to find the correct names, addresses, and bill information. Addresses and numbers for local officials can be found in your phone book, and for current members of congress in numerous reference books at your library or by calling the Capitol Hill switchboard at (202) 224–3121. You can also contact the League of Women Voters at (800) 836–6875. To find out specific bill information, contact the Senate or House Status Office through the Capital Hill switchboard or the office of your congressperson or local legislator.

Once you have prepared a letter, leverage your efforts by getting others involved. Make copies of your letter and give them to friends and acquaintances who share your views. Encourage them to prepare similar letters and to make copies to give to their friends to do the same.

Mount a petition drive: Because it contains a large number of signatures, a petition carries significantly more weight than an individual letter. At heart, however, a petition is simply a letter with additional signatures. For maximum effectiveness, petitions concerning local issues should contain hundreds of names. A petition being sent to Congress, though, should have a thousand or more.

Getting people to sign a petition is very similar to registering voters. Set up a table near a busy public place, and/or arm volunteers with clipboards and flyers briefly stating the purpose of the petition. In either case, volunteers should politely stop passers-by with a short "pitch" concerning the importance of the petition. These volunteers should also be prepared to answer questions about the issue from potential signers. As with voter registration drives, signs, music, eye-catching T-shirts, and other attention-getting devices can be used to attract the attention of passers-by.

Petitions are particularly important in supporting a new bill in your local legislature or in Congress. In lobbying for passage of a bill, it is important to get involved long before a piece of legislation comes before the full legislature for a vote. Very few bills make it that far; the vast majority die quietly in an assortment of subcommittees and committees. Of the more than 20,000 bills introduced in each session of Congress, fewer than 10 percent make it out of committee, according to political scientist August Bequai. "For a congressional bill to be enacted into law," Bequai says, "it must either have a powerful constituency and/or little opposition."

Therefore, it is important to lobby the members of the bill's committee as well. A large petition drive from your district or state can have an impact on legislators from other districts or states because it implies broad and varied support for an issue. For additional effect, call a press conference to announce the results of your petition drive and send clippings of positive press coverage along with the petition. You can also send copies of your petition to powerful legislators who might be able to sway committee members. In Congress, this would include the speaker of the House and House and Senate majority and minority leaders.

Finally, send a copy of your petition to the directors of governmental agencies that are likely to take a position for or against the legislation. For instance, the Environmental Protection Agency is likely to take a position on environmental legislation, the Federal Communications Commission on legislation concerning the media, the Department of Energy on nuclear power or energy conservation legislation, and the Department of the Interior on legislation concerning public lands or Native Americans.

Petitions can be powerful weapons. They can be used to influence Congress, local officials, the media, and even corporations. And remember that even though your petition may have only a hundred or a thousand names, others are also sending in petitions of their own. Together, in the eyes of the receiver, these petitions will represent the voices of a large constituency of voters and consumers seriously concerned about a particular issue or cause.

BECOME AN ORGANIZATIONAL BRIDGEBUILDER

To build greater political leverage, local grass-roots groups can combine their resources to champion a particular cause. For instance, a local Hispanic group fighting the expansion of a waste dump in its neighborhood can link up with neighboring community groups and city or state chapters of Greenpeace, the ACLU, or the Citizen's Clearinghouse for Hazardous Wastes. A group fighting discrimination in the funding of its neighborhood schools could solicit support from groups whose local chapters have been fighting for social justice and racial and gender equality. These include NOW, the NAACP, and SANE/FREEZE. Collaboration can greatly enhance the resources and visibility needed to win a community battle.

But although collaboration makes sense, it is one of the most difficult things to accomplish. Many groups do not want to divert time and resources from their own agendas to help other organizations. A group leader's ego or preoccupation with being seen as the dominant group can get in the way of cooperation. Differences in organizational style can also create difficulties. Because of these factors, many group leaders are resistant to seeking outside help, no matter how badly it is needed.

This is why "bridgebuilders" are required. Bridgebuilders are people who have no egos to bruise or turf battles to fight, who can develop and put forth workable plans for collaborative efforts between like-minded groups. Bridgebuilders can discuss with members of other organizations the likelihood of cooperation, how collaboration is in both groups' self-interest, and under what terms collaboration might take place. Bridgebuilders from two different organizations can draft a plan that defines the extent of joint cooperation between the groups and details specific goals, time frames, how decisions will be made, and the resources each group will provide.

With these ticklish concerns largely ironed out, each bridgebuilder can discuss the possibility of cooperation with his or her own group and lobby the group's leaders, along with its membership, to discuss the possibility of collaboration and agree to an exploratory meeting between the two groups.

SUPPORT STUDENT ACTIVISM

In just the past few years, Yale University students have supported a union strike against their administration, Columbia University students have blocked the university's administration building to protest the school's refusal to divest its South African stock holdings, gay and lesbian students at the University of Pennsylvania have held a "March against Homophobia" to protest on-campus harassment, and students from around the country have blocked the entrance to CIA headquarters in Washington to protest the agency's actions in Central America. In 1990, 13,000 students from around the country gathered at the University of Illinois for a convention of the Student Environmental Action Coalition (SEAC). And for over a decade, students have supported the ongoing boycott of Coors beer. In addition, on campuses across the country, progressive women and men hold an annual "Take Back the Night" demonstration, a week-long event that focuses attention on all forms of sexual harassment.

College campuses around the country continue to be hotbeds of progressive activity. Students have championed causes from fair wages and nuclear disarmament to women's and minority rights. They have formed or joined a number of progressive organizations, such as SEAC, Public Interest Research Groups (PIRGs), United Campuses to Prevent Nuclear War (UCAM), and the Progressive Student Network (PSN). In addition, many national progressive organizations have either student chapters or a large student membership.

Although student activists often have their hands full with campus-related issues, students are not averse to getting involved in broader activities. Students, for instance, were heavily involved in Carol Moseley Braun's campaign to become the Illinois Democratic nominee for the U.S. senate, virtually delivering a landslide vote for Braun in every major college town in the state. Students may also be interested in assisting on issues concerning the communities near their schools. For all these activities, they can use your support, including funding, speakers, literature, and assistance with the media. Contact progressive student groups at nearby universities or community colleges and discuss ways that you could lend each other assistance and support.

JOIN A PROGRESSIVE CHURCH OR SYNAGOGUE

Progressive religious institutions have long been leaders in the movements for peace, social justice, and civil rights. Groups like the National Council of Churches, the Interfaith Center for Corporate Responsibility, NETWORK, the Jewish Women's Caucus, Evangelicals for Social Action, Clergy and Laity Concerned, the American Friends Service Committee, and the National Council of Roman Catholic Bishops have taken stands on a broad range of progressive issues, including apartheid, peace, civil rights, hunger, nuclear disarmament, and the environment.

In addition, single-issue religious groups abound. Among these are Witness for Peace, Sojourners Peace Ministry, Quest for Peace, the Religious Task Force on South America, the Interfaith Hunger Appeal, the Presbyterian Hunger Program, Catholics for a Free Choice, and the Religious Coalition on Abortion Rights.

Religious institutions have tremendous influence over the attitudes of the public. By taking progressive stands on important issues, they can counter the onslaught of right-wing propaganda emanating from conservative think tanks, the government, and fundamentalist Christian leaders. Indeed, since the religious right dominates religious broadcasting, the role of progressive churches is especially critical.

If your church or synagogue refuses to take a progressive stand, find one that does. Not only will it give you another outlet for getting involved, but you will also receive spiritual enrichment from sermons exhorting you to put your faith in action. In addition, you will have the opportunity to build new and motivating relationships with like-minded fellow parishioners.

CHAPTER NINE

Dollars for Change

Bringing about fundamental change in America will require not only political reform, but also major changes in the way business is conducted. Social costs such as environmental destruction and unemployment must become part of each business's profit/loss equation, and a business's contributions to a just society—through fair labor practices, environmental preservation, and other socially beneficial practices—must become the key to consumer acceptance, and therefore corporate profits.

Corporations today are largely unaccountable to the public for their actions. This is ironic, since they are dependent on consumers and investors for their very survival. But, in spite of this dependence, many corporations pollute the environment, discriminate against women and people of color, exploit their labor forces, and use consumer dollars to fund right-wing think tanks.

The men who run America's major corporations, as a group, are the most powerful men in the country. Their control over trillions in corporate assets, their enormous political influence, and their control over production and employment practices give them a greater influence on the average American's quality of life than any other group, including the federal government. It is largely big business, which carefully nurtures an intimate relationship with the political elite, that ensures that

America remains the most capitalistic of the industrialized nations. It is largely big business that determines labor market policies, the level of environmental pollution, and the degree to which America exploits the Third World. And through its direct and indirect influence on government policy, big business also plays a major role in shaping federal and state tax and spending policies.

To counter this imbalance of power, the Left must do more than replace pro-business politicians with progressive alternatives. It also must use its enormous economic clout through socially responsible consumption and investment.

Socially responsible consumption and investment is one of the most powerful strategies the Left has for promoting social and environmental awareness in corporate America. Every individual who believes in social change can make a positive contribution to a just society on a daily basis by spending and investing his or her money in a socially responsible way. Your dollars can work consistently to promote ethical business practices and encourage changes in the way America does business.

To promote a new style of business, consumers must move their financial support from unprincipled corporations to more socially responsible businesses. They must support businesses that provide equal employment opportunities for women and minorities; that do not abuse the environment; that donate an above-average portion of their profits to charity; that support their surrounding communities; that do not exploit the Third World or support repressive foreign regimes; and that have strong employee relations and worker benefits programs.

While you may feel that your limited dollars can't make a big difference, collectively, you and your progressive counterparts can make a tremendous impact. In a 1990 Roper poll, 52 percent of those surveyed said they would pay 10 percent more for a product made by a socially responsible company, and 67 percent indicated that a company's social responsibility ratings were important. In addition, every concerned individual can influence how businesses, friends, local governments, churches, and pension plans spend and invest their money.

SOCIALLY RESPONSIBLE CONSUMERS

Ironically, socially responsible consumption has been the instrument least used by individuals to promote change. People who are truly concerned about world peace and social justice will readily purchase products made by nuclear weapons producers or invest in companies that do business in South Africa. People who are incensed by corporate insensitivity toward the needs of working mothers will readily purchase the products of the worst offenders. And many who are concerned about the destruction of the nation's forest stock up on paper towels, writing tablets, and other goods made by environmental "rapists."

Even though it is often overlooked, consumer activism can be extremely effective. In the past, it has been conducted mainly in the form of boycotts. One of the most famous and successful consumer boycotts was the civil rights movement's boycott of the Montgomery Bus Company in 1955. When that company was almost bankrupted by four months of severely reduced ridership, it finally succumbed and changed

THE FIFTEEN WORST CORPORATE POLLUTERS	
CORPORATION	TOTAL POLLUTION RELEASED IN POUNDS
Du Pont	338,416,705
Monsanto	201,858,822
American Cyanamid	189,040,601
Shell Oil	172,572,098
BP America	151,255,881
Freeport McMoran	150,465,176
AMAX	112,914,726
Allied-Signal	99,517,146
ASARCO	98,162,489
Vulcan Chemicals	92,831,594
General Motors	87,443,103
Occidental Petroleum	86,816,729
3M	83,233,924
Eastman Kodak	82,153,751
Phelps Dodge	80,545,334

Pounds of total pollution released include air, water, land, underround, public sewage, and off-site transfers, as reported to the EPA.

its racist practices. More recently, People for the Ethical Treatment of Animals (PETA) has campaigned very effectively against fur products and animal testing. PETA's actions have prompted mail order retailers such as Spiegel and Land's End to remove furs from their catalogs. In addition, consumer giants Avon and Colgate-Palmolive have ended or reduced their use of animals for testing purposes in response to consumer pressure.

Another national boycott is currently under way against General Electric to protest the company's production of nuclear weapons and its pollution of the environment. The boycott's sponsor, INFACT, estimated that the boycott had 3.5 million supporters in 1989 and cost General Electric more than $100 million in sales between 1986, when it started, and mid-1990.

Another INFACT-initiated boycott is being conducted against Nestle and American Home Products for their promotion of baby formula in Third World countries. The use of infant formulas in the Third World promotes disease, since formula is often mixed with contaminated water and deprives babies of the natural immunities in breast milk. The infant-formula boycott has been running on and off for well over a decade. It has generated a high level of commitment among its supporters, as this letter to Nestle testifies:

> My children love Nestle Quick. My husband and I are virtually addicted to Nescafe. But we will no longer be buying these or your other products. We have learned about the suffering your advertising of infant formula causes. You are a large company. Individually, we don't have much power over your actions. But our outrage joins with that of many others and together we will boycott Nestle products until you change.

The passion and commitment shown by the author of this letter is the attitude we all must take toward socially responsible consumption. If we are outraged by the ways in which some corporations spoil the environment, support war and Third World oppression, and discriminate against working mothers, women, and minorities, then we must give up our "Nescafe" for different brands until corporations change their unacceptable practices.

COLLECT INFORMATION

The first step in becoming a socially responsible consumer is collecting the necessary information. A good starting place is the annual consumer guide *Shopping for a Better World*, published by the Council on Economic Priorities (CEP). This $4.95 book, widely available at bookstores, provides social responsibility ratings for 166 corporations that account for more than two thousand products. The council rates companies in ten areas: charitable giving, advancement of minority employees, advancement of female employees, use of animals in product testing, community outreach, regard for the environment, family benefits, investments in South Africa, workplace issues such as safety and labor relations, and willingness to disclose company information to the public. It also notes involvement in the military or nuclear industries and other socially relevant information. *Shopping for a Better World* provides an easy and effective way to begin consuming responsibly. For $25, you can become a member of CEP and receive a copy of *Shopping for a Better World* each year and the monthly *Research Reports*, which offers more information of interest to socially responsible consumers. For more information, write CEP at 30 Irving Place, New York, NY 10003, or call (212) 420–1133.

When reading through *Shopping for a Better World*, you may note that few corporations rate highly in all ten areas. There are some people who believe there are no "good" big corporations. If, however, you choose to drive a car or use consumer products that are not available from alternative sources, you will undoubtedly have to compromise. Your purchase decisions may come down to finding the least bad supplier. Eventually, as companies realize the advantages of doing business in a socially responsible way, they will push each other to improve, just like healthy competition can lower prices.

The Kellogg Company, for instance, has high ratings in nine out of ten categories, but retains operations in South Africa. Compared to another cereal manufacture, RJR Nabisco, however, Kellogg's record is exemplary. In addition to manufacturing and actively marketing cigarettes, RJR received no top ratings at all and got poor ratings for its reluctance to disclose information (it couldn't be rated in five of the ten categories) and for its record on the environment.

CEP's rating system makes shopping for common consumer products simple. The vast majority of food products, personal care items, and

over-the-counter medicines, for example, are produced by a handful of
giant consumer companies. Once you know the ratings of these companies and how to read product labels to identify the "parent" manufacturing company, you have the information you need to purchase "ethical" products.

For example, Ralston Purina, maker of Oatmeal Goodness, Wonder,
Homepride, Beefsteak, and Bread Du Jour bread products, received high
or good ratings across the board. Flowers Industries, however, the
maker of Sunbeam Buttermaid, Hometown, Nature's Own, Evangeline
Maid, Cobblestone Mill, and Rich Grain bread products, rated poorly in
two categories and refused to provide sufficient information to be rated
in the others except South Africa, where is does do business. Likewise,
among makers of personal care products, Carter-Wallace, maker of
Arrid, Nair, Sea & Ski, Block-Out, and Mischief brands of personal-care
products was poorly rated because it lacks women in top management
positions, uses animals for testing, and lacks family benefits for its employees. Procter & Gamble, however, maker of Secret, Sure, Clearasil,
Cover Girl, Max Factor, Noxema, and Crest brands, received top marks
for charitable giving, advancing women and minorities, workplace issues, family benefits, community outreach, disclosure of information,
and reductions in animal testing.

It is also important to keep abreast of the various boycotts called by
progressive organizations. To find out which companies are being boycotted and why, read *Co-op America Quarterly*. It includes "Boycott
Action News," a section that reports on ongoing boycotts against major
corporations. Currently, labor groups are protesting unfair labor practices at Hormel, Holly Farms/Tyson Foods, and Castle and Cooke/Dole.
Labor groups are also protesting against Grand Metropolitan (Pillsbury,
Green Giant, Burger King, and Haagen Dazs) for exploiting Mexican
workers and the environment. Animal rights groups are protesting animal testing at L'Oreal and Gillette and the use of leather from endangered kangaroos by Puma, Adidas, Browning, and Florsheim. Anti-
apartheid groups are protesting Coca-Cola, Shell, and Kellogg for their
continued investment in South Africa. As noted earlier, boycotts are
also underway against Nestle (Carnation, Beech-Nut, Libby's, Hills
Brothers, Stouffer's) and American Home Products (SMA baby formula, Advil, Dristan, Anacin) for continuing to promote infant formulas in Third World countries. Environmental groups are protesting Mitsubishi, Georgia-Pacific, Scott Paper and Weyerhaeuser for policies de-

structive to forests. And gay and lesbian groups are protesting Cracker Barrel Restaurants and the United Way (for donations to the Boy Scouts of America) for discriminatory practices.

Co-op America Quarterly, published by Co-op America, also offers help in finding alternatives to traditional consumerism. This publication includes information on supporting small and employee-owned businesses and shopping through cooperatives, as well as other information on making our economy more just and sustainable. Co-op America also offers insurance and credit cards, as well as a catalog that sells socially responsible products. For further information, write Co-op America at 2100 M Street NW, Suite 403, Washington, D.C. 20063, or call (800) 424-COOP.

Another publication that offers information on company policies is *Catalyst*, a quarterly consumer newsletter. Recent issues of *Catalyst* have included a list of the largest defense contractors, the worst polluters (Du Pont was number one), and the U.S. companies most heavily involved in worldwide deforestation. *Catalyst* also includes information about smaller socially responsible companies and products and discusses issues of concern to consumers. For information, write *Catalyst* at 64 Main Street, Montpelier, VT 05602, or call (802) 223–7943.

SUPPORT ALTERNATIVES TO CORPORATE AMERICA

Small Companies. In addition to purchasing carefully from America's corporate giants, you can look for small, innovative companies to support. There are a growing number of small businesses that provide quality products and use a significant portion of their profits to make the world a better place. Ben and Jerry's Homemade is one well-known example; this ice cream manufacturer donates 7.5 percent of its pretax income to charitable causes, including 1 percent for peace. Tom's of Maine, a manufacturer of cruelty-free personal-care products, also gives 7.5 percent of its pretax earnings to charity and has five women on its board. Another high-profile progressive company is The Body Shop, a manufacturer and retailer of natural cosmetics. The Body Shop sells only cruelty-free products and is involved in a number of charitable projects in the Third World, including preserving the Amazon rain forest.

Other socially responsible smaller companies include Aveda, Brookside Soap, Clientele, Auria Cacia, Body Love Natural Cosmetics, Alexandra Avery, Earthrise, and Ecco Bella. These are cosmetics and personal-care products companies whose products use mostly natural ingredients. Barbara's Bakery, Cherry Hill Cannery, Dolefam, Earth's Best, Eden Foods, Falcon, Stoneyfield Farms, Imagine Foods, Mayacamas Fine Foods, Paul Penders, and Newman's Own are socially responsible food producers. And Earth Care Paper, Biobottoms, Shaklee, Big Sky Artisans, and Real Goods Trading Company are progressive companies offering consumers a variety of goods from recycled paper to cleaning supplies to baby clothing.

Although the products of these and other small, progressive companies are not always widely available, many do sell by mail. In addition, many of their products can be found in health food stores or other specialty retailers. But to help give more consumers easier access to socially responsible products, let your local retailers know that there is demand for them. Some retailers—including Walmart, the largest retailer in the country—have responded to consumer demand by creating special sections for environmentally friendly products.

Co-ops and Farmers' Markets. We are hearing more and more about the dangers of pesticides and hormones in meats and vegetables, especially in the products of agribusinesses. But in most cities and towns, there are co-ops and farmers' markets where naturally produced

---

TOP 25 DEFENSE CONTRACTORS

McDonnell Douglas	Honeywell
General Dynamics	Litton Industries
General Electric	IBM
Raytheon	TRW
General Motors	Unisys
Lockheed	United Technologies
Texas Instruments	Martin Marietta
Tenneco	Boeing
Textron	Grumman
Allied-Signal	GTE
FMC	Rockwell International
Gencorp	Westinghouse Electric

vegetables, and sometimes meats, are sold by small farmers or farming cooperatives. By shopping at these, you will not only purchase healthier foods, but you will also be doing your part to support sustainable agriculture and family farms. Look in your phone book or newspaper activity guide to see if there is a market near you.

Credit Cards. You can also be socially responsible while using your credit card or making long-distance phone calls. A company called Working Assets, for instance, offers long distance telephone service that donates one percent of your charges to peace, economic justice, human rights, and environmental organizations. It even allows you to make some phone calls to corporate or political leaders at no charge.

In addition, Working Assets, Co-op America, and the International Wildlife Coalition offer credit cards that contribute a portion of your purchase amount toward wildlife preservation, advocacy for a sustainable society, or to progressive nonprofit organizations such as the National Coalition for the Homeless, Planned Parenthood, and Rainforest Action Network.

USE YOUR INFORMATION

Once you have the information you need to choose products based on company practices, make sure you use that information to make an impact beyond your personal purchases. Share your knowledge with friends and acquaintances.

In addition, take your new consumer knowledge into appropriate institutional settings, such as your job, your religious organization, and any community groups you may belong to. For example, anyone who is responsible for purchasing office supplies can refuse to purchase White Out or Bic Pens, both of which are produced by Gillette. Likewise, anyone involved in the purchase of computer equipment can oppose the purchase of products from major defense contractors such as Hewlett Packard or IBM.

If you really want to expand your consumer power, form a socially responsible consumers' group in your community, religious group, or workplace. Assign each member the task of investigating the ratings of companies in a certain category, such as appliances, dairy products, or pet foods. Meet regularly to share information, and consider producing a small newsletter to share with those who are uncommitted. You can even follow the nuclear freeze movement and campaign to make your institution or community a "Socially Responsible Consumer Zone."

Finally, be sure to write letters to companies that you choose to support, as well as to those that you don't. Tell them how their socially responsible policies, or lack thereof, influence the buying decisions of ordinary consumers like yourself. By doing this, you will be alerting the corporate brass that consumers are holding them accountable for more than just the price or the color of their products. And as this sinks in, corporate leaders will come to understand the importance of corporate ethics and social responsibility to the bottom line.

SOCIALLY RESPONSIBLE INVESTING

Socially responsible investing is the next step in becoming a socially responsible consumer. Socially responsible investing means investing

---

CALVERT SOCIAL INVESTMENT FUND

SOCIAL CRITERIA

The Calvert Social Investment Fund invests in companies that:

1) Deliver safe and useful products and services in ways that sustain our natural environment.

+ Products or services that solve social problems
+ Products that are intrinsically useful
+ Energy from renewable sources
+ Progressive policies vis-a-vis the environment
+ Sensitivity to the issue of animal rights
− No tobacco, alcohol, gambling, or pornography
− No nuclear energy
− No observable patterns of illegal pollution or environmental records worse than the industry average

2) Are managed with participation throughout the organization in defining and achieving objectives

+ Employee stock ownership and profit sharing plans
+ Quality circles or incentive production teams

---

your money with the same care that you use to spend it. It means depositing your savings in economically sound, socially responsible banks
and savings institutions; investing in government credit obligations
such as housing bonds or other federal or local bonds that are earmarked
for socially responsible developments; and buying stocks and bonds
based on a company's social responsibility ratings, not just its expected
economic return.

While some socially responsible investors simply avoid investing in
"bad" companies, others work to change companies through shareholder resolutions, a technique pioneered by the late University of Chicago professor and organizer Saul Alinsky in the 1960s. Shareholder activists today are challenging corporate leadership on a variety of issues,
including investments in South Africa, animal testing, destructive environmental policies, and nuclear weapons production. In 1990, according
to the Interfaith Center for Corporate Responsibility, over 300 socially
responsible shareholder resolutions were filed with more than 180 companies.

---

3) Negotiate fairly with their workers, provide an environment
supportive of their wellness, do not discriminate on the basis of
race, religion, age, disability or sexual orientation. . . .
  + Unionized firms with good labor relations
  + Non-union firms with innovative policies
  − No regular violators of EEO, OSHA, or FLRB standards
  − No companies on AFL-CIO or other labor boycott
  lists

4) Foster an awareness of commitments to human goals. . . .
  + Active commitments to community affairs

5) Other
  − No company doing business directly or indirectly in
  South Africa
  − No top 100 weapons system contractors
  − No companies involved in nuclear weapons
  − No companies with more than 10% in weapons sys-
  tems

The amount of money invested in socially responsible investments today, James Goodno reports in *Dollars & Sense*, is estimated at $625 billion. This figure includes a number of union, university, and religious pension funds (including the Teachers Insurance and Annuity Association of America/College Retirement Equity Fund; the Presbyterian and United Methodist churches; and Smith College, Columbia University, and Swarthmore College); individual investors; and mutual funds and money market accounts with social-responsibility criteria.

The criteria that investors use to screen investments vary, but many exclude companies doing business in South Africa; companies that are major weapons or nuclear energy producers; companies that are major environmental polluters; companies with poor labor relations records; and companies whose major business is alcohol, tobacco, or gambling.

The vast sum of socially invested dollars *has* had an impact on business ethics. One of SRI's most notable achievements has been convincing U.S. corporations to stop doing business in South Africa. Between 1984 and 1989, the number of U.S. companies in South Africa dropped from over 300 to just 124. Hospital Corporation of America was prompted by a shareholder resolution to adopt a policy discouraging the use of infant formula in its hospitals, and a shareholder resolution led Monsanto not to renew its contract to operate a nuclear weapons facility.

Socially responsible investments often outperform other investment vehicles. From 1976 to 1989, the Good Money Industrial Average —an index of thirty socially responsible stocks compiled by *Good Money* magazine to mirror the Dow Jones Industrial Average—has outpaced the Dow Jones in ten of fourteen years, generating a cumulative return of 646.6 percent versus the Dow's 174.1 percent. Another socially responsible stock index, the Domini Social Index, reports *Dollars & Sense*, outperformed the Standard and Poor's 500 (19 to 18 percent) in the twelve-month period ending April 30, 1991, and as of June 1991, the Calvert socially responsible money market fund had one of the highest yields in the country.

HOW TO BECOME A SOCIALLY RESPONSIBLE INVESTOR

There are a number of socially responsible mutual funds that an investor can use to invest responsibly. The largest socially responsible fund manager, Calvert, manages more than $600 million through its equity, corporate bond, and money market funds. Other funds, such as the Working Assets Money Market Fund, the Pax World Fund, the Parnassus Fund, and the New Alternatives Fund, offer socially responsible investors a number of vehicles and strategies for money management. A list of socially responsible money managers is provided in chapter 10.

Socially responsible investors who prefer to invest on their own have a number of investment publications available to help them. *Good Money, Clean Yield, Franklin Research,* and *Catalyst* are publications that focus on the social responsibility as well as the profit performance of publicly traded corporations. There are also a number of stockbrokers and investment advisers who specialize in socially responsible investments; their names can be found in many of the magazines mentioned here.

SRI also includes carefully choosing the financial institutions you use. Instead of depositing your funds into a large bank that uses them for who knows what, invest them in banks, credit unions, or revolving loan funds that invest in the community and in worker-owned or minority businesses. In Chicago, South Shore Bank has used investors' funds to rehabilitate more than ten thousand housing units in low to moderate income neighborhoods since 1975. In Durham, North Carolina, Self-Help Credit Union has financed more than fifty-three worker-owned businesses since 1984. The Vermont National Bank created the Socially Responsible Banking Fund, which has loaned $31 million to small businesses, sustainable agriculture, and affordable housing projects.

To determine whether a financial institution is socially responsible, request a copy of its Community Reinvestment Statement. This document reveals what the institution has identified as the credit needs of the community and what services it is providing to meet those needs. In addition, ask the institution how many of its loans are to small businesses and low-income housing projects.

Better yet, if you can afford a reduced yield, invest in a revolving loan fund that makes loans to small worker-owned businesses, co-ops, low-income housing projects, or other community development projects. Investors in these funds are typically asked to accept below-market interest rates so that the funds can, in turn, lend to borrowers at below-market rates. The Jubilee Housing Loan Fund, for example, funds the purchase and renovation of buildings for low-income housing in

Washington, D.C., and the Women's Economic Development Corporation, in Minnesota, funds small but growing businesses started by women.

There is even a socially responsible insurance company. Consumers United Insurance Company, in Washington, D.C., is the largest employee-owned life and health insurer in the country. Unlike most insurance companies, it permits the use of alternative care providers and covers domestic partners; it also offers nondiscriminatory, unisex insurance rates. Even more, premium reserves are used to make socially responsible investments.

THE DECENCY DECADE

Insurance, mutual funds, small progressive companies, and credit cards are a sample of the many ways that people can become socially responsible consumers and investors. Use them all to bring about change in the conscience of corporate America. Become part of what social trends forecaster Faith Popcorn calls the "Decency Decade." Popcorn, a business consultant, has put her corporate clients on notice:

> The consumer will want to know who you are before buying what you sell. . . . Who you are will mean publicly stating your environmental policy, your stance on health care and child care, how (or if) you deal with an apartheid country. . . . In the '90s, you've got to have a Corporate Soul.

CHAPTER TEN

Resource Guide

BRINGING ABOUT ECONOMIC AND SOCIAL CHANGE will require active participation by everyone who embraces the progressive agenda. To help you get involved, this chapter provides a list of organizations with local chapters; alternative political parties; alternative media sources; information on socially responsible companies; and national progressive organizations you can join or otherwise support.

What you may find most noticeable about these lists are the many progressive organizations that are not included. This is primarily because the organizations listed are only those national groups with multi-issue agendas. The Rainforest Network and People for Ethical Treatment of Animals, for example, are not listed because of their narrow focus. The Earth Island Institute, however, is listed because its stated agenda includes the environment, Third World development, and advocacy for a new economic order in America.

There are also thousands of local activist groups that are not listed. You can find information about these groups, however, through your local alternative newspaper or by asking around in your community. Information about the more narrowly defined, national organizations can be found in books such as Brad Erickson's *Call to Action* or Richard Zimmerman's *Making A Difference*.

Be sure to use this chapter. Contact some of these organizations to find one or more you'd like to work with. Peruse copies of some of the alternative publications and subscribe to the ones you like best. And keep abreast of which corporations are socially irresponsible or being boycotted and refuse to purchase their products.

NATIONAL PROGRESSIVE ORGANIZATIONS WITH LOCAL BRANCHES

The following organizations have local branches that are actively involved in working for social justice in their communities. Their organizational priorities differ somewhat, but most advocate a reduced military budget, greater government funding for social needs, greater citizen empowerment, environmental protection, and economic and social equality.

Citizen's Clearinghouse for Hazardous Wastes
P.O. Box 926
Arlington, VA 22216
(703) 237-2249
CCHW is a national clearinghouse for more than 1,700 grass-roots environmental and social justice groups of all races and income levels. Concerns include eliminating industrial pollution in the community and workplace, fighting environmental racism, supporting progressive candidates in local elections, and promoting community empowerment.

Jobs with Peace
76 Summer St.
Boston, MA 02110
(617) 338-5783
This group organizes peace, environmental, women's rights, civil rights, and labor activists in grass-roots campaigns to redirect military spending toward housing, job-skill training, environmental clean-up, public works, education, and health programs. Jobs with Peace has local chapters in communities through the United States.

National Organization for Women (NOW)
1000 16th St., NW
Washington, DC 20036
(202) 331-0036

This multi-issue organization operates on both the local and national levels to promote women's rights, social programs for children and families, gay rights, environmental protection, economic conversion, and civil rights. Local chapters are actively involved in organizing and supporting progressive political candidates.

SANE/FREEZE
1819 H St., NW, Suite 1000
Washington, DC 20006-3603
(202) 862-9740
A peace and justice organization that advocates nuclear disarmament, Third World development, and diverting military spending to help solve the country's pressing social and environmental problems. SANE/FREEZE has over 1,600 groups in communities across the country.

Students for Environmental Action (SEAC)
Box 1168
Chapel Hill, NC 27514
(919) 967-4600
An activist student organization advocating environmental protection, peace, racial and gender equality, and economic justice. SEAC has more than 1,000 chapters nationwide.

ALTERNATIVE POLITICAL ORGANIZATIONS AND THIRD PARTIES

21st Century Party
1600 Wilson Blvd., Suite 707
Arlington, VA 22209
(800) 394-2178
This newly formed party is an outgrowth of NOW's Commission for Responsive Democracy. The party platform centers on NOW's call for a new Bill of Rights for the 21st century that includes freedom from all forms of discrimination; freedom from violence, including the threat of nuclear war; adequate food, housing, health care, and education as a basic right; and the right to a clean and safe environment.

Campaign for a New Tomorrow
Box 27798
Washington, DC 20038-7798
(202) 736-1747
Composed of African-American, labor, farm, peace, and environmental
activists, the party is sponsoring the 1992 presidential campaign of Ron
Daniels, former executive director of the Rainbow Coalition. Daniels
has been endorsed by the Wisconsin Labor/Farm party and the Pennsylvania Consumer party.

Congressional Black Caucus
House Annex 2
Washington, DC 20515
(202) 226-7790
The leading congressional group supporting economic conversion, racial
and gender equality, environmental protection, labor market reform,
and a stronger social welfare state. Currently working with others in
Congress to form a coalition of progressive legislators.

Democratic Socialists of America (DSA)
15 Dutch St., Room 500
New York, NY 10273
(212) 962-0390
A political organization whose primary agenda is to promote a more socially democratic economic and political system in America. Largely by
working through the Democratic party, DSA advocates labor market reform, environmental protection, equal rights, national health care, and
economic conversion. Has local chapters in more than eighty cities
throughout the country.

The Greens/Green Party, USA
Box 30208
Kansas City, MO 64112
(816) 931-9366
Active since 1984, this national political party has more than 200 local
chapters. Issues of concern include the environment, social justice
through a new economic order, and gender and racial equality.

The New Party
324 Belleville Ave.
Bloomfield, NJ 07003
(201) 743-1105
A newly formed social democratic party that expects to begin supporting candidates in state and local elections in 1993. Modeled after
Canada's New Democratic party, the New Party plans to support progressives who run as Democrats and field alternative candidates when
the Democratic candidate is unacceptable.

Progressive Labor Party
Box 1510
Highland Park, NJ 08904
(609) 561-6259
Currently unnamed and still in the process of formation, this party's
goal is to articulate and represent the needs of working people by con-
fronting corporate power and advocating national health care, parental
leave, and a "Superfund" to retrain workers displaced due to military
cutbacks or environmental regulations.

PROGRESSIVE RESEARCH AND ADVOCACY ORGANIZATIONS

This is a list of national, progressive, multi-issue organizations. It includes research institutes, grass-roots advocacy organizations, and lobbying groups. Most of them are membership organizations that provide
newsletters, issue updates, and other resources to their members. Progressives can assist them in their efforts by becoming members, by
making financial donations, and in some cases by becoming actively involved.

American Association of University Women
1111 16th St. NW
Washington, DC 20036-4873
(202) 785-7737
An advocacy organization concerned with pay equity, sexual harassment, abortion rights, discrimination, education, and health.

American Civil Liberties Union (ACLU)
132 W. 43rd St.
New York, NY 10036
(212) 944-9800
A legal advocacy organization that lobbies and litigates against government intrusion on individual rights guaranteed by the Constitution and
against censorship and gender and race discrimination.

American Friends Service Committee
1501 Cherry St.
Philadelphia, PA 19102
(215) 241-7000
An activist organization that works for economic conversion, peace,
Third World development, and economic and social justice.

Amnesty International
322 8th Ave.
New York, NY 10001
(212) 633-4200
An international human rights organization that fights for the release
of political prisoners and for the abolition of torture and the death penalty.

Bread for the World
802 Rhode Island Ave., NE
Washington, DC 20018
(202) 269-0494 or (800) 82-BREAD
A Christian activist organization dedicated to ending Third World hunger and lobbying for tax relief for America's working poor and greater
funding for social programs. Has local chapters nationwide.

The Center for Budget and Policy Priorities
777 N. Capitol St., NE
Washington, DC 20002
(202) 408-1080
A research and advocacy organization that alerts and educates the public
and legislators on poverty, national budget concerns, and other issues
facing the economically disadvantaged.

Center for Economic Conversion
222-C View St.
Mountain View, CA 94041
(415) 968-8798
This resource and education organization promotes economic alternatives to excess military spending.

Center for Policy Alternatives
1875 Connecticut Ave., NW, Suite 710
Washington, DC 20009
(202) 387-6030
A research and advocacy organization that works with more than 1,500 state legislators to promote economic conversion, environmental protection, and economic justice at the state level.

Center for Third World Organizing (CTWO)
3861 Martin Luther King Jr. Way
Oakland, CA 94609
A network of activists and scholars that provides resources and training to community organizers in poor communities of color. Issues addressed include industrial pollution, health and education, gender and racial bias, immigration, housing, and jobs.

Children's Defense Fund
122 C St., NW
Washington, DC 20001
(202) 628-8787
This research and advocacy organization concerns itself primarily with the economic, social, and educational needs of children and teens. Addresses issues such as poverty, parental leave and child care, health care, and economic conversion.

Clergy and Laity Concerned (CALC)
198 Broadway
New York, NY 10038
(212) 964-6730
An interfaith organization concerned with peace, economic and racial justice, demilitarization, and ending Third World exploitation. CALC has local chapters across the country.

Earth Island Institute
300 Broadway, Suite 28
San Francisco, CA 94133
(415) 788-3666
An activist and education organization concerned with the environment, Third World exploitation, and promoting the connections between the environment and economic and social justice.

Economic Policy Institute
1730 Rhode Island Ave., NW, Suite 200
Washington, DC 20036
(202) 775-8810
A research organization that educates decision makers and the public on labor issues and working class economics, income inequality, education, tax policy, and the need for an industrial policy in America.

Educators for Social Responsibility
23 Garden St.
Cambridge, MA 02138
(617) 492-1764
A research and education organization that offers workshops and resources to parents and teachers on educating the young about human rights, peace, foreign policy, and social justice.

Fairness and Accuracy in Reporting (FAIR)
130 W. 25th St.
New York, NY 10001
(212) 633-6700
A research and advocacy group that monitors and reports on inaccurate reporting by the mainstream news media.

Food First/Institute for Food and Development Policy
145 Ninth St.
San Francisco, CA 94103
(415) 864-8555
A research and advocacy organization working to end Third World hunger, resolve the Third World debt crisis, and demilitarize America's foreign aid program.

Fund for the Feminist Majority
1600 Wilson Blvd., Suite 704
Arlington, VA 22209
(703) 522-2214
An organization dedicated to supporting progressive women political candidates and advocating racial and gender equality, abortion rights, social justice, and citizen empowerment.

Gray Panthers
311 S. Juniper St., Suite 601
Philadelphia, PA 19107
(202) 387-3111
A national organization of senior citizens fighting for the rights of the elderly and the environment. Advocates shifting federal funds from military spending to social programs and an end to ageism and other forms of discrimination and injustice.

Greenpeace USA
1436 U St., NW
Washington, DC 20009
(202) 462-1177
An international direct-action organization that promotes environmental protection and preservation, Third World development, economic conversion, peace, and nuclear disarmament.

Institute for Policy Studies/Transnational Institute (IPS)
1601 Connecticut St., NW
Washington, DC 20009
(202) 234-9382
A research and education organization concerned with promoting economic and social justice in America and the Third World.

Learning Alliance
494 Broadway
New York, NY 10022
(212) 226-7171
An educational organization that provides local organizers and activists with information and other tools needed to advocate for change in their communities.

National Gay and Lesbian Taskforce
1517 U St., NW
Washington, DC 20009
(202) 332-6483
An advocacy group that lobbies for equal rights for gays and lesbians, greater government spending on AIDS research, and increased services for people with AIDS.

People for the American Way
2000 M St., NW, Suite 400
Washington, DC 20036
(202) 467-4999
A lobby and advocacy group concerned with a range of issues from censorship and education to civil rights.

Planned Parenthood Federation of America
810 Seventh Ave.
New York, NY 10019
(212) 785-3351
An international organization which advocates the constitutional sanctity of the right to privacy, reproductive freedom, and equal rights for women and the poor.

Public Citizen
2000 P St., NW, Suite 300
Washington, DC 20036
(202) 833-3000
A research and advocacy group concerned with consumer and environmental protection, citizen empowerment, and corporate accountability.

Women's International League for Peace and Freedom (WILPF)
1213 Race St.
Philadelphia, PA 19107
(215) 563-7110
An advocacy and legislative lobby organization concerned with human rights, social justice, world peace, and military disarmament.

World Policy Institute
New School of Social Research
777 United Nations Plaza, 5th Floor
New York, NY 10017
(212) 490-0010
A research organization that collects and disseminates information on disarmament, human rights, social justice, the environment, economic conversion, and Third World development.

Worldwatch Institute
1776 Massachusetts Ave., NW
Washington, DC 20036
(202) 452-1999
A research and education organization whose interests include the environment, economic conversion, and Third World development.

LEGISLATIVE INFORMATION AND
CANDIDATE RATINGS

AFL-CIO
Legislative Department
815 16th St., NW
Washington, DC 20006
(202) 637-5000
The AFL-CIO produces a congressional report card, called the Voting Record, on how members of Congress vote on labor and other issues of concern to working Americans.

Americans for Democratic Action
1625 K St., NW, Suite 1150
Washington, DC 20006
(202) 785-5980
ADA produces a congressional report card that measures how members of Congress vote on legislation ranging from handgun control and campaign reform to funding for social programs and military spending. From this voting record, ADA compiles a list of the top liberal senators and representatives in Congress.

Center for National Independence in Politics
129 N. W. 4th St., Suite 204
Corvallis, OR 97330
(503) 754-2746
This bipartisan group sponsors Project Vote Smart, a voter's information hotline (800-786-6885) that provides "instant access" to voting
records, issue positions, and performance evaluations from a variety of
organizations. It covers presidential, congressional, and gubernatorial
elections.

Greenpeace Activist Network
1436 U St., NW
Washington, DC 20009
(202) 462-1177
Provides free information on important upcoming legislation and on
letter-writing campaigns.

League of Conservation Voters
2000 L St., NW, Suite 804
Washington, DC 20036
(202) 785-VOTE
A nonpartisan political action committee that rates members of Congress and presidential candidates on their environmental voting record.

League of Women Voters
1730 M St. NW
Washington, DC 20036
(202) 429-1956
A nonpartisan organization that rates congressional candidates on their
voting record regarding issues affecting women, children, families, and
the environment.

National Women's Political Caucus
1275 K St. NW, #750
Washington, DC 20005
(202) 898-1100
This organization produces voting guides that are useful in assessing
both Democratic and Republican presidential candidates' credentials
with respect to their stance on the spectrum of women's issues.

Sierra Club Activist Network
730 Polk St.
San Francisco, CA 94109
Provides action alerts on upcoming environmental legislation and provides callers with names and addresses of legislators.

RESOURCES FOR SOCIALLY RESPONSIBLE CONSUMPTION AND INVESTING

Calvert Social Investment Fund
4550 Montgomery Avenue
Bethesda, MA 20814
(800) 368-2748
Socially responsible mutual fund.

Catalyst
64 Main St., 2nd Floor
Montpelier, VT 05602
(802) 223-7943
Quarterly newsletter providing information on socially responsible companies, mutual funds, and community development and revolving loan funds.

Clean Yield
Box 1880
Greensboro Bend, VT 05842
(802) 533-7178
Monthly stock market newsletter for socially responsible investors.

Consumer United Insurance
2100 M St., NW
Washington, DC 20063
(800) 255-4397
Socially responsible life and health insurance company.

Co-op America
2100 M. St., NW, Suite 310
Washington, DC 20063
(800) 424-COOP

Produces *Co-op Quarterly*, which contains "Boycott Action News."
Also publishes a catalog of socially responsible products and is a good
source for information on companies that sell nontoxic and cruelty-free
products and socially responsible investment vehicles.

Council on Economic Priorities
30 Irving Place
New York, NY 10003
(800) 822-6435
Publishes *Shopping for a Better World* and other valuable information
on corporations' level of socially responsibility.

Good Money
P.O. Box 363
Worchester, VT 05682
(800) 535-3551
A bimonthly newsletter for socially responsible investors that is con-
cerned with monitoring activities of large, publicly traded corporations.

Green Consumer Letter
(800) 955-GREEN
Monthly newsletter on environmentally responsible consumer products.

Interfaith Center for Corporate Responsibility
475 Riverside Drive
New York, NY 10115
(212) 870-2936
Coordinates socially responsible shareholder resolutions against major
corporations. Contact for information on upcoming shareholder actions
resolutions and on corporate practices.

Investor Responsibility Research Center
1755 Massachusetts Ave., NW
Washington, DC 20036
(202) 939-6500
A research organization that publishes a number of publications on corporate social responsibility, U.S. companies' practices in South Africa,
and other issues of concern to socially responsible investors.

National Association of Community Development Loan Funds (NACDLF)
151 Montague City Rd.
Greenfield, MA 01301
(413) 774-7956
Trade association for community loan funds that lend to worker-owned businesses and community development projects. Contact to find out about loan funds in your community.

National Federation of Community Development Credit Unions
29 John St., Room 903
New York, NY 10038
(212) 513-5191
Trade association for financial cooperatives located in low-income communities. Contact to find community development credit unions in your area.

New Alternatives Fund
259 Northern Blvd.
Great Neck, NY 11021
(516) 466-0808
Socially responsible mutual fund.

Parnassus Fund
244 California St., Suite 200
San Francisco, CA 94111
(415) 999-3505
Socially responsible mutual fund.

Pax World Fund
224 State St.
Portsmouth, NH 03801
(800) 767-1729
Socially responsible mutual fund.

Social Investment Forum
430 First Ave.
Minneapolis, MN 55401
(612) 333-8338

Professional association of investment funds, financial advisors, and investors active in the field of socially responsible investing. Contact for a listing of socially responsible advisers in your area.

Working Assets
701 Montgomery St.
San Francisco, CA 94111
(800) 52-APPLY
Offers a socially responsible long distance service, Visa card, and money market fund.

ALTERNATIVE MEDIA

NEWS AND POLITICAL
COMMENTARY PUBLICATIONS

The Advocate
Box 4371
Los Angeles, CA 90078-4371

Dissent
Foundation for the Study of
Independent Social
Ideas, Inc.
521 Fifth Ave.
New York, N.Y. 10017

Dollars & Sense
One Summer St.
Somerville, MA 02143-9969
(617) 628-8411

Guardian
33 W. 17th St.
New York, NY 10011
(212) 691-0404

In These Times
2040 N. Milwaukee
Chicago, IL 60647
(312) 772-0100

The Nation
72 Fifth Ave.
New York, NY 10011
(212) 242-8400

National Catholic Reporter
115 E. Armour Boulevard
Kansas City, MO 64111
(816) 531-0538

The Progressive
Box 421
Mt. Morris, IL 61054-0421
(608) 257-4626

Z Magazine
116 St. Botolph St.
Boston, MA 02115-9979

Sojourners: The Women's Forum
42 Seaverns Ave.
Jamaica Plain, MA 02130
(202) 636-3637

Tikkun
5100 Leona St.
Oakland, CA 94619
(414) 482 0805

World Policy Journal
World Policy Institute
New School for Social Research
777 United Nations Plaza
New York, NY 10164-0339
(212) 490-0010

CULTURE AND POLITICS

Mother Jones
Foundation for National Progress
1663 Mission St.
San Francisco, CA 94103
(415) 558-8881

Village Voice
842 Broadway
New York, NY 10003
(212) 475-3300

Utne Reader
Box 1974
Marion, OH 43305
(612) 338-5040

ENVIRONMENTAL PUBLICATIONS

Animal's Agenda
c/o Humane Alternative Products
8 Hutchinson St.
Concord, NH 03301

Buzzworm
2305 Canyon Blvd., Suite 206
Boulder, CO 80302

E Magazine
P.O. Box 6667
Syracuse, NY 13217
(800) 825 0061

FEMINIST PUBLICATIONS

Ms. Magazine
230 Park Ave.
New York, NY 10169
(212) 551-9595

New Directions for Women
108 West Palisade Ave.
Englewood, NJ 07631
(201) 568-0226

On the Issues
Box 3000, Dept. oT1
Denville, NJ 07834

Sage: A Scholarly Journal on
Black Women
Box 42741
Atlanta, GA 30311-0741.

ETHNIC
PUBLICATIONS

AKWE:KON
Northeastern Indian Quarterly
American Indian Program
300 Caldwell Hall
Cornell University
Ithaca, N.Y. 14853

Black Scholar
485 65th St.
Oakland, CA 94609
(415) 547-6633

Emerge
Box 7127
Red Oak, IA 51591

Native Nations
Box 1201
Radio City Station
New York, NY 10101-1201
(212) 765-9510

ALTERNATIVE RADIO

American Dialogues
Robert Foxworth
8033 Sunset Blvd., #967
Los Angeles, CA 90046
(213) 550-3949

Common Ground
Stanley Foundation
216 Sycamore St., Suite 500
Muscatine IA 52761
(319) 264-1500

Consider the Alternatives
5808 Greene St.
Philadelphia, PA 19144
(215) 848-4100

National Federation of
Community Broadcasters
666 11th St. NW, Suite 805
Washington, DC 20001
(202) 393-2355

New Voices
Public Interest Video Network
1642 R St., NW
Washington, DC 20001
(202) 797-8997

Pacifica (Program Service)
3729 Cahuenga Boulevard West
North Hollywood, CA 91604
(818) 985-2711

Pacifica National News Bureau
702 H St., NW
Washington, DC 20001
(202) 783-1620

Radio for Peace International
Box 10869
Eugene, OR 97440
(503) 741-1794

Second Opinion
Erwin Knoll (host)
c/o The Progressive
409 E. Main St.
Madison, WI 53703

Undercurrents
130 W. 25 St.
New York, NY 10001
(212) 691-7370

WINGS
Women's International News
Gathering Service
Box 5307
Kansas City, MO 64131
(816) 361-7161

LOCAL ALTERNATIVE
NEWS WEEKLIES

Advocate—Connecticut
Austin Chronicle
Baltimore City Paper
Boston Phoenix
Chicago Reader
City Pages—Minneapolis
Cleveland Edition
Creative Loafing—Atlanta
Dallas Observer
East Bay Express—Berkeley
Easy Reader—Los Angeles
Gambit—New Orleans
Illinois Times—Springfield
The Independent—Durham
In Pittsburgh
Isthmus—Madison
L.A. Weekly
Los Angeles Reader
Metro—San Jose
Metro Times—Ann Arbor/
Detroit
Miami New Times

New Times—Phoenix
New York Press
Palo Alto Weekly
Philadelphia Welcomat
Philadelphia City Paper
Riverfront Times—St. Louis
Sacramento News and Review
San Antonio Current
San Diego Reader
San Francisco Bay Guardian
SF Weekly
Santa Barbara Independent
Sante Fe Reporter
Seattle Weekly
Shepard Express—Milwaukee
Syracuse New Times
Times of Acadia—Lafayette, LA
Tucson Weekly
Vanguard Press—Burlington
Washington City Paper
Westword—Denver
Wilmette Week—Portland, Oregon

Notes

CHAPTER 1

1. William Greider, *Who Will Tell the People* (New York: Simon and Schuster, 1992), p. 12.
2. Ayn Rand, as quoted in *Time*, February 29, 1960; in George Seldes, compiler, *The Great Thoughts* (New York: Ballantine Books, 1985), p. 347.
3. Charles Murray, *Losing Ground* (New York: Basic Books, 1984); George Gilder quote from David Barash, *The L Word* (New York: Morrow, 1992), p. 23; Ronald Reagan and New Right comments from Susan Faludi, *Backlash* (New York: Crown, 1991), pp. 66, 232.
4. Michael Harrington, *The Next Left* (New York: Henry Holt, 1986), p. 11.
5. Robert Kuttner, *The Life of the Party* (New York: Viking, 1987), pp. 13–14.
6. Leslie Dunbar, *Reclaiming Liberalism* (New York: Norton, 1991), p. 45.
7. Carl N. Degler, ed., *The New Deal* (Chicago: Quadrangle Books, 1970), p. 13.
8. Harrington, p. 8.
9. Mickey Kraus, *The End of Equality* (New York: Basic Books, 1992), p. 9.
10. Harrington, pp. 7, 15.
11. Kuttner, pp. 5, 7.
12. Patricia Schroeder, "A Rendezvous with Reality: The New Global Economy," in Robert Levin, ed., *Democratic Blueprints* (New York: Hippocrene, 1991), pp. 107, 117.
13. Paul Simon, "Let's Put America Back to Work," in Robert Levin, ed., *Democratic Blueprints* (New York: Hippocrene, 1988), p. 120.
14. Jim Hightower, "Grass Roots Economic Development: From the Ground

Up," in Robert Levin, ed., *Democratic Blueprints* (New York: Hippocrene, 1988), p. 366.

15. Sheila Collins, *The Rainbow Challenge* (New York: Monthly Review Press, 1986), p. 35.

16. Jeremy and Carol Grunewald Rifkin, *Voting Green* (New York: Doubleday, 1992); the Woman's Political Action Group; *The Women's Voting Guide* (Berkeley: Earthworks Press, 1992), p. 73.

17. Michael Pertschuk and Wendy Schaetzel, *The People Rising* (New York: Thunder's Mouth Press, 1989), pp. 303–305.

18. L. A. Kauffman, "Tofu Politics," *The Nation*, September 16, 1991; excerpted in *Utne Reader*, March/April 1992, pp. 72–75.

19. Collins, pp. 193–194.

20. Collins, p. 92.

21. Adolph Reed, Jr., *The Jesse Jackson Phenomenon* (New Haven: Yale, 1986), p. 86.

22. Russ Bellant, *The Coors Connection* (Boston: South End Press, 1991), pp. xiv and xv.

23. Deb Preusch and Tom Barry, "The AFL-CIO Meddles Abroad," *Utne Reader*, July/August 1989, p. 26.

24. Ellen Ryan, "Growing Politics in the Backyards of America," *Utne Reader*, November/December 1991, p. 87.

25. Brad Erickson, "Forward on All Fronts," in Brad Erickson, ed., *Call To Action* (San Francisco: Sierra Club, 1990), p. 5.

26. Elizabeth Larsen, "Youth Environmental Movement Flowers," *Utne Reader*, March/April 1991, pp. 30–31.

27. Collins, pp. 319–324.

28. Roger Peace, *A Just and Lasting Peace* (Chicago: Noble, 1991), pp. 134–148.

29. Marc Levinson, "Don't Look for the Union Label: It's Camouflaged," *Newsweek*, May 18, 1991, p. 54; Brian Ahlberg, "Green Around the Blue Collar?" *Utne Reader*, July/August 1991, pp. 44–45.

30. Matthew Rothschild, "Is it Time for a Third Party?" *The Progressive*, October 1989, excerpted in *Utne Reader*, September/October 1990, pp. 56–63.

31. Howard Kohn, "Who's on Third?" *Mother Jones*, July/August 1992, pp. 43–44.

32. Martha Burk, "What If We Built a Party and American Voters Came?" *In These Times*, December 18–24, 1991, p. 16.

33. Ron Verzuh, "The New Democrats: Canada's Thriving Third Party," *Utne Reader*, September/October 1990, pp. 60–61; David Barsamian, "Free Trade and Canada," *Z Magazine*, May 1992, pp. 39–41.

CHAPTER 2

1. Sheila D. Collins, *The Rainbow Challenge: The Jackson Campaign and the Future of U.S. Politics* (New York: Monthly Review Press, 1986), p. 49.

2. Thomas Byrne and Mary D. Edsall, *Chain Reaction* (New York: Norton, 1991), pp. 9, 12.

3. Susan Faludi, *Backlash: The Undeclared War Against American Women* (New York: Crown, 1991), pp. 66, 67.

4. Barbara Ehrenreich, *Fear of Falling: The Inner Life of the Middle Class* (New York: Pantheon, 1989), p. 59.

5. Robert Reich, *Tales of a New America* (New York: Vintage, 1988). pp. 33, 35, 36.

6. David Barash, *The L Word* (New York: Morrow, 1992), p. 81.

7. Reich, p. 172.

8. Ehrenreich, pp. 48–49.

9. Reich, p. 173.

10. Robert Kuttner, *The Life of the Party: Democratic Prospects in 1988 and Beyond* (New York: Viking, 1987), p. 7.

11. Collins, p. 35.

12. Jerome Himmelstein, *To the Right: The Transformation of American Conservatism* (Berkeley: University of California Press, 1990), pp. 66–70.

13. E. J. Dionne, *Why Americans Hate Politics,* (New York: Simon & Schuster, 1991) pp. 55–60. The term neoconservative was first coined by Michael Harrington.

14. Gillian Peele, *Revival and Reaction: The Right in Contemporary America* (New York and London: Oxford University Press, 1984), p. 20.

15. Peele, p. 20.

16. Ehrenreich, pp. 146–154; Peele, pp. 19–49.

17. Russ Bellant, *The Coors Connection: How Coors Family Philanthropy Undermines Democratic Pluralism* (Boston: South End Press, 1991), pp. 27, 63, 128; Himmelstein, pp. 145–150.

18. Himmelstein, pp. 147–148; Martin A. Lee and Norman Solomon, *Unreliable Sources* (New York: Lyle Stuart, 1990), p. 83.

19. Bellant, *Coors,* p. 2.

20. Bellant, *Coors,* pp. 5, 15–17, 22–28. Eighty percent of House Republicans affiliated with Republican Study Committee from Peele, p. 134.

21. Bellant, *Coors,* pp. 38–43.

22. Himmelstein, p. 150.

23. Himmelstein, p. 123.

24. Thomas Bodenheimer and Robert Gould, *Rollback! Right-wing Power in U.S. Foreign Policy* (Boston: South End Press, 1989), p. 207.

25. Himmelstein, p. 201.

26. Russ Bellant, *Old Nazis, the New Right, and the Republican Party* (Boston: South End Press, 1988), pp. 60–61.

27. Bellant, *Nazis,* pp. 4, 123–131.

28. Bellant, *Nazis,* p. 26.

29. Bellant, *Coors,* pp. 21, 39–40.

30. Bellant, *Coors,* pp. xv, 6–9, 39–40.

31. Bellant, *Coors,* pp. 18–19, 22, 60.

32. Faludi, p. 241.
33. Bellant, *Coors*, pp. 19–21.
34. Bellant, *Coors*, p. 57.
35. Haynes Johnson, *Sleepwalking Through History* (New York: Anchor Books, 1991), pp. 170–185.
36. Johnson, p. 183.
37. Johnson, p. 183.
38. Himmelstein, pp. 201–202.
39. James Kilpatrick, "The Reagan Presidency: A Pattern of Significant Change," *Nation's Business*, January 1983, reprinted in Paul Boyer, ed., *Reagan as President* (Chicago: Ivan Dee, 1990), p. 43.
40. Kuttner, p. 28.
41. Kuttner, p. 111.
42. Mark Green, "Rating Reagan: Trendlines, Faultlines," *The Nation*, November 7, 1981, reprinted in Paul Boyer, ed., *Reagan as President* (Chicago: Ivan Dee, 1990), p. 39.
43. Kuttner, p. 114.
44. Louis Harris, *Inside America* (New York: Vintage, 1987), p. 297.
45. Thomas Ferguson and Joel Rogers, *Thunder on the Right* (New York: Hill and Wang, 1986), p. 15.
46. Kuttner, pp. 115–116.
47. Ferguson and Rogers, pp. 16–17.
48. Harris, pp. 235–236.
49. Harris, pp. 318; 251–252.
50. Larry Schwab, *The Illusion of a Conservative Reagan Revolution*, (New Brunswick, N.J.: Transaction, 1991), p. 28.
51. Harris, pp. 306; 191–192.
52. E. J. Dionne, *Why Americans Hate Politics* (New York: Simon & Schuster, 1991), excerpted in *Utne Reader*, November/December 1991, p. 83.
53. Dionne, p. 80.
54. Kuttner, p. xiv.

CHAPTER 3
1. Michael Wolff et al., *Where We Stand* (New York: Bantam, 1992). America's GDP per person ranks eighth, p. 11. America's rate of increase in worker productivity from 1951–1987 falls behind Germany, France, Japan, Italy and the United Kingdom, pp. 144–145. America's standard of living as measured by the United Nations Human Development Index ranks seventh, p. 203.
2. Michael Harrington, *The New American Poverty* (New York: Holt, Rinehart and Winston, 1984), p. 92.
3. Harrington, *Poverty*, p. 72, 92.
4. Monika Bauerlein, "Why Doesn't the U.S. Have a Family Policy?" *Utne Reader*, September/October 1991, p. 18.
5. Henry J. Aaron, ed., *Setting National Priorities: Policy for the Nineties* (Washington, D.C.: Brookings Institution, 1990), p. 38, 39.

6. "A Long-Term Tax Increase Is Urged," *The New York Times*, January 27, 1992, p. C5.

7. Kevin Phillips, *The Politics of Rich and Poor* (New York: Random House, 1990), p. 9. In compiling its survey, *The Los Angeles Times* used data supplied both by individual governments and by the World Bank. Phillips also points out, on pp. 146–153, that income disparity during the 1980s increased in Britain and Japan as well.

8. "U.S. Among Worst in Inequality," *Dollars & Sense*, July/August 1992, p. 23.

9. Wolff, p. 23.

10. Phillips, p. 180.

11. Wolff, p. 151.

12. Helen Cordes, "How Much Dough for the Big Cheese?" *Utne Reader*, March/April 1992, p. 17.

13. "Census Says 1 in 5 Earns Poverty Wage," *Chicago Tribune*, May 12, 1992, p. 14.

14. Robert Reich, *The Resurgent Liberal* (New York: Times Books, 1989), p. 62. Before the Tax Reform Act of 1986, corporations' share of the federal tax burden had dropped to 6.2 percent in 1983.

15. Wolff, p. 21.

16. Reich, *Liberal*, p. 80.

17. Wolff, p. 153.

18. Sue Murray, "The Silent Epidemic," *Utne Reader*, July/August 1992, p. 21.

19. Barbara Brandt, "Less Is More: A Call for Shorter Work Hours," excerpted from a paper by the Shorter Work-Time Group of Boston in *Utne Reader*, July/August 1991, p. 82.

20. Michael Harrington, *The Next Left* (New York: Henry Holt, 1986), p. 131.

21. Annetta Miller, "Are We Really That Lazy?" *Newsweek*, February 17, 1992, p. 42.

22. Brandt, p. 85.

23. Robert Heilbroner and Lester Thurow, *Economics Explained* (Englewood Cliffs, N.J.: Prentice Hall, 1982), p. 238.

24. Heilbroner and Thurow, p. 238.

25. Robert Kuttner, *The Life of the Party* (New York: Viking, 1987), pp. 227–229.

26. Reich, *Liberal*, pp. 68–69.

27. Donald L. Barlett and James B. Steele, *America: What Went Wrong?* (Kansas City: Andrews and McMeel, 1992), pp. 31–35.

28. Thomas Bodenheimer and Robert Gould, *Rollback!* (Boston: South End Press, 1989), p. 156.

29. Phillips, p. 70. Kuttner, writing in *The Los Angeles Times*, reported that companies had invested 12.2% of total income in plants and machinery before the tax cut. After the cut, new investment fluctuated between 11% in 1983 and 12.6% in 1985. Friedman, in his 1988 book *Day of Reckoning*, wrote that net business investment during the 1983–1986 economic

recovery was below the average level of the past three decades.

30. *The Progressive*, December 1991, p. 9. Industrial waste percentage, Wolff, p. 285.

31. Craig Canine, "The Second Coming of Energy Conservation," *Harrowsmith*, March/April 1989, reprinted in *Utne Reader*, January/February 1990, p. 117.

32. Holly Sklar, "Washington DC: Divide and Conquer," *Z Magazine*, March 1992, p. 15.

33. Wolff, pp. 11, 202.

34. Bodenheimer and Gould, pp. 150–151.

35. Charles Wilber and Kenneth Jameson, *Beyond Reaganomics* (Notre Dame: University of Notre Dame Press, 1990), p. 103.

36. David Barash *The L Word* (New York: Morrow, 1992), p. 129.

37. Harrington, *The Next Left*, pp. 21–25.

38. Reich, *Liberal*, p. 74.

39. Canine, p. 117.

40. Phillips, p. 75.

41. Haynes Johnson, *Sleepwalking Through History* (New York: Anchor, 1991), p. 111.

42. Walter Karp, *Liberty Under Siege: American Politics, 1976–1988* (New York: Henry Holt, 1988), pp. 154–156.

43. William Greider, *Who Will Tell the People* (New York: Simon and Schuster, 1992), p. 91.

44. Karp, p. 161.

45. Thomas and Mary Edsall, *Chain Reaction* (New York: Norton, 1991), p. 159.

46. Barlett and Steele, pp. 46, 49; Philip Mattera, *Prosperity Lost* (Reading, Mass.: Addison Wesley, 1991), p. 50.

47. Greider, p. 95.

48. Barlett and Steele, p. 48.

49. Neil Longman and Phillip Howe, "The Next New Deal," *The Atlantic Monthly*, April 1992, p. 98; Greider, pp. 92–94.

50. Greider, p. 92.

51. Greider, p. 93.

52. Edsall, p. 159. The authors point out that from 1980 to 1985, "the combined effective tax rate — including federal income, Social Security, excise, and corporate taxes —" went from 8.4 to 10.6 percent for the bottom 20 percent of all households.

53. Harrington, *Next Left*, p. 110.

54. Wilber and Jameson, pp. 98–99.

55. David Moberg, "Union Busting, Past and Present," *Dissent*, Winter 1992, p. 76.

56. Mattera, p. 143. National Committee on Pay Equity data taken from 1987 Census Bureau study that measured changes in incomes from 1973 and 1986.

57. Robert Reich, "Why the Rich are Getting Richer and the Poor Poorer," *Utne Reader*, January/February 1990, p. 47.

58. Wilber and Jameson, pp. 98–99.

59. "Census Says 1 in 5 Earn Poverty Wage," *Chicago Tribune*, May 12, 1992, p. 14.

60. Reich, "Why the Rich," p. 43–44.

61. James Nathan Miller, "What Really Happened at EPA," *Reader's Digest*, July 1983, p. 61.

62. James Coates, "Coors Connection Unearthed by Probe of EPA," *Chicago Tribune*, March 7, 1983, pp. A1, A5.

63. Carl Pope, "The Politics of Plunder," *Sierra*, November/December 1988, reprinted in Paul Boyer, ed., *Reagan as President* (Chicago: Ivan Dee, 1990), p. 183.

64. Johnson, p. 171.

65. Greider, p. 115.

66. Karp, p. 164–166.

67. Steven Waldman, "Watching the Watchdogs," *Newsweek*, January 11, 1988, p. 40.

68. Greider, p. 143.

69. Steven Waldman, "Putting a Price Tag on Life" and "Watching the Watchdogs," *Newsweek*, February 20, 1989, p. 20 and January 11, 1988, p. 40.

70. Greider, p. 143.

71. Arthur E. Rowse, "Deregulatory Creep," *The Progressive*, May 1992, p. 28, 31.

72. Barlett and Steele, pp. 106–113.

73. "The Darwinian World of Banking," *U.S. News & World Report*, February 24, 1992, p. 4.

74. Stephen Pizzo, "The New Looters," *Mother Jones*, January/February 1992, p. 13.

75. Lawrence J. Korb, "The 1991 Defense Budget," in Henry J. Aaron, ed., *Setting National Priorities* (Washington, D.C.: Brookings Institution, 1990), p. 117.

76. Benjamin M. Friedman, *Day of Reckoning* (New York: Vintage, 1988), p. 282.

77. Wilber and Jameson, p. 118.

78. John E. Jacob, "The Government and Social Policy," lecture to John F. Kennedy School of Government, Harvard, May 1, 1986, reprinted in Paul Boyer, ed., *Reagan as President* (Chicago: Ivan Dee, 1990), p. 151.

79. Bill Turque et al., "Where Did All the Money Go?" *Newsweek*, July 1, 1991, pp. 25–30.

80. Susan Dentzer, "A Wealth of Difference," *U.S. News & World Report*, June 1, 1992, p. 45.

81. Phillips, p. 10.

82. Phillips, p. 17.

83. Jim Hightower, "Share the Wealth," in Brad Erickson, ed., *Call to Action: Handbook for Ecology, Peace and Justice* (San Francisco: Sierra Club, 1990), p. 107.

84. Thurow and Heilbroner, p. 238.

85. William Julius Wilson, *The Truly Disadvantaged* (Chicago: University of Chicago, 1987), p. 154.

86. Harrington, p. 170.

87. Reich, *Liberal*, p. 59.

88. Robert B. Reich, "Training A Skilled Work Force," *Dissent*, Winter 1992, p. 46.

89. Robert L. Borosage, "Imagine Peacetime," *Mother Jones*, January/February 1992, p. 20.

90. Reich, *Liberal*, p. 129.

91. Robert Levin, ed., *Democratic Blueprints: 40 National Leaders Chart America's Future* (New York: Hippocrene, 1988), pp. 124–127.

92. Jeremy Rifkin and Carol Grunewald Rifkin, *Voting Green* (New York: Doubleday, 1992), p. 136.

93. Bodenheimer and Gould, pp. 158–159.

94. Henry Aaron, ed., *Setting National Priorities* (Washington D.C.: Brookings Institution, 1990), p. 63. The study cited by Schultz suggests that public investment increases output at a rate as much as four times that of private investment. Schultz questions the magnitude, but believes that "carefully selected" infrastructure investment can improve productivity and output.

95. Bodenheimer and Gould, pp. 218–219.

96. Jay Walljasper, "Who Says Socialism Doesn't Work?" *Utne Reader*, September/October, 1990, p. 158.

97. Wolff, pp. 175, 203, 213.

98. Wolff, pp. 26, 32, 50, 51, 55, 56. Swedish export figure from Walljasper, "The Crisis and Promise of Swedish Socialism," *Utne Reader*, January/February 1992, p. 149.

99. Wolff, pp. 16, 18, 279, 280, 287, 289, 294. Reduction in pesticide use from Walljasper, "The Crisis and Promise of Swedish Socialism," p. 150.

100. Joanne Barkan, "End of the 'Swedish Model'?" *Dissent*, Spring 1992, p. 194.

101. Walljasper, "The Crisis and Promise of Swedish Socialism," p. 149.

102. Sandy Tolan with Jerry Kramer, "Life in the Low-Wage Boomtowns of Mexico," *Utne Reader*, November/December 1990, pp. 42–50.

103. Brian Ahlberg, "Green Around the Blue Collar?" *Utne Reader*, July/August 1991, pp. 44–45.

CHAPTER 4

1. Troy Segal, "The Riots: 'Just As Much About Class As About Race,'" *Business Week*, May 18, 1992, p. 47.

2. Tom Mathews, "The Siege of L.A.," *Newsweek*, May 11, 1992, p. 36.

3. Mike Tharp and David Whitman, "Hispanics' Tale of Two Cities," May 25,

1992, p. 40; Betsy Streisand, "Equal-Opportunity Looting," *U.S. News & World Report,* May 18, 1992, p. 25.

4. Segal, p. 47.

5. Thomas Sancton, "How to Get America Off the Dole," *Time,* May 25, 1992, p. 44.

6. Sancton, p. 47.

7. For more details concerning these statistics and other information about the working poor, see chapter 5.

8. David T. Ellwood, *Poor Support* (New York: Basic Books, 1988), pp. 137–138.

9. Sancton, p. 46.

10. Ruth Conniff, "Cutting the Lifeline," *The Progressive,* February 1992, p. 29.

11. Conniff, p. 26.

12. Thomas and Mary Edsall, *Chain Reaction* (New York: Norton, 1991), p. 152.

13. Sancton, p. 45.

14. Edsall, p. 148.

15. Danny Duncan Collum, "Whites: How to do the Right Thing 'for' Blacks," *Sojourners,* August/September 1990, excerpted in *Utne Reader,* May/June 1992, p. 87.

16. Dionne, *Why Americans Hate Politics* (New York: Simon & Schuster, 1991), p. 306.

17. Barbara Koeppel, "Paul Sweezy," *The Progressive,* May 1992, p. 36.

18. David Barash, *The L Word* (New York: William Morrow, 1992), pp. 82–83.

19. Barbara Ehrenreich, *Fear of Falling* (New York: Pantheon, 1989), p. 25.

20. Edsall, p. 193.

21. Thane Peterson, "Can Corporate America Get Out From Under Its Overhead?" *Business Week,* May 18, 1992, p. 102.

22. Robert Reich, "Training a Skilled Work Force," *Dissent,* Winter 1992, p. 42.

23. Reich, "Training," pp. 43–45.

24. Peter Dreier and John Atlas, "The Scandal of Mansion Subsidies," *Dissent,* Winter 1992, p. 93.

25. Neil Howe and Phillip Longman, "The Next New Deal," *The Atlantic,* April 1992, p. 90.

26. Holly Sklar, "Washington D.C.: Divide and Conquer," *Z Magazine,* March 1992, pp. 16–17.

27. Philip Mattera, *Prosperity Lost* (Reading, Mass.: Addison Wesley, 1990, 1991), p. 35.

28. Daniel Cantor and Juliet Schor, *Tunnel Vision* (Boston, South End Press: 1987), p. 61.

29. Brad Edmondson, "The Deep, Dark Secret of Our Government," *Utne Reader,* March/April 1989, p. 14. Edmondson takes Volcker's quote from William Greider's book *Secrets of the Temple* (New York: Simon and Schuster: 1987).

30. Vicente Navarro, "The Class Gap," *The Nation*, April 8, 1991, p. 436.
31. Susan Dentzer, "A Wealth of Difference," *U.S. News & World Report*, June 1, 1992, p. 45.
32. Mattera, p. 16.
33. Robert Reich, *Tales of a New America* (New York: Times Books, 1987), pp. 9–10.
34. Sylvia Nasar, "Those Born Wealthy or Poor Usually Stay So, Studies Say," *New York Times*, May 27, 1992, p. 1.
35. Ehrenreich, p. 256.
36. Galbraith, *The Culture of Contentment* (New York: Houghton Mifflin, 1992), p. 22.
37. Galbraith, p. 26.
38. Joseph Julian and William Kornblum, *Social Problems* (Englewood Cliffs, N.J.: Prentice Hall, 1986), p. 286.
39. Bella Abzug and Mim Kelber, "Women: Still the Second Sex," in Brad Erickson, ed., *Call to Action* (San Francisco, Sierra Club: 1990), pp. 56–57.
40. Julian and Kornblum, p. 271.
41. Susan Faludi, *Backlash* (New York: Crown, 1991), p. xiii.
42. Amanda Troy Segal, "Corporate Women," *Business Week*, June 8, 1992, pp. 76, 77.
43. Faludi, p. 232.
44. Bellant, *The Coors Connection* (Boston: South End Press, 1991), pp. 56–57; Faludi, p. 234.
45. Faludi, p. 369.
46. Faludi, p. xvii.
47. James Garbarino, *Toward A Sustainable Society* (Chicago: Noble, 1992), pp. 173, 191.
48. Ann Lewis, "Return of the Gender Gap — Just in Time for November," *Ms.*, January/February 1992, p. 90.
49. Lisa Grunwald, "If Women Ran America," *Life*, June 1992, pp. 39–42.
50. Garbarino, p. 174.
51. Maudlyne Ihejirika, "Lending Gap Hits Home for Blacks," *Chicago Sun-Times*, June 3, 1992, p. 1. A Federal Reserve study showed that lenders turned down white applicants 14.4 percent of the time, Hispanics 21 percent of the time, and African-Americans 34 percent of the time. A local Chicago study showed that whites earning between $50,000 and $75,000 were turned down 9 percent of the time, while the rejection rate for whites earning under $24,000 was 28 percent. The rejection rate for African-Americans earning $50,000-$75,000 was 25 percent.
52. Arthur Ashe, "Can Blacks Beat the Old-Boy Network?" *Newsweek*, January 27, 1992, p. 40.
53. Christopher Farrell et al., "The Economic Crisis of Urban America," *Business Week*, May 18, 1992, pp. 40–41.
54. Tharp and Whitman, p. 40.
55. Farrell, p. 40.
56. Farrell, pp. 41, 40.

57. Karl Grossman, "From Toxic Racism to Environmental Justice," *E Magazine*, May/June 1992, pp. 30–35.

58. Steve Whitman, "The Crime of Black Imprisonment," *Z Magazine*, May 1992, p. 69.

59. Jake Lamar, "The Trouble With You People," *Esquire*, February 1992, reprinted in *Utne Reader*, May/June 1992, pp. 82–83.

60. Ehrenreich, p. 216.

61. Julian and Kornblum, p. 239.

62. Julian and Kornblum, p. 277.

63. "Values in the Classroom," *Newsweek*, June 8, 1992, p. 26.

64. Donna Minkowitz, "Why Heterosexuals Need to Support Gay Rights," *Village Voice*, in *Utne Reader*, March/April 1991, pp. 98–99.

CHAPTER 5

1. Paul Lewis, "Environment Aid for Poor Nations Agreed at the U.N.," *New York Times*, April 5, 1992, p. A1.

2. "Draft of Environmental Rules: 'Global Partnership,'" *New York Times*, April 5, 1992, p. A6.

3. James Garbarino, *Toward A Sustainable Society* (Chicago: Noble, 1992), p. 34.

4. Holly Sklar, "Washington D.C.: Divide and Conquer," *Z Magazine*, March 1992, p. 15.

5. "George Bush's Poverty Woes," *U.S. News & World Report*, January 6, 1992, p. 43.

6. Christopher Farrell et al., "The Economic Crisis of Urban America," *Business Week*, May 18, 1992, p. 38.

7. Holly Sklar, "Reaffirmative Action," *Z Magazine*, May 1992, p. 10.

8. Sklar, "Reaffirmative," p. 10.

9. David Ellwood, *Poor Support: Poverty in the American Family* (New York: Basic Books, 1988), pp. 193–194.

10. Thomas Sancton, "How to Get America Off the Dole," *Time*, May 25, 1992, p. 45.

11. "Planet, Its People Sicker Than Ever," *Nashville Banner*, May 14, 1992, p. 7.

12. "More Bad News in the Air," *Newsweek*, February 17, 1992, p. 26.

13. Paul Lewis, "Island Nations Fear a Rise in the Sea," *The New York Times*, February 16, 1992, p. A3.

14. Helen Caldicott, *If You Love This Planet: A Plan to Heal the Earth* (New York: Norton, 1992), pp. 25–26.

15. Thomas Lovejoy, "Deforestation," *1992 Earth Journal* (Boulder, Colo.: Buzzworm Books, 1992), p. 89; Randall Hayes, "Rainforest Conservation," *1992 Earth Journal*, p. 126.

16. Caldicott, p. 43.

17. Jeremy and Carol Grunewald Rifkin, *Voting Green* (New York: Doubleday, 1992), pp. 189–190.

18. Caldicott, p. 46.

19. Caldicott, p. 44.
20. "East Africa," *1992 Earth Journal* (Boulder, Colo.: Buzzworm Books, 1992), p. 156.
21. Donald G. McNeil Jr., "The Withering Woods," *The New York Times*, November 3, 1991, sec. 4, p. 2.
22. Rifkin, p. 243.
23. Caldicott, p. 70.
24. Lester Brown, Christopher Flavin, and Sandra Postel, *Saving the Planet* (New York: Norton, 1991), p. 26.
25. Nancy Green, *Poisoning Our Children: Surviving in a Toxic World* (Chicago: Noble Press, 1991), p. 136.
26. Caldicott, pp. 64–65.
27. Caldicott, p. 71.
28. Karl Grossman, "Environmental Justice," *E Magazine*, May/June 1992, pp. 31–32.
29. Jack Rosenburg, "Toxic Beagles," *E Magazine*, May/June 1992, pp. 24–28.
30. Dick Thompson, "Living Happily Near a Nuclear Trash Heap," *Time*, May 11, 1992, p. 53.
31. Deeann Glamser, "N-Cleanup Turns Bomb Town to Boom Town," *USA Today*, March 26, 1992, p. 8A.
32. Peter Hong, "The Toxic Mess Called Superfund," *Business Week*, May 11, 1992, p. 32.
33. Caldicott, p. 66.
34. Green, p. 36.
35. Green, pp. 124–128.
36. Green, pp. 87–94.
37. Green, pp. 46–47.
38. Franklin Delano Roosevelt, June 16, 1933, quoted in George Seldes, compiler, *The Great Thoughts* (New York: Ballentine, 1985), p. 354.
39. Sklar, "Washington, D.C.," p. 14.
40. Coretta Scott King, Murray H. Finley, and Calvin H. George, "On the Road Again...A Six Point Agenda Toward A Full-Employment Economy," in Robert Levin, ed., *Democratic Blueprints* (New York: Hippocrene, 1988), p. 418.
41. Sklar, "Reaffirmative," p. 10.
42. Ellwood, p. 145.
43. Sancton, p. 47.
44. Ellwood, pp. 137–139. Ellwood's analysis is based on 1986 welfare, Medicaid, and food stamp policies. His break-even hourly wage was $5 an hour, while the minimum wage in 1986 was $3.35 per hour.
45. Faludi, p. 364.
46. Sancton, p. 47.
47. DeMott, p. 132.
48. Sklar, "Washington," p. 16.
49. Jonathan Kozol, *Savage Inequalities* (New York: Crown, 1991), from Ruth

Sidel's review, "Separate and Unequal," *The Nation*, November 18, 1991, pp. 620–622.

50. Barbara Kantrowitz, "A Head Start Does Not Last," *Newsweek*, January 27, 1992, pp. 44–45.

51. William Julius Wilson, *The Truly Disadvantaged: The Inner City, the Underclass, and Public Policy* (Chicago: University of Chicago Press, 1987), p. 154.

52. Ellwood, p. 238.

53. Hong, p. 32.

54. Jon Krakauer, "Brown Fellas," *Outside*, December 1991, p. 70.

55. Craig Canine, "The Second Coming of Energy Conservation," *Harrowsmith*, March/April 1989, excerpted in *Utne Reader*, January/February 1990, p. 117.

56. Michael Lemonick, "The Big Green Payoff," *Time*, June 1, 1992, pp. 62, 63.

57. Teresa Opheim, "Can We Have Both Spotted Owls and Jobs?" *Utne Reader*, May/June 1992, p. 42.

58. Lemonick, p. 62.

CHAPTER 6

1. Lawrence J. Korb, "The 1991 Defense Budget," in Henry J. Aaron, ed., *Setting National Priorities* (Washington, D.C.: Brookings Institution, 1990), p. 117.

2. Christopher Lasch, "The Cost of Our Cold War Victory," *The New York Times*, July 13, 1990, reprinted in James Ridgeway and Jean Casella, eds., *Cast a Cold Eye* (New York: Four Walls Eight Windows, 1991), p. 19.

3. Marcus G. Rakin, "The Road to Reconstruction," *The Nation*, April 22, 1991, p. 512.

4. John Steinbruner, "Revolution in Foreign Policy," in Henry J. Aaron, ed., *Setting National Priorities* (Washington, D.C.: Brookings Institution, 1990), p. 65.

5. Douglas Walker, Ann Wolfberg, and Ann McDaniel, "Gates' Biggest Challenge," *Newsweek*, September 23, 1991, p. 24.

6. Bill Hall, "Intervention and History," in Brad Erickson, ed., *Call to Action* (San Francisco: Sierra Club, 1990), p. 91.

7. Laurence Shoup and William Minter, *Imperial Brain Trust* (New York: Monthly Review Press, 1990), p. 274.

8. Michael Wolff, *Where We Stand* (New York: Bantam, 1992), p. 222; intelligence budget, John Barry with Tom Morganthau, "Remaking the CIA," *Newsweek*, May 27, 1991, p. 19.

9. Tim Wall, "Jamaica's Free Market Tempest," *In These Times*, February 26, 1992, p. 6; Francis Moore Lappé, Rachel Schurman, and Kevin Danaher, *Betraying the National Interest* (New York: Grove, 1987), p. 140.

10. Brian Ahlberg, "Remembering Grenada," *Utne Reader*, November/December 1990, pp. 30–31.

11. Lappé, pp. 27–34.

12. Lappé, p. 15.
13. Michael Blain, "Panama: Two Years Later," *Z Magazine*, December 1991, p. 93.
14. Lappé, p. 85.
15. Susan George, "Third World Debt Crisis," in Brad Erickson, ed., *Call to Action* (San Francisco: Sierra Club, 1990), pp. 84–87.
16. Daniel Cantor and Juliet Schor, *Tunnel Vision* (Boston: South End Press, 1987), p. 57.
17. George, p. 86.
18. George, p. 86.
19. Wolff, p. 223.
20. Noam Chomsky, "Middle East Diplomacy," *Z Magazine*, December 1991, p. 31.
21. Thomas Bodenheimer and Robert Gould, *Rollback!* (Boston: South End Press, 1989), pp. 26–33.
22. Lappé, p. 38.
23. Bodenheimer and Gould, p. 27.
24. Peter Dale Scott and Jonathan Marshall, *Cocaine Politics* (Berkeley: University of California, 1991), p. 5.
25. Bodenheimer and Gould, pp. 60, 70–72.
26. Scott and Marshall, p. 5.
27. Roger Peace, *A Just and Lasting Peace* (Chicago: Noble, 1991), p. 9.
28. Randolph Ryan, "U.S. Role in a Civilian Massacre," *The Boston Globe*, May 29, 1990, reprinted in James Ridgeway and Jean Casella, eds., *Cast a Cold Eye* (New York: Four Walls Eight Windows, 1991), pp. 80–81.
29. Lappé, p. 3.
30. Lappé, p. 59.
31. Peace, p. 267.
32. Robin Broad, John Cavanagh, and Walden Bello, "U.S. Plan for Latin Debt Relief is a Non-Starter," *The Los Angeles Times*, December 2, 1990, reprinted in James Ridgeway and Jean Casella, eds., *Cast a Cold Eye* (New York: Four Walls Eight Windows, 1991), p. 165.
33. James Brooke, "Venezuela's Two-Faced Boom: Riches and Riots," *The New York Times*, January 21, 1992, p. 11.
34. Broad, Cavanagh, and Bello, p. 165.
35. Richard Fagen, *Forging Peace* (New York: Basil Blackwell, 1987), p. 5.
36. Fagen, p. viii.
37. Peace, p. 259.
38. Fagen, p. viii.
39. Jeremy and Carol Grunewald Rifkin, *Voting Green* (New York: Doubleday, 1992), pp. 129–132.
40. Paul Krugman, *The Age of Diminished Expectations* (Cambridge: MIT Press, 1992), p. 149.
41. Fagen, pp. 60–61.
42. Fagen, pp. 61–69.
43. John Stockwell, *The Praetorian Guard* (Boston: South End Press, 1991), p. 62.

44. Stockwell, p. 22.
45. Lappé, p. 49.
46. Fagen, p. 59–74.
47. Alexander Cockburn, "U.S.-Backed Terrorism Won in Nicaragua, Not Democracy," *Wall Street Journal*, March 1, 1990, reprinted in James Ridgeway and Jean Casella, *Cast A Cold Eye* (New York: Four Walls Eight Windows, 1991), p. 24.

CHAPTER 7
1. Jeremy Gerad, "Walter Cronkite: This Is The Way It Is," *International Herald Tribune*, January 10, 1989.
2. Theodore Becker and Anthony Dodson, *Live This Book* (Chicago: Noble, 1991), p. 67.
3. Becker and Dodson, p. 69.
4. Helen Caldicott, M.D., *If You Love This Planet* (New York: Norton, 1992), p. 154.
5. G. William Domhoff, *Who Rules America Now?*, (New York: Touchstone, 1983), p. 110.
6. Robert Reich, *Tales of a New America* (New York: Times Books, 1987), pp. 8, 235.
7. Reich, p. 8.
8. Eric Hoffer, *The True Believer* (New York: Harper and Row, 1951; reprint, 1989), p. 4.
9. Herbert Schiller, *The Mind Managers* (Boston: Beacon, 1973), in Bertram Gross, *Friendly Fascism* (Boston: South End Press, 1980), p. 259.
10. Reich, p. 9.
11. Martin Lee and Norman Solomon, *Unreliable Sources* (New York: Lyle Stuart, 1990), p. 17.
12. Mark Hertsgaard, *On Bended Knee* (New York, Farrar Straus & Giroux, 1988; reprint, Schocken Books, 1989), p. 68.
13. Hertsgaard, p. 68.
14. Hertsgaard, p. 348.
15. Lee and Solomon, p. 76; Edward Herman and Noam Chomsky, *Manufacturing Consent* (New York: Pantheon, 1988), pp. 5–7; Caldicott, p. 182.
16. Lee and Solomon, pp. 82, 81.
17. Lee and Solomon, pp. 78–84.
18. Lee and Solomon, pp. 93–98, 141.
19. A. J. Liebling, *The New Yorker*, May 14, 1960, in George Seldes, compiler, *The Great Thoughts* (New York: Ballentine, 1985), p. 243.
20. Chomsky and Herman, p. 17.
21. Lee and Solomon, p. 85.
22. Lee and Solomon, pp. 143, 145, 229.
23. Lee and Solomon, p. 17.
24. Christopher Georges, "Confessions of an Investigative Reporter," *Washington Monthly*, March 1992, p. 38.
25. Lee and Solomon, pp. 197–198.
26. Herman and Chomsky, p. 33.

27. "The Top Ten Censored Stories of 1990," *Utne Reader*, July/August 1991, pp. 61–64; "The Top Ten Censored Stories of 1989," *Utne Reader*, September/October 1990, pp. 107–112.

28. Lee and Solomon, pp. 35–46.

29. Lee and Solomon, pp. 46 and 189.

30. Susan Faludi, *Backlash* (New York: Crown, 1991), p. 79.

31. Faludi, p. 77.

32. Lee and Solomon, p. 148.

33. Noam Chomsky, *Deterring Democracy* (New York: Hill and Wang, 1992), p. 76.

34. Chomsky, pp. 73–74.

35. Hertsgaard, p. 301.

36. Lee and Solomon, p. 151.

37. Hertsgaard, pp. 264, 270.

38. Lee and Solomon, p. 148.

39. Lee and Solomon, p. 150.

40. Hertsgaard, pp. 3, 5.

41. Hertsgaard, p. 144.

42. Lee and Solomon, p. 35.

43. Hertsgaard, pp. 138, 245.

44. Mark Green and Gail MacColl, *Ronald Reagan's Reign of Error* (New York: Pantheon, 1983).

45. Chomsky, p. 73.

46. Paula Rothenberg, "Critics of Attempts to Democratize the Curriculum are Waging a Campaign to Misrepresent the Work of Responsible Professors," *Chronicle of Higher Education*, April 10, 1991, reprinted in Paul Berman, ed., *Debating P.C.* (New York: Dell, 1992), pp. 265–266.

47. Bertram Gross, *Friendly Fascism* (Boston: South End Press, 1980), p. 277.

48. Cornel West, "Diverse New World," *Democratic Left*, July/August 1991, reprinted in Paul Berman, ed., *Debating PC* (New York, Dell, 1992), p. 329.

49. Ted Gordon and Wahneema Lubiano, "The Statement of the Black Faculty Caucus," *The Daily Texan*, reprinted in Paul Berman, ed., *Debating PC* (New York: Dell, 1992), p. 257.

50. Paula Bennett, "Canons to the Right of Them...," in Patricia Aufderheide, ed., *Beyond PC* (Saint Paul: Graywolf, 1992), pp. 165–170.

51. John Hurst, "Education for Social Change," in Brad Erickson, ed., *Call to Action* (San Francisco: Sierra Club, 1990), p. 200.

52. Katha Pollitt, "Why Do We Read?" *The Nation*, September 23, 1991, reprinted in Paul Berman, ed., *Debating PC* (New York: Dell, 1992), p. 205.

53. Dave Marsh, *50 Ways to Fight Censorship* (New York: Thunder's Mouth Press, 1991), pp. 8, 22, 73, 74.

54. Elizabeth Larsen, "Censoring Sex Information," *Utne Reader*, July/August 1990, pp. 96–97.

55. Marsh, p. xvi.

CHAPTER 8

1. Nancy Skinner, "Act Locally: Using the Powers of City Government to Effect Social Change," in Brad Erickson, ed., *Call to Action* (San Francisco: Sierra Club, 1990), pp. 19–21.

2. David Osborne and Ted Gaebler, *Reinventing Government* (New York: Addison Wesley, 1992), pp. 151–153.

3. Jeremy and Carol Grunewald Rifkin, *Voting Green* (New York: Doubleday, 1992), pp. 71, 85, 86, 264.

4. Sheila Collins, *The Rainbow Challenge: The Jackson Campaign and the Future of U.S. Politics* (New York: Monthly Review Press, 1986), pp. 314, 318–319.

5. Collins, pp. 309–314.

6. Roger Allison, "Environmental Integrity From the Bottom Up," *CrossRoads*, April 1992, pp. 25–27.

7. William Greider, *Who Will Tell the People* (New York: Simon and Schuster, 1992), pp. 223–235.

8. Greider, p. 228.

9. Matthew Rothschild, "Is It Time for a Third Party?" *Utne Reader*, September/October 1990, p. 57.

10. Howard Hawkins, "Left Greens and Independent Politics," *CrossRoads*, April 1992, pp. 44–47.

11. Eric Odell, "Movement on a Threshold," *CrossRoads*, April 1992, pp. 30–32.

12. Pat Bryant, "Milestones of Hope and Solidarity," *CrossRoads*, April 1992, pp. 2–4.

13. *Everyone's Backyard*, October 1991, December 1991, February 1992, June 1992.

14. Rob Karwath and David Silverman, "Braun Fulfills Reputation of Being a Star on the Rise," *Chicago Tribune*, March 18, 1992, p. 12; Frank James, "Braun Stirs Political Newcomers," *Chicago Tribune*, March 27, 1992, p. 1.

15. Robert Kuttner, *The Life of the Party: Democratic Prospects in 1988 and Beyond* (New York: Viking, 1987), p. 128.

16. Dave Marsh, *50 Ways to Fight Censorship* (New York: Thunder's Mouth Press, 1991), p. 88.

17. August Bequai, *Making Washington Work for You* (Lexington, Mass.: Lexington Books, 1984), p. 39.

18. Tony Vellela, *New Voices* (Boston: South End Press, 1988), pp. 62, 149, 178–180.

CHAPTER 9

1. Alice Tepper Marlin, Jonathan Schorsch, Emily Swaab, and Rosalyn Will, *Shopping for a Better World* (New York: Council on Economic Priorities, 1991), p. 11.

2. Myra Alperson, Alice Tepper Marlin, Jonathan Schorsch, and Rosalyn

Will, *The Better World Investment Guide* (New York: Prentice Hall, 1991), p. 223; Marlin et al., p. 31.

3. Alperson et al., pp. 86–87.

4. Craig Smith, *Morality and the Market* (London and New York: Routledge, 1990), p. 249.

5. Marlin et al.

6. "Boycott Action News," *Co-op America Quarterly*, Spring 1992, pp. 29–30, 33–34.

7. Ritchie P. Lowry, *Good Money* (New York: Norton, 1991), p. 27.

8. James Goodno, "Caring Capitalism?" *Dollars & Sense*, January/February 1992, p. 9.

9. Ritchie Lowry, pp. 21–23.

10. Ritchie Lowry, p. 29.

11. Susan Meeker-Lowry, *Economics as If the Earth Really Mattered* (Philadelphia: New Society, 1988), p. 30.

12. Ritchie Lowry, p. 47.

13. Goodno, p. 10.

14. Cindy Mitlo, "Doers' Profiles," *Co-op America Quarterly*, Summer 1991, pp. 6–8.

15. Susan Meeker-Lowry, pp. 140, 147.

16. Faith Popcorn, *The Popcorn Report* (New York: Doubleday, 1991), p. 159.

17. "Who Are the Worst Polluters in the Nation?" *Catalyst*, Fall 1990, p. 13.

18. Calvert Social Investment Fund, 1700 Pennsylvania Avenue, N.W., Washington, D.C. 20006.

19. Franklin Research and Development, "Top 25 Publicly-Traded Defense Contractors for Fiscal Year 1989," *Catalyst*, Fall 1990, p. 13.

Index

ABC
abortion rights, 10, 20, 81, 84
ACLU, 11, 89, 143, 184
Acquired Immune Deficiency
    Syndrome (AIDS), 3, 80, 149
activism, grass-roots, 147–164
ACT-UP, 6,
Adelman, Irma, 119
Adidas, 170
Advocate, The, 194
affirmative action, 20–23
Afghanistan, 112, 117
AFL-CIO, 11, 13, 189
African-Americans, 12–13, 19, 23,
    76, 150, 151, 153, 155
    poverty among, 84–85 discrimina-
    tion against, 84–86
Age of Diminished Expectations, The
    (Krugman), 123
Aid for Dependent Children (AFDC),
    56, 61, 68–70, 94, 101–102
airline industry, impact of

deregulation on, 54
Alabama, 150
Alaska National Wildlife Refuge, 44,
    108
Alinsky, Saul, 151, 175
Alliance of Small Island States, 95
Amazon, deforestation in, 96
American Association of University
    Women, 183
American Booksellers Association's
    Foundation for Free Expression,
    143
American Coalition for Life, 31
American Conservative Union, 24
American Dialogue, 196
American Enterprise Institute (AEI),
    26
American Friends Service Committee,
    163, 184
American Home Products, 168, 170
American Library Association,
    144–145

American Security Council, 30
Americans for Democratic Action, 189
Amnesty International, 80, 184
Amway Corporation, 26
Angola, 112, 118, 120
Animals Agenda, 195
Arias, Oscar, 116
Armstrong, William, 27
Artin, Stellan, 65
Ashe, Arthur, 84
Association of Retarded Citizens, 11
Atkinson Index, 41
Atlanta Journal-Constitution, 137
Atlantic Monthly, 49, 75
Atlantic Richfield, 133
Atlas, John, 74
AT&T, 133
Australia, income differentials in, 41
Avon Products, 168

Backlash (Faludi), 20–21, 82, 137
backlash, conservative, 20–22
Bagdikian, Ben, 133–134
Bakker, Jim, 28, 31
Baldwin-United Insurance, collapse of, 54
Baltimoreans United in Leadership Development (BUILD), 151
Bane, Mary Jo, 101
banking industry, see financial services industry
Barash, David P., 21–22
Barkin, Joanne, 65
Barlett, Donald L., 49
BCCI, 136
Beatrice Foods, 55
Becker, Theodore, L., 129
Bell, Daniel, 25
Belgian Congo (Zaire), 117, 118
Bellant, Russ, 30–31, 82

Bello, Walden, 119–120
Ben and Jerry's Homemade, 171
Bennett, Paula, 141
Bequai, August, 161
Berkeley, California, 11–12, 148, 149
Betz, Charles, 14
biodiversity, 97
blacks, see African-Americans
Black Scholar, 196
Block Bork Coalition, 11
Bodenheimer, Thomas, 62–63, 117
Body Shop, The, 171
Boeing, 56
Boren, David, 61
Bork, Robert H., 10–11, 26
Borosage, Robert L., 59
Boston, 85, 149
Boston Globe, 30, 76, 118
Boulding, Elise, 83
boycott campaigns, 13, 163, 167–168, 170
Boxer, Barbara, 9, 83
Bradlee, Benjamin, 138
Braun, Carol Moseley, 83, 155, 163
Brazil, 117
Bread for the World, 184
Britain, see England
Broad, Robin, 119–120
Brokaw, Tom, 138
Brooking Institution, 39, 62, 112, 134
Browning, boycott against, 170
Bryant, Pat, 153
Buchanan, Patrick, 32
Buckley, William, 24, 134
budget deficit, U.S., 45, 59
Bullard, Robert D., 85
Burford, Anne, 51
Burk, Martha, 17,
Bush administration, 30,
    deregulation policies of, 54,
    economic policies of, 52–53, 54

environmental policies of 43, 105–106, foreign policies of, 112–113, 117–120, 126

Bush, George, 3, 32–33, 47, 90, 52, 137

business development, grass-roots, 61

business, progressive, 171–172

Business Week, 41, 67, 73, 81

Butler, General Smedley D., 113

Buzzworm, 195

Caldicott, Helen, 7, 96–99, 130

California, 56

California's Peace and Freedom Party, 10, 17

Call to Action (Erickson), 179

Calvert Social Investment Fund, 174–176, 191

Campaign for New Tomorrow, 182

Canada
income and wage differentials in, 41, New Democratic Party, 17–18, social programs, 17–18, 40–41

Canine, Craig, 46

Cannon, Lou, 138

Canter, David, 75

Capital Cities/ABC, 132–133

capitalism, 39–47

carbon dioxide, 107

Carter, Jimmy, 29, 33, 34, 53, 137

Carter-Wallace, 170

Casey, William, 132

Castle and Cook, boycott against, 170

Catalyst, 171, 177, 191

Catholics for a Free Choice, 11, 163

Cavanagh, John, 119–120

censorship, 142–143

Census Bureau, U.S., 41, 69,

Center on Budget and Policy Priorities, 184

Center for Economic Conversions, 185

Center for National Independence in Politics, 190

Center for Policy Alternatives, 185

Center for the Study of the States, 56

Center for Third World Organizing, 185

Central Intelligence Agency, 112, 124, 162
budget of, 114, covert activities of, 114, 117–118, 120, 126– 127, illegal activities of, 117–118, 136

Chain Reaction, (Edsall), 20–21, 70

Chandler, Otis, 133

Chase Manhattan Bank, 26

chemical industry, toxic poisoning by, 98–99

Chicago, 98

Chicago Tribune, 51, 133, 155

children
child care, 61, 71, 102, infant mortality rates among, 93, poverty rates among, 92–93

Children's Defense Fund, 40, 93, 185

Chile, 114, 117, 118

China, People's Republic of, 79, 120

chlorofluorocarbons (CFCs), 106–107

Chomsky, Noam, 117, 134, 136, 137, 139

Christian Fundamentalist, see religion

Christianity Today, 30

Christian Reconstructionist, 30

Christian Voice, 30–31

Chrysler Corporation, 43

Circle K, 55

Citizens Budget Campaign 14,

citizen groups, see grass-root organizations

Citizen Trade Watch Committee, 15

Citizen's Clearinghouse for Hazardous Waste (CCHW), 153–154, 161, 180

Civil Rights Act, 6, 87

civil rights movement, 6, 12–13
class, "contented" and professional, 78–79
class division
 among the left, 12–13, class warfare, 67–77, 86–90, Reaganomics and, 72–77
classless society, myth of, 72–73, 77
class mobility, 77–78
Clean Yield, 177, 191
Clergy and Laity Concerned, 163, 185
Clifford, Clark, 138
Coalition for America, 26
Coalition on Revival (COR), 31
Cocaine Politics (Scott and Marshall), 117
Cockburn, Alexander, 126
Colby, William, 118
cold war, 111–112
Colgate-Palmolive, 168
Collins, Sheila D., 12, 20, 150
Collum, Danny, 71
Commission for Racial Justice, 85, 153
Common Ground, 196
Communities Organized for Public Service, San Antonio, 151
community government, 147–149
Congress, U.S., 43, 48–49, 51–52, 159–161
Congressional Black Caucus, 15, 182
Congressional Budget Office, 55
Congressional Quarterly, 48
Connecticut, 56
Conniff, Ruth, 69–70
conservation policy, see environmental policy
Conservatism, 1–2, 5
Conservative Caucus, 82
Consider the Alternatives, 196
consumerism, socially responsible, 10, 191–194
Consumer United Insurance

Company, 178, 191
Conyers, John, 9
Coolidge, Calvin, 48
Co-op America, 170–171, 173, 191
co-ops, 172–173
Coors Connection, The, 82
Coors Family, 12, 25, 26, 51, 163
corporate influence, 147, 165–166
 on foreign policy, 113–114, on the media, 132–134, on the New Right, 26, on the Republican party 17–18, 29
corporate investment
 in corporate buy-outs, 43, 52–53, in the Third World, 43–44, 52–53, 73, in worker training, 74,
corporate social responsibility, 61–62, 165–166, 173–174, 178
corporate socialism, 43, 55–56
Costa Rica, 116, 136
Council on Competitiveness, 54
Council on Economic Priorities (CEP), 169–170, 192
Council for National Policy (CNP), 27, 30–31, 82
Cox Enterprises, 134
Cracker Barrel Restaurants, boycott against, 171
crime, 85
Cuba, 112, 117, 120
Culture of Contentment, The (Galbraith), 78

death squads, in the Third World, 117–118
Deaver, Michael, 31–32
debt, national, 2, 45
DDT toxins, 99
Dees, Morris, 89
Defense Department, U.S., 136
defense industry, 56, 172
defense spending, 55–56

deforestation, 96–97
Degler, Carl, 6
Dellums, Ron, 9;
Demarco, Susan, 57
Democratic Party, 45, 155
    business influence on, 16, 48–49,
    disenchantment with, 16–17, 33,
    35–37, elite in, 18, move to the
    right, 36–37, progressives in,
    155–159, 163
Democratic Socialist of America, 17,
    182
DeMott, Benjamin, 103
Department of Energy, 161
Department of Housing and Develop-
    ment (HUD), 32
Department of the Interior, 161,
deregulation, see Reagan administra-
    tion
Deterring Democracy, (Chomsky),
    137
Devos, Richard, 26, 27
Dewey, John, 129–130
Diet for a New America, (Robbins),
    99
Dingell, John, 53
Dionne, E. J., 25, 35–36
disability insurance, 56, 61
discrimination, see gay and lesbian
    rights, gender bias and racism
disinformation, media, 129–139,
    143–145
Dissent, 74, 194
Dixon, Alan, 155–156
Dollars and Sense, 176, 194
Domhoff, William G., 130
Dominican Republic, 117
Domini Social Index, 176
domino theory, 113
Donaldson, Sam, 131
Dow Chemical, 26, 51
Downey, Thomas, 102

Dreier, Peter, 74
drinking water, contamination in,
    97–98
drug trafficking, CIA, 117–118
Dumanoski, Dianne, 141
Dunbar, Leslie. 5
Du Pont, pollution by, 171
Duvalier, Francois, 118

Eagle Forum, 26
Earth First!, 6
Earth Island Institute, 14, 179, 186
Earth Journal, 1992, 96
Earth Summit, 1992 Conference on
    Environment and Development,
    91–92
Eastern Airlines, collapse of, 3, 54
economic conversion, 59–61
economic planning, 43–44, 58
Economic Policy Institute, 186
Economic Support Funds, 115
Economics Explained, 58
economics, progressive, 57–62
Edelman, Marian Wright, 40
Edsall, Thomas B. and Mary, 20–21,
    70, 72
education, 59
    eurocentric bias in, 87–88, 132,
    139–142, funding bias in, 75,
    103–104, need for multi-cultural,
    140–142, 145, spending cuts in,
    75, 77–78
Educators for Social Responsibility,
    186
Egypt, 115, 116
Ehrenreich, Barbara, 7, 16, 21, 72–73,
    77–79, 87, 136
elections
    local, 147–148, 155–159, partici-
    pation in, 64, 1980 presidential,
    28–29, 1984 presidential, 33, 1986
    Congressional, 34

Ellis, Tom, 27
Ellwood, David T., 69, 94, 101–102, 105
El Salvador, 13, 112, 118, 148
E Magazine, 195
employment, in the U.S., 60–61
Endangered Species Act, 108
England
    domestic spending policies, 40, income differentials in, 41, labor policies in, 46
Equal Employment Opportunity Commission (EEOC), 81–82
environment, worsening of, 95–100
environmentalist, 5, 92, 106, 109
environmental protection policies, U.S., 44, 107–109, 149
Environmental Protection Agency (EPA), 62, 95, 109, 161
    erosion of protection, 47, 51, 100, 105–106, 136, scandals in, 31, 51–52
Ephesians 5:23, 88
Equal Pay Act, 87
Erickson, Brad, 14, 179
Esquire, 86
Ethiopia, 96, 112
Eugenics and Race (Pearson), 29–30
Evangelicals for Social Action, 163
export allowances, 56
Exxon, 51

Fagen, Richard, 120
Fairness and Accuracy in Reporting, (FAIR), 133, 186
Falwell, Rev. Jerry, 4, 27, 28, 30, see also Moral Majority
Faludi, Susan, 20–21, 27, 31, 82, 102, 137
families, single parent, 68–71, 85, 101–102
farm crisis, 75

farm policy, 56
fascist, in the Republican party, 31
Fear Of Falling, (Ehrenreich), 78–79
Federal Deposit Insurance Corporation (FDIC), 55
Federal Reserve, 75
Feinstein, Dianne, 83, 155
feminism, 4, 5, 23, 87, 137
    New Right's response to, 4, 28, 82
Fernandez, Eduardo, 120
50 Ways to Fight Censorship, 142
financial services industry, 2, 55, 75–76
Finland, 44, 47
First Executive Insurance, collapse of, 55
Florsheim Shoes, 54, 170
Flower Industries, 170
Focus on the Family, 143
Food and Drug Administration (FDA), 100, 109
Food First, 186
food stamps, 59–60
Forbes, 57
Ford Foundation, 149
Ford, Gerald, 34
Ford, Henry, 45–46
Ford Motor Company, 26
foreign policy, U.S.
    covert activities, 113–114, 117–118, 120, foreign aid, 114–117, 119–120, objectives of, 111–114, progressive alternatives, 121–124, also see cold war
Forest Service, U.S. 96–97
Fort Collins, Colorado, 149
Fortune, 138
France
    domestic spending policies in, 40, economic planning in, 43, 47, labor market policies in, 42, income and wage differentials in, 41

Franklin Research, 177
Free Congress Foundation, 26
free trade agreements, 15, 52–53, 61
Freedom to Read foundation, 143
Friedman, Benjamin, M., 44
Friends of the Earth, 11
Fuerst, J.S., 104–105
full employment policies, 9, 22, 43, 60, 70
Fund for the Feminist Majority, 187

Gaebler, Ted, 149
Galbraith, John Kenneth, 78–79, 130
Gallup Poll, 34–35
Galston, William, 33
Garbarino, James, 83, 92
Gates, Robert, 112
gay and lesbian rights, 80, 171
gender bias, 12, 21, 67–71, 79–83, 86–89, 135
General Dynamics, 133
General Electric, 56
  boycott of, 168, ownership of NBC, 132–133, political influence of, 26,
George, Christopher, 135
George, Susan, 116
Georgia-Pacific, 170
Germany, Unified and former West Germany, 2
  domestic spending policies in, 40, economic planning in, 43, energy policies in, 44, 46, 107, labor market policies of, 46, income and wage differentials in, 41, standard of living in, 44
Gibbs, Lois Marie, 7, 154
Gilder, George, 4, 25, 27
Gillette, 170, 173
Glazer, Nathan, 25
global warming, 95, 106–107
Goldwater, Barry, 25
Goodlee, Lee, 12

Good Money, 176, 177, 192
Good Money Industrial Average, 176
Goodno, James, 176
Gorbachev, 29
Gould, Robert, 62–63, 117
Grand Metropolitan, boycott of, 170
grassroots movements, see movements
Gray Panthers, 187
Great Depression, 8,
Great Society, see Johnson, Lyndon
Green Consumer Letter, 192
Green, Mark, 33, 139
Green, Nancy, Sokol, 97–99
Green Party, USA, 10, 18, 150, 152, 153, 182
greenhouse effect, see global warming
Greenpeace, USA, 161, 187, 190
green taxes, 108–109
Greider, William 1, 7, 48, 53, 75, 151
Grenada, 13, 115
Gordon, Ted, 141
Gross, Bertram, 140
Guardian, 194
Guatemala, 117, 118
Gulf Coast Tenants Association, 153

Haiti, 118
Hanford nuclear weapons reservation, 98
Harkin, Tom, 9, 10
Harrington, Michael, 4, 6, 8, 23, 39–40, 45, 50, 58
Harris poll, 34–35
Harvard University, 75
Hayden, Tom, 19
Haymarket Square, Chicago, 72
hazardous waste sites, 59, 98, 154
Head Start, 6, 104–105
health insurance, subsidized, 22, 39, 59, 61, 70–71,
health risk

in industry, 42, from toxins, 97–100, of working class, 76

Heath Anthology of American Literature, 141

Heilbroner, Robert, 43, 58

Helms, Jesse, 26

Heritage Foundation, 26, 30, 31, 47, 81, 134

Herman, Edward, 134, 136

Hersh, Seymour, 131

Hertsgaard, Mark, 131, 138–139

Hewlett Packard, 173

Hightower, Jim, 7, 9, 16, 57

Himmelstein, Jerome, L., 24, 27, 29, 32

Hispanics, 84, 151, 153, 155

Hoffer, Eric, 130

Holly Farms, boycott of, 170

homosexuality, see gay and lesbian rights

Hoover, Herbert, 8, 33

Hormel, boycott of, 170

House of Representatives, U.S., see Congress, U.S.

House Republican Study Committee, 26

housing programs, 59, 75, 103, 149

Housing and Urban Development (HUD), scandal in, 136

Houston Post, 136

Howe, Neil, 49, 75

Hunt, Nelson Bunker, 27

Hurst, John, 140–142

Hussein, Saddam, 112

Hyde, Henry, 102

IBM, 52, 173

illiteracy, 84

Imperial Brain Trust, (Shoup and Minter), 113–114

income, U.S.

decline in, 22, 41, 50–51, 77–78, executive pay, 41 inequitable distribution of, 41, 49, of women, 69, 80, of working-class, 68–71

India, 80

Indonesia, 112, 118

Industrial Areas Foundation (IAF), 150, 151

industrial policy, see economic planning

INFACT, 168

INF disarmament treaty, 29

infant formula, boycott against, 168

infant mortality, 44, 93

infrastructure, U.S., 59–60, 62–63, 102–103

Institute for Food and Development Policy, 115

Institute for Peace and International Security, 121

Institute for Policy Studies, 59, 187

Intercessors for America, 26

Interfaith Center for Corporate Responsibility, 163, 175, 192

Interfaith Hunger Appeal, 163

Interior Department, U.S., 52

Internal Revenue Service (IRS), 102

International Monetary Fund, 114, 116

International Policy Forum, 26

International Wildlife Coalition, 173

In These Times, 194

Investor Responsibility Research Center, 192

Iran, 112, 117, 120

Iran-Contra scandal, 136

Iraq, 112

Ising, Beth, 14

Israel, 115

Italy, 40–41

ITT, 52

Jackson, Jesse, 7, 16, 36, 71, 150
Jamaica, 114–115
Jameson, Kenneth, P., 50
Japan, 2, 73
   domestic spending policies in,
   40–41, economic planning in, 43,
   energy policies in, 44, 46, 107,
   labor market policies in, 46,
   income and wage differentials in,
   41, standard of living in, 44
Jefferson, Thomas, 129
Jencks, Christopher, 102
Jewish Women's Caucus, 163
job exportation, 43–44, 54–55, 73
job-training programs, 60, 70–71,
   149
Jobs with Peace campaign, 14–15,
   149, 180
John Birch Society, 24, 32
John Olin Foundation, 25–26
Johnson, Haynes, 32
Johnson, Lyndon, B., 8, 33, 137
   Great Society and War on Poverty
   programs, 6, 23
Jubilee Housing Loan Fund, 177
Julian, Joseph, 81, 87

Kadane, Kathy, 118
Kauffman, L.A., 11–12
Kellog Company, 169
Kennedy, John F., 6, 8, 19, 137
Kilpatrick, James J., 32, 33
Kimberly-Clark, 52
King, Coretta Scott, 101
King, Martin Luther, Jr., 6, 9, 19, 23
King Rodney, 67, 84
Kirkpatrick, Jeane, 25
Klein, Lawrence, 63
Kodak, 52
Korea, 111–112, 119–120
Kornblum, William, 81, 87
Kozol, Jonathan, 85, 104

Krakauer, Jon, 106
Kraus, Mickey, 8,
Krieble, Robert, H., 26
Kristol, Irving, 25
Krugman, Paul, 123–124
Kuttner, Robert, 4–5, 7–9, 23, 33, 36,
   44, 58

labor market policy
   global, 42–44, Reaganomics and,
   50–51, in U.S., 42–44
labor unions, U.S., 13, 36, 124
   boycotts by, 170, conservative
   attack on, 50–51, 72–74, decline
   of, 42, labor legislation, 23, 60
LaHaye, Tim, 81
Lamar, Jake, 86
Lands End, 168
Lappe, Frances Moore, 115, 118
Larsen, Reed, 27
Lasch, Christopher, 111
Lavelle, Rita, 51
League of Conservation Voters, 190
League of Women Voters, 160, 190
Learning Alliance, 187
Lee, Martin, A., 133–135, 136
Left, The
   accomplishments of, 5–7,
   composition of, 5–7, failings of,
   35– 37, New Left, 19–20, also see
   liberalism and the progressive left
Leontief, Wassily, 58
lesbians, see gay and lesbian rights
Lessin, Nancy, 42,
Lewis, Ann, 82
Lewis, Paul, 91
liberalism
   among the professional class, 21,
   backlash against, 20–21, economic
   policies of, 8–9, public support
   for, 4
Libya, 112

Liebling, A. J., 134
Life, 81
Locite Corporation, 26
Longman, Phillip, 49, 75
L'Oreal, 170
Los Angeles, 67–68, 98
Los Angeles Times, 41, 132–133, 134, 135
Losing Ground (Murray), 27
Louisiana, 98, 153
Love Canal, 98, 154
Lubiano, Wahneema, 141
Luxembourg Income Study, 92

McCarthy, Eugene, 19
McCarthy, Joseph, 2
McElvaine, Robert S., 45
McGovern, George, 120–121, 122
McLaughlin Group, The, 134
McNeil, Donald G., 96–97
MacColl, Gail, 139
Macy's, 3, 54
MacNeil/Lehrer NewsHour, 134
Making A Difference, (Zimmerman), 179
Malcolm X, 19,
Malek, Fred, 30
Mandate for Leadership, 47
Manhattan Institute, 27
Manufacturing Consent, 134
maritime-marine industry, 56
Marmor, Theodore, 68
Marsh, Dave, 142–143
Marshall, Jonathan, 117
Marshner, Connaught (Connie), 31
marxism, 5–6,
Mattera, Phillip, 75
Mazzocchi, Tony, 16
media
    bias in, 131–139, corporate
    ownership of, 132–134, govern-
    mental influence on, 131, 135

Medicare and Medicaid, 6, also see
    subsidized health insurance
Memorex, 52
Messe, Edwin, 31
Metropolitan Organization (TMO), 151
Mexico, U.S. factories in, 52–53, 42–43
middle-class
    backlash against liberalism, 20–22,
    33, 35, declining economic
    fortunes of, 49–50, tax burden
    shifted to, 49
Mills, C. Wright, 78
Milner, Henry, 64
minimum wage, 6, 70–72, 73, 101–102
Minkowitz, Donna, 80
Minneapolis, 149
minorities, see people of color
Minter, 113
Missouri Rural Crisis Center, 150
Mitterrand, Francois, 47
Mitsubishi, boycott of, 170
Mobil Oil Corporation, 26, 133
Mondale, Walter, 33
Montgomery Bus Company, boycott
    of, 167
Moon, Rev. Sun Myung, 30
Moral Majority, 26, 31
Morris, Cynthia, 119
Mother Jones, 55, 195
Mountain States Legal Foundation, 51
movements, 6
    civil rights, 6, grass-root move-
    ments, 5, 14– 15, 150–154, labor,
    6, peace, 6–7, student left, 6, 21,
Moynihan, Daniel Patrick, 25, 42
Ms., 83, 195
Murray, Charles, 4, 27
Myerson, Adam, 134
mythology, American, 130–131

NAACP, 6, 11, 13, 80, 162
Nader, Ralph, 7, 16, 19
Nation, The, 11, 33, 76, 112, 126, 194
National Association of Christian
    Educators, 30
National Association of Community
    Development Loan Funds, 193
National Association for the Educa-
    tion of Young Children, 105
National Coalition for the Homeless,
    173
National Catholic Reporter, 194
National Committee for Full
    Employment, 101
National Committee on Pay Equity,
    50

National Congressional Club, 26
National Conservative Political
    Action Committee, 32
National Council of Churches, 11, 163
National Council of Roman Catholic
    Bishops, 163
National Endowment for the Arts,
    142
National Federation of Community
    Broadcasters, 196
National Federation of Community
    Development Credit Unions, 193
National Gay and Lesbian Task Force,
    11, 188
National Highway Traffic Safety
    Commission, 52
National Housing Institute, 74
National Labor Relations Board
    (NLRB), 6, 50, 60, 73
National Lawyers Guild, 11
National Organization for Women
    (NOW), 12, 16, 18, 150, 151–152,
    161, 180–181
National People of Color Environ-
    mental Summit, 153

National Pro-Family Coalition, 31
National Public Radio (NPR), 134
National Right to Work Committee,
    26
National Safe Workplace Institute, 42
National Toxics Campaign, 150
National Women's Political Caucus,
    190
nationalism, 130
Nation's Business, The, 33
Native Americans, 19, 84, 150, 152,
    154
Navarro, Vicente, 76
NBC, see General Electric
NBC Nightly News, 138
neo-conservatism, 24–25
neo-nazis, 26, 29–30
Nestles, boycott of, 168, 170
NETWORK, 163
New Alternatives Fund, 177, 193
New American Poverty, The
    (Harrington), 39
New Deal, 6, 8–9, 33, 72
New Directions for Women, 195
New Jersey, 103–104
New Party, The, 183
New Republic, The, 8
New Right
    agenda of, 28, censorship by,
    142–143, feminism attacked by, 4,
    81, formation of, 34, leaders of,
    26–28
New School for Social Research, 59
New Voices, 196
Newsweek, 52, 68, 135, 138
New York City, 84
New York Times, 26, 91, 111, 117,
    120, 133, 135, 138
Next Left, The (Harrington), 8,
Nicaragua, 112, 117, 118, 125–127,
    148
Nixon, Richard, 33

Noriega, Manuel, 112
Northeastern Indian Quarterly, 196
North, Oliver, 20, 27, 136
Norway, 44
Novack, Michael, 25
Novack, Robert, 134
nuclear free zones, 10, 149
Nuclear Regulatory Commission, 136

Oak Ridge, Tennessee, 98
Occupational Safety and Health
    Administration (OSHA), 46,
    52–53, 62, 76
Odell, Eric, 152
Office of Management and Budget,
    52–54
Olin Foundation, 25, 27
On Bended Knee (Hertsgaard) 131
One On One, 134
On the Issues, 195
Operation Push, 13
opinion polls, 34–35, 166
    on abortion rights, 35
    on affirmative action, 35
    on environment protection, 34
    on foreign affairs, 34–35
    on government regulations, 34
    on government spending, 34
Organization of Chinese Americans,
    11
Osborne, Dave, 149
Outside Magazine, 106
ozone layer, depletion of, 95,
    106–107, 136

Pacifica, 196
Pacific Northwest, 108
Pakistan, 118,
Panama, 96, 115
parental leave, 40, 71
Parnassus Fund, 177, 193
Pax World Fund, 177, 193

payroll tax, see taxation
peace dividend, 59–61, 62
Peace, Roger C. III, 118
Pearson, Roger, 30
Peele, Gillian, 25
Pentagon, see Defense Department,
    U.S.
people of color, 20–24, 28
People for the American Way, 188
People for the Ethical Treatment of
    Animals, (PETA), 168, 179
Persian Gulf War, 112
Peru, 116
pesticides, 99–101
Peterson, Thane, 73
petition drives, 159–161
Pfizer, 26
Philadelphia Inquirer, 30, 49
Philippines, 118
Philip L. Graham Fund, 26
Phillips, Howard, 29, 81
Phillips, Kevin, 41, 48, 57
Pinochet, Augusto, 118
Piven, Frances Fox, 16
Pizzo, Stephen, 55
Planned Parenthood, 173, 188
Podhoretz, Norman, 25
Poisoning Our Children (Green), 97
Policy Alternatives for the Caribbean
    and Central America, 120
political action committees (PACs), 27
political involvement, 156–164
Politics of Rich and Poor, The,
    (Phillips), 41
Pollitt, Kathy, 141
political parties, see Democratic Party,
    Green Party, Progressive Vermont
    Alliance, Republican Party,
Politics of Rich and Poor, The
    (Phillips), 41
pollution, industrial, 95–100, see also
    environment, state of

Poor Support (Ellwood), 101
Popcorn, Faith, 178
Population Crisis Committee, 81
Population Reference Bureau, 84
poverty, 91–94, 100–105
    among children, 44, 92–93,
    eradication of, 59, 100–105,
    among women, 68–71, 101–102,
    among working-class, 68–71
Presbyterian Hunger Program, 163
press, see media
Proctor & Gamble, 170
productivity growth, U.S., 45, 62–63
Progressive, The, 52, 69, 194
Progressive Labor Party, 182
Progressive Left
    counterrevolution by, 15–16,
    definition of, 7–10, economic
    agenda of, 8–10, 57–63, foreign
    policy agenda, 121– 124, ideals of,
    7, political agenda of, 9–10, third
    party movements in, 16–18
Progressive Student Network, 163
Progressive Vermont Alliance, 10, 14,
    17, 151
Project Censored, 136
Project Vote, 159
Public Broadcasting Service (PBS),
    134
Public Citizen, 51, 52, 188
Public Interest Research Groups, 163
Puma, 170

Quality of Life Alternative Budget, 15
Quayle, J. Danforth, 27, 53, 106
Quayle, James, 27
Quest For Peace, 163
Quinn, Jane, 135

racism, 12, 20, 67–71, 83–89,
    140–141, 153
Racism and Sexism: An Integrated

    Study (Rothenberg), 139
Radio for Peace International, 196
Rainbow Challenge, The (Collins), 20
Rainbow Coalition, 10, 17, 150–151
Rainbow Institute, 150
Rainforest Action Network, 173, 179
Rakin, Marcus, 112
Ralston Purina, 170
Rand, Ann, 3–4
Reader's Digest, 26
Reagan administration, 2–3, 8, 32,
    47–56, agenda of, 29, 47–48,
    attack on labor by, 73–77,
    defense spending by, 55–57,
    industry deregulation by, 51–53,
    environmental policies of,
    105–106, foreign policy of,
    114–115, 117–118, 119–120,
    125–127, scandals in, 31–32,
    social spending cuts by, 56
Reagan's Reign of Error, 139
Reagan, Ronald, 10, 20, 25, 30
    assertions of, 21, 70, false
    popularity of, 137–139
    incompetence of, 137–139,
    political agenda of, 29, 33,
    supporters of, 28–29, 33–34
Reed, Adolph, Jr., 13,
Reich, Robert B., 20–21, 23, 46,
    50–51, 58–60, 74, 77, 130
Reinventing Government, 149
religion, 88
    liberal activism in the church, 150,
    151, 163–164, Religious Right, 26,
    27–28, 30–31
Religious Coalition on Abortion
    Rights, 163
Religious Task Force on South
    America, 7, 163
Rensenbrink, John, 152
Republican Party, 28–29, 45
    corporate favoritism in, 17, 48–49

Revco Drugs, 55
revolving loan funds, 177–178
Rifkin, Jeremy and Carol Grunewald,
  96–97
Right, The,
  attack on feminism, 81–82,
  composition of, 28–29, fall of,
  29– 33, growth of, 24–28, New
  Right, 25–27, propaganda of, 3–4,
  28–29
RJR Nabisco, 52, 169
Robbins, John, 99
Robertson, Pat, 31
Roosevelt, Franklin D., 101
Rothenberg, Paula, 139–140
Rothschild, Emma, 48
Rowse, Arthur E., 54
Rules for Radicals, 151
Rushdoony, R.J., 30
Ryan, Ellen, 13,
Ryan, Randolph, 118

Sage, 195
Sanders, Bernie, 7, 14, 151
Sandler, Marion, 81
SANE/FREEZE, 7, 11, 162, 181
San Francisco, 149
Santa Monica, California, 149
Sassy, 143
Savage Inequalities, 85, 104
Savimbi, Jonas, 112
savings and loan (S&L) crisis, 8, 32,
  55, 135
Scaife, Richard Mellon, 25
schools, see education
Schlafly, Phyllis, 4, 27, 30, 81
Schlesinger, Arthur, 48
Schmoke, Kurt, 151
Schor, Juliet, 42, 75
Schroeder, Patricia, 7, 9
Schultze, Charles, L., 62
Scott Paper, 170

Scott, Peter Dale, 117
Scribbs Howard, 134
Seattle, 150
Second Opinion, 197
Segal, Troy, 67–68
Self-Help Credit Union, 177
Senate, U.S., see Congress, U.S.
Shiller, Herbert, 130
Shopping for a Better World,
  169–170
Shorter Work-Time Group, 42
Shoup, Lawrence, 113
Siegal, Norman, 88
Sierra Club, 7, 11, 51, 190
Simon, Paul, 9,
Simon, William, 25–26, 60
Simplicity Pattern, 54
sister cities, 10, 148, 149
sixties era, 6, 8, 19–20
Sklar, Holly, 75, 92–93, 102, 104
slavery, 5
Smeal, Eleanor, 16
Smithkline Beckman, 26
Smith Richardson Foundation, 26, 27
Social Democratic Party, Sweden,
  63–65
social democracy, 5, 17
socialism, 5–6, 18, 47
Social Investment Forum, 193
social justice, 5, 36
socially responsible consumerism,
  165–174
socially responsible investing,
  174–178
Social Security, 6, 49, 56, 59
social-welfare programs
  international comparisons, 39–40,
  progressive, 59–61
Sojourners, 71, 195
Soldiers of Fortune, 27
Solomon, Norman, 133–135, 136
Solomon, Peter, 48

Somoza family, 125–126
South Africa, 40, 84, 148, 162, 167, 169, 170
South Shore Bank, 177
Soviet Union, 111–112
Spain, 43
species extinction, 97
Speigel, 168
Stahl, Leslie, 138
State News Service, 118
Steele, James B., 49
Steinbruner, John D., 112
Steinem, Gloria, 19
Stockwell, John, 125
Strauss, Franz Josef, 26
student activism, 162–163
Student Environmental Action
    Coalition, (SEAC), 14, 152–153,
    162–163, 181
Sulmont, Denis, 116
Superfund, 106
supply-side economics, see
    Reaganomics
Supreme Court, 10, 82
sustainable society, development of,
    92
Swaggart, Jimmy, 28, 31
Sweden, 2, 63–65, 80
    domestic spending policies in, 40,
    economic planning and full-
    employment policies in, 43,
    46–48, 149, income equality in,
    41, standard of living in, 44, 63–65
Sweden: Social Democracy in
    Practice (Milner), 65
Sweezy, Paul, 71
Switzerland, 2, 44

21st Century Party, 181
Taiwan, 119–120
tax policy, U.S.
    business and wealthy favored in,

41–42, 48–49, 74–75, need for
    more progressive taxation, 23,
    41–42, 58–60, payroll taxes, 49,
    62, 74, 101
Teaching Tolerance, 88
Thatcher, Margaret, 47, 138
Third World, 7, 61, 73, 154, 168, 170,
    also see foreign policy, U.S.
Third World debt crisis, 114–116,
    123–124
Third World development, 122–123
Thurow, Lester, 43, 48, 58, 77
Tikkun, 195
timber industry, 56
Time, 69, 94, 98, 107, 108
Times Mirror Company, 26
Time Warner, 133
Tobin, James, 48
Mustafa K. Tolba, 95
Toward A Sustainable Society
    (Garbarino), 81, 92
toxic poisoning, 97–100, 109, 150,
    153, also see hazardous waste
trade deficit, U.S., 45, 116
Transnational Institute, 116
trickle-down economics, see
    Reaganomics
trucking industry, 54
Trump, Donald, 20
Tunnel Vision (Schor and Cantor), 75
Turkey, 115

underclass, 94
Undercurrents, 197
unemployment insurance, 6, 60–61
Unification Church, see Moon, Sun
    Myung
unions, see labor unions
Unisys, 52
UNITA, 112
United Campuses to Prevent Nuclear
    War, 163

United Church of Christ, 153
United Nations, 41, 44, 63, 95,
    121–122, 126
United Nations Children's Fund
    (UNICEF), 119
United States Steel Corp., 3
United Technologies, 52
United Way of America, 170
University of California, Davis, 98
University of Illinois, 162
University of Pennsylvania, 162
Unreliable Sources (Lee and
    Solomon), 133, 135
U.S. News and World Report, 68
U.S. Steel, 3
Utne Reader, 14, 64, 195

vacation time, government mandated,
    42–43
Valerio, Michael, 26
Venezuela, 120
Vermont, 151
Vermont National Bank, 177
Vietnam, 20, 112, 118
Viguerie, Richard, 32
Village Voice, 89, 195
Vladeck, David, 54
Volcker, Paul, 76
voter registration, 158–159
Voting Rights Act, 6

wages, see income and minimum
    wages
Wallace, George, 29
Walljasper, Jay, 63–65
Wall Street, see financial service
    industry
Wang Computer, 3
Washington Jewish Monthly, 30
War on Poverty, see Johnson, Lyndon
Washington Monthly, 135
Washington Post, 26, 30, 133–134,

    135, 138
waste, hazardous, see toxic poisoning
Watt, James, 51–53
Wealth and Poverty, (Gilder), 27
Wedtech scandal, 31
Weiler, Paul, 50
welfare, see AFDC
welfare reform, 69–71
Welles, Chris, 134
Wellstone, Paul, 9
West, Cornel, 140
wetlands, 97
Weyerhaeuser, boycott of, 26, 170
Weyrich, Paul, 26–27
Where We Stand (Wolff), 41
Whitman, Steve, 84
Whole Food Market, 11–12
Who Will Tell The People (Greider),
    54
Who Rules America Now?
    (Domhoff), 130
Why Americans Hate Politics,
    (Dionne), 35
Wilbur, Charles K., 50
Wildmon, Donald, 27
Willer, Barbara, 105
Wilson, William Julius, 58, 105
Winship, Christopher, 68
Wisconsin, 69–71
Wisconsin Labor/Farm party, 10, 17
Wise Use, 106
Wolff, Michael, 41
Wolfson Center for National Affairs,
    59
Women's Economic Development
    Corporation, 178
Women's International League for
    Peace and Freedom, 188
Women's International News
    Gathering Service, 197
women's rights, see gender bias
Word of God church (WOG), 30–31

workers, working class,
  class warfare, 72–76, conservative
  backlash among, 22–24, declining
  wages of, 41 76, Democrats and,
  35–37 poverty and, 41, 101
Working Assets, 173, 177, 194
World Bank, 114, 119
World Court, 122, 126
World Policy Institute, 189
World Policy Journal, 195
World Resource Institute, 96
Worldwatch Institute, 189

World War II, 72
Worster, Donald, 141

Xerox, 133

Yale University, 162
Yeakel, Lynn, 83, 155
Young Americas for Freedom, 24
YWCA, 11

Zimmerman, Richard, 179
Z Magazine, 75, 84, 92, 194